DATE DUE

DEC 1 6 1995	
APR 2 4 1996	

GAYLORD   'ED IN U.S.A.

D1213076

PARENTS IN CONTEMPORARY AMERICA

A sympathetic view

The Dorsey Series in Sociology

Consulting Editor
Charles M. Bonjean
The University of Texas at Austin

Parents in contemporary America

A sympathetic view

E. E. LeMasters, professor emeritus
School of Social Work
University of Wisconsin–Madison

John DeFrain, associate professor
Department of Human Development
    and the Family
University of Nebraska–Lincoln

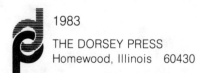
1983

THE DORSEY PRESS
Homewood, Illinois   60430

ISBN 0-256-02679-3

Library of Congress Catalog Card No. 82–72877

Printed in the United States of America

1 2 3 4 5 6 7 8 9 0   ML   0 9 8 7 6 5 4 3

*For our wives
and our children*

The relationship between parents and children is no less difficult, no less fraught with drama, than that between lovers. The growing child, developing into an independent individual, surprises and annoys its parents. What once was a charming plaything becomes an adversary.

ANDRÉ MAUROIS
Lelia: The Life of George Sand

Insanity is hereditary.
You get it from your kids.
popular bumper sticker

Preface

When the first edition of this book was conceived and written in the late 60s, the author was long on experience as a professor at the embattled University of Wisconsin–Madison. The Vietnam War threatened to tear the country apart, and parents in contemporary America then struggled to maintain their balance between the demands of the state and the demands of their children.

While Professor LeMasters was a participant-observer from his vantage point in Madison, John DeFrain, of a much younger generation, was a participant-observer as a student and young father in Lincoln and Seattle. DeFrain sometimes reported events of the times for a local newspaper and just as often was involved in them.

Parents in Contemporary America has survived now into its 4th edition. The United States has changed significantly since the first edition came out, and the book also has changed significantly to reflect the vast transitions of the times.

In this edition, then, the book has the added perspective of a younger person, age 36, joining that of an older person, age 72. The older person has helped nurture his sons Bill and Gary to adulthood and remains with his wife Billie. The younger person is in the thick of the struggle, taking the days one at a time with his wife Nikki as they raise Amie, Alyssa, and Erica.

The issues have changed also as the book reflects them. Battles over money have taken the headlines from wartime battles, which many people are trying to forget and many others never will be able to. OPEC and inflation and tax cuts and the Reagan administration's attempts to dismantle 50 years of work to extend human services are now in the news. Research on parenthood and families has come up with a lot more for us to talk about in the area of sex roles and androgyny. There is also added emphasis on voluntary childlessness, child abuse and neglect, the challenges of single parenthood and stepparenting, and the crisis parents face when adult children return home because of divorce or financial difficulty to a formerly empty (and comfortably so) nest. Furthermore, a new emphasis on family strengths in research and clinical practice has added a breath of fresh air to the study of parenthood. Besides an awareness of the problems of parents, in the spirit of the times we will continue to note the fact that most parents in spite of tremendous odds are doing a pretty good job.

As the first author said in the Preface to the 3d edition of this book:

> . . . In many cases the efforts of mothers and fathers today are to be considered heroic. That some of them produce children who are well organized and constructive is almost a miracle. That others fail is to be understood.
>
> In many ways this book is a defense of American parents against their critics. I feel that the case against parents in our society has been overstated, and I am trying to restore some balance to the discussion. That the book is controversial is admitted. It is hoped that the debate will prove constructive rather than destructive.

Robin M. Williams, Jr., of Cornell University, the Consulting Editor in Sociology and Anthropology for The Dorsey Press, was the first editor to see any merit in the original manuscript of this book. The first author again wishes to thank him for this consideration. It would appear that his faith in the book has been vindicated. Heartfelt thanks also to Nikki DeFrain, Harriet and Orville DeFrain, Charlotte Jackson, Nick Stinnett, Julie Claybaugh, George E. Hart III, Russ Porter, and Richard Straker.

E. E. LeMasters
John DeFrain

Contents

Chapter 1

Parents in contemporary America

In his autobiography, Norbert Wiener, one of the true geniuses of our time, confesses his humility in his attempts to cope with the baffling complexities of parenthood. He writes: "Thus, like all families, we had our problems to consider and our decisions to make. I am neither certain of the correctness of the policies I have adopted nor ashamed of any mistakes I might have made. One has only one life to live, and there is not time enough in which to master the art of being a parent."[1]

In writing this book, the authors were inspired (or motivated) by hundreds of interviews with parents who echoed the feelings of Norbert Wiener—a man who could design a computer modeled on the human brain but who found parenthood a mystery and a confusion.

Many of the parents we talked with—perhaps a majority—were quite competent in their jobs and in the other areas of their lives, yet they felt insecure and inadequate as parents.

Talking with these fathers and mothers, the writers found themselves haunted by the questions: *Why* do these people find parenthood so difficult? How can a man run a corporation and fail miserably as a father?[2] How can a woman be regarded as a superior teacher in a suburban school system and be told by her daughter that she is a poor mother?

1

Max Lerner, in an interesting book, has written: "It is evident that in no other culture has there been so pervasive a cultural anxiety about the rearing of children."[3] The writers share this feeling, and this book may be regarded as our attempt to account for this cultural complex.

This book is neither intended to be an attack on parents in contemporary America nor is it intended to be an attack on the institution of parenthood. The authors have too many children and too much good feeling about the joys of rearing children (in spite of the innumerable challenges and frustrations we outline here) to throw our babies out with the bath water.

Instead, we believe we are settling an important score by defending parents, by presenting a more sympathetic view of them. Parents, in short, have the most difficult task in the world—to rear happy, healthy children in an incredibly complex environment. The vast majority of parents love their children and do the very best job they can in spite of the odds against them. Our society puts this tremendous responsibility almost totally on the parent, even though parents, in reality, are only one influence, albeit a major one, among many influences on the development of children. Our economic system, schools, religious organizations, mass media, peer groups, and many other institutions and pressure groups impinge on a child's world; most often these influences are positive ones and helpful to the parent in the task of socializing children. But oftentimes these influences can be negative and counter to the direction parents are working so diligently.

This book is not a cookbook for parents. It speaks of much broader issues, on a societal level rather than the particular problems parents face in their individual families. You will find no discussions of bedwetting, sibling rivalry, teenagers and pimples, or coping with empty-nest syndrome. There are literally hundreds of how-to books for parents on the market today; a visit to any bookstore, bus depot book rack, or drug store magazine stand will give the eager parent a veritable smorgasbord of books and magazines from which to choose—all with excellent discussions on specific troubles.

What we have to offer in this book that is very important, however, is our fervent belief backed up by adequate documentation that parents in contemporary America have been given a bum rap, so to speak. They take all the blame and get precious little praise for their efforts in behalf of the young. Few books have seriously addressed this issue, because it is much easier for writers as well as parents and anybody else to focus on the trees rather than the forest. The well-being of a society in general, however, has a tremendous effect on the well-being of its individuals in particular; and so, we here choose to look at the social system as a whole and how it affects the institution of parenthood.

In this first chapter, we wish to explore some of the features of our society that seem to pose problems for parents. In subsequent chapters, most of these variables will be analyzed in depth—here we wish to only sketch them in.

The reader should remember that this book does not attempt to deal with the *personal* or *individual* problems that any given father or mother might have—on the contrary, we are concerned with the problems that *most* American parents seem to have. In other words, it is a sociological, not a psychiatric, study.

In reviewing the literature on parents, it seems to us that the vast majority of the material is concerned with children—not with parents. We are impressed by an observation of Orville Brim that most family writers seem to think that parents operate in a social and cultural vacuum because so little is said about the social situations confronting fathers and mothers.[4]

In this book, then, we wish to look long and hard at the social system—or systems—in which American parents operate; we want to analyze the problems that plague *most* of these fathers and mothers—not just the inadequate ones; we want to talk to fathers as well as mothers, to lower- and upper-class parents as well as middle-class ones.

Not much will be said about children—the libraries are full of books about them.

We will begin, in this first chapter, by noting some of the features of our society that constitute the social framework in which American fathers and mothers must function.

Sociological factors that affect parents

In his classic paper, "The Sociology of Parent-Youth Conflict,"[5] Kingsley Davis discussed 11 variables that he believed to be related to the problems that American parents have. These are as follows:

The rate of social change. It seems obvious that parents in a relatively static society would have less difficulty than those in one in which social change is rapid and deep—as in the United States.

In a slowly changing society, parents would be closer to their children—the generation gap would be minimized. In such a society, parents need only to produce children like themselves. The models do not change so often or so drastically as they do in contemporary America, where families find themselves hurtling through one social or technological revolution after another.

The decelerating rate of socialization of the parent in contrast to that of the child. Davis is referring to the fact that the learning curve of the parent is almost the exact opposite of that of the child. During adolescence, for example, when the boy or girl is in the process of discovering sex, the parent may be well past the peak of his or her interest in sex. As one middle-aged father once lamented to us: "I must have reached my sexual peak as a Boy Scout. How do I relate to my 14-year-old son now? He runs around like a bull elk in rut." In terms of learning theory, the child reaches a peak of psychological and social change at a time when the average parent is learning and changing less and less.

If the child is learning about the same things that the parent learned earlier, no great problems may arise; but in societies such as the United States, social change is so rapid, and so deep, that the new generation does not learn the same things the parents learned. One exasperated mother put it this way: "How in the hell am I supposed to help my kids with their homework when even *adding* and *subtraction* have changed? This new math makes me feel *old!*"

It will be seen in later chapters that rapid and deep social change poses serious problems for American parents.

A combination of physiological and psychological differences between parent and child. This is a sort of *gestalt* effect—the parent is not only different physiologically from the child, but also psychologically and culturally. The difference is enormous and all-pervasive.

Adult realism versus youthful idealism. Davis argues that as parents mature they tend to compromise their ideals—they still teach them to their children but only partially believe in them—or they have become cynical about the practicality of their ideals.

Youth, in contrast, takes ideals seriously and are upset when they find their parents giving only lip service to ideals such as racial equality, world peace, or the elimination of poverty. It does not help to tell the child, "Wait until you are as old as I am and then you will understand." This only widens the gap between parents and child.

The nature of parental authority. Davis cites Simmel to the effect "that authority is bearable for the subordinate because it touches only one aspect of his life."[6] But in a primary group such as the family, parental authority extends over all phases of the child's life. The wise parent, of course, limits his exercise of authority as much as he can—but in the last analysis the father and/or mother is responsible for all phases of the child's life as long as the youngster is not of legal age.

Conflicting norms. In a rapidly changing, pluralistic society, children can often challenge parents as to what constitutes moral or good behavior. Should a youth resist the draft? Smoke marijuana? Engage in premarital sex? Not only do the two generations hold different norms, but *within* each generation the standards also vary. This greatly complicates the enforcement of discipline.

Competing authorities. Parents are not the only source of wisdom and propriety in modern society. The schools, the mass media, and the youth peer groups all tell the youth what he or she should think and behave. Fathers and mothers are always in competition with these forces when they seek to influence their children. Children quickly become adept at playing one parent against another: "But Mom, Dad says it's okay. . . ." When they go into the world outside the home, they have innumerable new possibilities for this tactic.

Poor age grading. We lack a series of clear steps by which boys and girls move from the status of a child to that of an adult. A male college student put it this way: "The local movie theater decided I was an adult when I was 12 and has been charging me adult prices ever since. The Bureau of Motor Vehicles gave me the nod to drive a car at 16—but if I had been living in Texas I could have driven at 14. The draft board says I mature at 18, but until the new law was passed, the bars, the marriage license bureau, and the voting authorities thought I was a kid until 21. It is very confusing."

Concentration within the small family. Davis argues that in larger family systems authority and its related feelings are more diffused among several adults than in our intense nuclear system.

Not only are the parent-child feelings very intense in our society, but the smallness and detachment of our family units make them vulnerable to dissolution, thus adding to parent-child tensions.

Riesman[7] argues that the margin for parental error shrinks as the family system becomes smaller—each child becomes more crucial. An only child put it in these words: "I am all the children my parents have. If I get into trouble, *all* of their children are in trouble. It is not a very comforting thought."

Vertical social mobility. The adult status of children in our social class system is not finally settled at birth. The child may eventually occupy a social position quite different from that of the parents. This means, essentially, that the parents do not know for what set of roles they are preparing the child. Furthermore, they are often unable to comprehend the social world their child will ultimately have to cope with. An analogy here would be a professional training program in which the faculty did not know whether the graduates would become physicians, dentists, or veterinarians.

Sex tension. Davis contends that sex "tensions not only make the adolescent capricious, but create a genuine conflict of interest between the two generations."[8] In short, the young are bent on releasing that tension; the old aim at thwarting or redirecting the energy generated by that tension.

These, then, are the features of Western society that Davis believed to be sociological factors in creating parent-youth conflicts. Since 1940, when Davis was writing, American society has undergone deep and pervasive changes—some of which may have simplified the role of parent, while others made it more difficult. Let us look, first, at the negative impact of recent social change on American parents, and then we will close the chapter with a review of the positive aspects of recent social change as it affects parents.[9]

Negative aspects of recent social change on parents

Higher standards for parents

It is our belief that parents today are being judged by higher standards—by their children, by professionals such as schoolteachers, psychologists, and social workers, and by parents themselves.

There seems to be no way to prove or disprove this empirically. It appears logical, however, to assume that in a society in which other standards are being raised, those applied to parents would be elevated also. We refer to school standards enforced on elementary and secondary students, higher living standards, and others.

During the first author's own lifetime, it seems quite obvious that parents in the 1920s were not expected to have their children's teeth straightened—only the very wealthy ever did that. But today even blue-collar parents are expected to make sure that the teeth of their offspring are not crooked. And, as he labors on this fourth edition of *Parents in Contemporary America*, the second author wonders how he'll come up with the $6,000 necessary to put braces on all three of his girls' teeth—not to mention violin and ballet lessons, art instruction, summer camp, theatre training, *ad infinitum*.

Illustrations of this sort are endless. What was good enough for children in 1900 or 1920 is not good enough today—and this means that many fathers and mothers are judging themselves more harshly. This may be a crucial factor in explaining why American fathers and mothers feel so inadequate.[10]

The concept of progress

In most human societies, according to social scientists, it is enough if parents produce and rear children as good as the parents are—biologically and socially.[11] But in contemporary America, this is not good enough: The children have to be *superior* to the parents. The concept of progress is a fundamental tenet of the American credo. This may be functional for the society, but it may also help to produce a negative self-image in parents.

The cult of the child/The cult of youth

Max Lerner writes about the "cult of the child" in American society[12]—parents are expendable, but children are "precious"—the salt of the earth. To the extent that this is true of our society, it has to have a negative impact on parents as well as on all other older persons; it means that any person not a child is a second-class citizen. This may be one of the reasons why people in the United States do not want to become old—they know what that means.

Recent developments, such as the glibly-labeled "gray power movement," are an attempt by the mature to balance out our societal notions regarding youthfulness versus aging. "Older and better" has become a popular counterslogan in the tension between maturity and designer jeans. Clearly, there is a place also for "the cult of age."

Judgment by professionals

It is one thing for parents to be judged by their peers (other parents), but it is quite a different experience to have your efforts evaluated by professionals. It seems that, increasingly, fathers and mothers in our society have to submit to the judgment of teachers, school counselors, social workers, clinical psychologists, speech therapists, psychiatrists, physicians, nurses, and a host of other experts if anything happens to the child. The professionals are often nonparents and often younger than the parents they sit in judgment on. This provides added dimensions for tension between the professional and the parent.

This was certainly not the case when our parents and our grandparents were rearing their children. In those days a parent could hold up his head if he did what other parents in the community regarded as right and decent, even if his child did get into difficulty. A grandmother of ours—the mother of 15 children—had a rebellious son who ran away from home at the age of 14 and was not seen again for 10 years. As we recall family history, nobody called this woman a bad mother; after all, her other 14 children had not found it necessary to run away from home. It was simply felt in the community that some boys are more restless than others and that these things had to be expected. This was judgment by our grandmother's peers.

A few years ago a friend of ours also had a boy run away—he simply took off at age 16 and was not heard from for 18 months. Meanwhile, the parents had consulted a child-guidance clinic and came away burdened with guilt. They were led to believe that boys do not run away from good parents. Now, how can we make this judgment? How do we know this is true?

It would be interesting to know how many boys have left home in America since 1800. This was apparently quite common during frontier days, when restless sons would decide to "go west."[13]

It is a fact that the boy who ran away from our grandparents eventually came home and always claimed that he left home not because of anything his parents had ever done but because he wanted to see the world. It is also true that he was very close to his parents once he had returned to his native community.

Ivan Nye, for example, in his excellent review of research on the age-old problem of runaways, notes that the youth are motivated by three groups of reasons for running away:

1. Positive reasons. There is a desire to explore, to see the world and meet new people and have new experiences. Possibly 20 percent of the runaways are motivated by these thoughts.
2. Negative experiences. The youth may be fed up with school or his or her parents. The disagreements are generally over issues of control. Possibly 75 percent of the runaways cite these reasons for leaving.
3. Pushouts. These youths are thrown out, abandoned, or severely and repeatedly beaten by parents. Possibly 5 percent of the runaways fit in this general category.

Clearly, as Nye's review of research literature indicates, bad parents are not necessarily responsible for a youth's leaving home.[14]

We live in a world of specialists, some of whom are very helpful to parents. But fathers and mothers are *amateurs* in their parental roles, not professionals. In a book that has received wide acclaim, Alvin Toffler makes this statement: "Despite the increasing complexity of the task, parenthood remains the single preserve of the amateur."[15]

Our criminal courts provide that an accused person be judged by a jury of his or her peers. It seems to us that parents are entitled to the same consideration.

Marital instability

Fathers and mothers are usually assumed to operate as a team in rearing their children. This may still be true for a majority of American parents, but it is no longer true for a sizable minority. In 1975 the United States recorded for the first time more than 1 million divorces. During that year, there were also 2 million marriages. The ratio of marriages to divorces has hovered around the 2 million to 1 million mark ever since. If this trend continues for an extended period of time, 5 out of 10 marriages will end in divorce. More than one in six families is headed by a single parent.[16]

Rearing children is difficult in our society with the best of marriages. For couples whose marriages are failing or have already broken, there are added challenges to meet.[17]

New roles for American mothers

Since grandmother's day, American mothers have taken on new community roles and new economic roles—they raise money for Red Cross, run the PTA, teach Sunday school, and more than 4 in 10 of them are employed outside the home.[18] In many ways they have more responsibility than their mothers and grandmothers ever had. Maybe some of them try to do too much, but that is the world they find themselves living in.

America is no longer a rural society

Parents do not operate in a social vacuum—they struggle to rear their offspring in a laboratory that consists of the world they live in. One can hardly imagine that being a father or mother was not easier in the rural America of 1850 or 1900 than it is today in Chicago or Los Angeles or any other major urban center.[19] The contemporary parent has less knowledge of the various facets of the urban scene—and his or her children have more choices to make.

On the farm, children could be kept busy with chores, while in the city they have little of social import to do. The long school vacations pose very real problems for urban parents, but on the farm these recesses simply provided more hands to do all the things that have to be done on a farm.

In Chapter 11, the impact of urbanization on parents will be discussed at greater length. Here we simply note that the critics of American parents need to remember that the child-rearing laboratory is vastly more complex today than it was 50 years ago.

Rise of the mass media

Parents today are only one of several powerful influences on their children—at least this is so once the youngsters are old enough to read the comics, go to movies, listen to the radio, or watch television. Madison Avenue would like to have us believe that television does not influence children, but parents are skeptical. It is a bit difficult to grasp why advertisers would spend hundreds of millions of dollars on television programs for children if they didn't influence anybody.[20]

Parents and children today are so immersed in messages from the mass media that they are scarcely aware of it.

It seems clear that neither Hollywood nor the local rock 'n' roll radio station worries about whether they support the values that parents are struggling to promote. The mass media are commercial enterprises and they promote what sells. If this happens to be sex and violence, as in the movies or on television, that is not their concern—parents are supposed to see that their children avoid such movies and programs. And some parents, of course, are able to do just that. But many others are not so skillful or so fortunate. Monitoring children's viewing habits is a time-consuming task, added to an already overloaded schedule dictated by the parenting role.

We were reminded of this recently when we took time to read an information sticker on a cigarette machine. It read: "Minors are prohibited by state law from purchasing cigarettes from this machine. *Parents will please cooperate.*" The machine was in a corner at the back end of a fast-food emporium. Young teens purchased these cancer-causing symbols of independence and maturity, stuffed them greedily in their pockets, and sneaked past the youthful and bored cashier at the front of the hangout. Parents should cooperate! How? In an earlier America, cigarette vending machines were illegal; you had to prove your age to buy cigarettes over the counter.

It is perfectly obvious that the legislators who authorized these machines were primarily interested in only one thing—the easier sale of cigarettes. They were certainly not concerned about helping parents prevent or control smoking among teenagers.

Why not have a beer machine, or a martini dispenser, with the same hypocritical sticker stating "Parents will please cooperate"?

Emergence of the youth peer group

One of the most dramatic developments of modern urban America has been the phenomenal rise to power and influence (also affluence) of the youth peer group.[21] In rural America young people might spend one evening a week together, but most of their time was absorbed by the work on the farm. Today, however, high school students and other young people may spend several hours *daily* within a subsociety often labeled "teenage society." These young people have their own mass idols, their own music, their own clothes, their own language, their own code of ethics. In a very real sense they have created their own world.

Parents find that to buck this youth peer group is not an easy matter. More will be said about this later, but it needs to be remembered that this youth peer group is a new force in American society that parents (as well as university administrators) have to reckon with.[22] It is the writers' belief that only the more skillful and tenacious parents can challenge the youth peer group with any consistent success.

Parents today have to deal with the experts on child rearing

After World War I, psychiatry, sociology, anthropology, and psychology (the behavioral sciences) became very prominent in the United States.[23] The psychiatric casualties of the war and concern about the causes of war led the more intelligent members of our society to turn to the sciences in an effort to understand human behavior.

This development soon raised serious questions about the methods parents were using to rear their children.

Two specific threads in this new behavioral science tended to bother parents: (1) Freudian theory, which revolutionized the concept of what children were like and took the position, we believe erroneously, that what parents did (or did not do) in the first five years of the child's life would shape the person forever and (2) the conclusion of sociology and anthropology that children were born with few (if any) instincts, that their eventual behavior would essentially reflect the socialization they received (or did not receive) from their family and other social institutions. This extremely plastic view of the child frightened the more intelligent parents and left them apprehensive. Later on, if their child did not turn out well, they were saddled with guilt.

The writers feel that these new behavioral sciences have not, as yet, been of much help to parents. Much of the research has not been good enough to stand up over the years, with the result that the recommendations to parents on child-rearing methods have changed from one decade to the next.[24] This has resulted in the term *child-rearing expert* becoming almost a national joke in our society.

There were undoubtedly many different factors involved in the

developments discussed earlier, just as there were many different results—both positive and negative. But one result was that
traditional parental methods, based on hundreds of years of experience, were discarded (or at least downgraded) before a mature
and reliable science of child rearing became available. Thus, a
great many of the more progressive parents were caught between
the old and the new. To a considerable extent, this situation still
prevails.

Confusion over the nature of discipline

There has been an upsurge of interest and research in the area of
child abuse in the past decade. Child abuse, of course, is tremen-
dously important and has been overlooked far too long. A full-scale
public debate has begun over the nature of discipline. What is reasonable? What is unreasonable?

At the heart of the matter is the question as to whether or not
spanking is a useful tool in shaping children's behavior or whether it
is abusive, as some professionals assert. In fact, some have gone so
far as to say that societal acceptance of spanking is the greatest
boon our child abuse statistics could ever find, for spanking often
gets out of hand and real damage is done.

In the center of the whirlwind are parents. Most of them know that
kindness and love are the greatest tools they have in their task of
rearing children. And most of them know, also, that children are
very difficult to control and, without some way of getting their attention, they can easily run amok. Where is the balance, and what are
the disciplinary techniques to effect this balance?

The development of well-defined and practical approaches to
discipline will do a lot to end this confusion. The behaviorists, in
accentuating positive reinforcement of desirable behaviors and
substituting neutral consequences for negative ones, have made a
step in the right direction. The timeout has offered respite to many a
weary parent, for example. The child is taken out of the negative
situation and isolated for a short period until the smoke clears. In the
DeFrain household, the timeout room happens to be a very boring
bathroom where the transgressor sits for three to five minutes cool-
ing off, while mom or dad retires to living room or kitchen also to
cool off.

Until the debate includes not only philosophy but brass-tacks solutions, parents' heads will continue to swim.

Poor preparation for parental roles

In a study of young parents,[25] the first author was impressed by the frequency of the comment, "We didn't know what we were getting into." Even though this sample included only couples who had wanted a baby, the actual process of becoming parents had posed problems and stresses they had not anticipated.

It seemed to us that these couples had received very inadequate preparation for the parental role. Most of the husbands felt that they had had no preparation whatsoever for the father role, and even a majority of the wives felt that their preparation for the role of mother had been quite inadequate.

One obvious factor in this feeling of not being prepared for the parental role was the almost complete failure of our high schools and colleges to include this subject in their courses of study.

Another factor, less obvious, was that these parents had grown up in relatively small families and had had very little experience caring for younger brothers and sisters.[26]

A third factor was the existence in our culture of a very real "romantic complex" about children (especially babies) and parenthood. If you interview parents whose children are 15 to 20 years of age, they will usually admit that the parent role is perhaps the most challenging thing they have ever done in their lives—exciting, thrilling, exhausting, and (at times) heartbreaking. These are not bitter or cynical parents; they are just realistic. They remind the writers of war veterans: They find the experience unforgettable but are not enthused about doing it again.

Young parents lack any of this feeling of what parenthood involves. And when they begin to find out, they often experience a temporary state of shock or disbelief. As one young mother, an honors graduate from a famous women's college, put it to us: "I just couldn't believe that the baby could upset me the way she did. But when she cried so much during the first few weeks and the doctor couldn't find out what was wrong, I thought I would lose my mind." We have heard this story time after time.

The complexity of the parent role

In addition to not being prepared for the role of parent, many young fathers and mothers have expressed to the writers their consternation at discovering the role of parent to be more baffling and more frustrating than they had anticipated. This same sentiment is echoed by a number of writers on the family.

In a study of 571 mothers, Helena Lopata concluded that "the concern over this role (parenthood) is very high." She also states that the birth of the first child is "the event causing the greatest discontinuity in American middle-class women."[27]

A well-known student of the American family, Virginia Satir, has this to say about the role of parent: "Parenting is probably the most crucial, challenging, and interesting job for each adult engaged in it."[28]

In one of her famous analyses of American society, Margaret Mead observed that parents rear their children with "the sidewise look"—that is, they are not quite sure how they should rear their offspring so they keep a watchful eye on how other parents are bringing up their children.[29] This stance, of course, betrays insecurity and doubt on the part of these fathers and mothers.

Riesman points out that modern parents are more apprehensive than their ancestors in thinking about child rearing: "Increasingly in doubt as to how to bring up their children, parents turn to other contemporaries for advice."[30]

Robert Frost, the poet who was once rated one of the most loved men in America, had a son who committed suicide. Frost's trials as a parent are useful in elaborating on the notion of the complexity of the parent role. "I took the wrong way with him," Frost once wrote. "I tried many ways, and every single one of them was wrong. Something in me is still asking for the chance to try one more."

He also had a daughter who had to be committed to a state mental hospital. A third child, Lesley, once told him "that he was the kind of artist who should never have married, or at least who should never have had a family."[31]

And Bertrand Russell, a prolific genius of mathematics and philosophy who remained politically and intellectually active up until his death in his early 90s, noted in his autobiography that he, too, "failed as a parent and could hardly keep on advising others."

Russell had written books on marriage and child rearing and had founded a progressive school for children in his native England. His son and daughter-in-law shocked him after one Christmas dinner together. They announced they were "tired of children." Russell wrote that "They left, taking the remainder of the food, but leaving the children, and did not return." Russell, who loved children, could not understand such behavior; even though quite elderly, he and his fourth wife took the grandchildren and cared for them. How could he rear children who would desert their own? he asked himself.[32]

Comedian Bill Cosby put it so succinctly: "We decided to have children because we liked what they look like. You see 'em on TV and you say, "Ohhh, let's have one of those.' And you don't realize this is gonna be with you half your life."[33]

Finally, a five-year study on the needs of children in America sponsored by the Carnegie Corporation concluded that the plight of the American parent must be improved before the nation's children can be helped. We concur.

The study called for a national commitment to full employment and a system of income supports guaranteeing families with children a minimum income. According to the Carnegie Council on Children, the supports could be managed through a credit income tax or by modifying current support systems. The council also recommended the destruction of widespread job barriers and promotion ceilings for women and minority groups and greater use of flexible daily, weekly, and annual work schedules. The Reagan administration may halt the march of progress toward the inception of these ideas in our national policy—but only temporarily.[34]

This concludes the discussion of features of our society that the writers believe pose problems for parents.

In order to balance the picture somewhat, let us look briefly at some of the developments in contemporary America that have been supportive to fathers and mothers in this crucial role.

Positive features of American society in relationship to parents

Modern medicine

There can be no doubt that the substantial progress made in understanding and controlling childhood diseases has lifted some of the fear and agony from the hearts and shoulders of parents. One has only to remember back a few years when polio stalked the land to appreciate this type of progress.

The dramatic decline in infant mortality since 1920 has alone saved millions of parents from tragedy and despair.

As a branch of modern medicine, child psychiatry has undoubtedly helped some parents; but the writers feel that other parents have actually been damaged by the inadequate scientific base upon which psychiatric diagnoses are made.

Greater affluence in the society

In an urban society, parenthood is an expensive business. Since more parents have more money in the 1980s than ever before in our society, they should be in a better position to finance their child-rearing efforts.

This is undoubtedly true, yet only a few interviews with affluent parents are needed to uncover some of the hazards of this affluence. One father said to the first author: "It worries me that kids today get almost everything they want just by asking for it. My wife and I have tried not to spoil our children, yet I am afraid they have not learned the value of a dollar. Things come too easy for them these days." This father had grown up in a family of modest means and was concerned that some of the lessons he had learned as a child were being denied his children.[35]

Better means of contraception

Obviously, modern means of contraception have been a great boon to parents—or potential parents. But it has been estimated that more than one out of three couples using a method of birth control will face an unplanned pregnancy in spite of medical advances.[36] When we think of the problems parents often experience when their child was wanted and planned for, one can only imagine the consequences when a child is unwanted. We've personally seen enough cases of infant and child abuse after unplanned pregnancy to believe it to be quite common, especially with younger parents.

Miscellaneous positive factors

Most American parents are no longer immigrants reared in a society quite different from the one in which they are trying to rear their children.[37] Most of the fathers and mothers today have another advantage in that they grew up in an urban community; they are not migrants from the farm trying to rear their sons and daughters in the strange world of the city.[38]

Striking exceptions can be found to this statement—southern black parents recently moved to the urban jungles of the North and the West; southern rural whites from Appalachia and elsewhere trying to make a new start in Chicago or Detroit or some other city where the jobs are supposed to be; American Indians resettled in Chicago or Denver or some other city; anxious workers and their families migrating to Alaska and the often elusive bounty of the North Slope oil boom; Puerto Rican and Cuban parents trying to make the long jump from the island to the mainland; and Vietnamese making a quantum leap from Southeast Asia to the United States. These parents and their problems are very real and very dramatic, but they comprise a relatively small proportion of all American parents.[39]

Most fathers and mothers today have more education than their parents had—and in a society that places so much stress on formal education, one would like to think that this should be an advantage.

Some general observations

Earlier in the chapter, the point was made that modern America lacks consensus-based, clearly articulated age-grading steps, which would define for both young people and their parents the specific point in the maturation cycle occupied by the child at any given time. When such age grading exists, for example, that children enter the first grade at six years of age, the parent and the child both know what the next step in growth consists of and when it will occur. An even better example, mentioned earlier, is the legal age of driving an automobile, a step clearly enunciated in most of the 50 states.

Based on the writers' personal experiences as parents and on interviews with other parents, situations of this nature which have been clearly defined appear to produce relatively little conflict between parents and their children. But in many other areas, such as dating and the hours to be observed in dating, there seems to exist considerable leeway and variation in many local communities. This produces a situation in which parents and young people must bargain and haggle. This, in itself, may be desirable, but it places parents who do not possess great skill in handling their children at a considerable disadvantage. In an ideal social system, even the average person can manage his role assignments—this is the plan for most armed-forces units, for example—but the absence of age grading sets up situations that only the superior parent can manage.

Another observation that might be pertinent at this point is the fragmentation of family functions in our society. Other social institutions, such as the school, have been expanding their responsibilities since World War I, which means that it is not always clear whether parents or teachers (or somebody else) are supposed to do certain things for children.[40] A good example of this may be found in the area of sex education: In some school systems young people are given excellent courses in human reproduction, the part that sex plays in marriage, and other aspects of human sexuality. In such communities, the function of parents in sex education might be limited to the inculcation and/or discussion of values. But, in other communities, the parent would have to assume the entire responsibility for sex education—or else concede it to the adolescent peer group and the mass media.

Contrast the confused state of sex education in American society with that in Sweden, which has a uniform nationwide compulsory sex education program for all school children from the first grade through secondary school.[41]

The transfer of functions from the family to some other social organization does not necessarily represent social decline, nor does it foretell the demise of the American family. Soap was once made in the home, for example, whereas today it is usually purchased at a store. We doubt that this transfer accounts for the current divorce rate. Such transfer of functions, however, does produce a more specialized type of family, as Jesse Pitts has pointed out.[42]

One of the reasons why many parents feel inadequate in contemporary America is the pervasive nature of negative news stories about fathers and mothers. One seldom reads or hears or sees any items about successful parents—we only know about those that have failed. It is as if the only business news available would be that about firms that have gone bankrupt, whereas, in truth, most of the news about private corporations in our society today tells how successful they have been in the current year.

A few outstanding newspapers, such as the *Christian Science Monitor*, still make a determined effort to report positive news about the American family, but, for the most part, the stories about parents and their children in the mass media are tragic and sad. They may make some parents feel superior, but it hardly encourages most of us to think that we are on a winning team.

A recent example in our own experience comes to mind. Nick Stinnett, Greg Sanders, Karen Strand, and the second author recently completed a nationwide study of strong families, focusing on success in marriage and parenthood, rather than failure. A writer for a national magazine called up to find out what the latest devel-

opments were in our various research projects. We mentioned studies on divorce, death in the family, and the strong families project, a
major undertaking with more than 300 families involved all over the
United States. The reporter jumped at the divorce study and wrote it
up quickly; the strong family study sparked no interest whatsoever.
"New York's not interested in *that!*" was the remark. Our faith in
"New York's" judgment was reestablished a few weeks later when
reporters from *Ladies' Home Journal*, *Families*, and *Redbook*,
among many others, saw the importance of a focus on family
strengths and wrote articles.[43]

Constants and variables in parenthood

In the paper by Davis,[44] a distinction is made between the con-
stants (or universals) in parenthood and the variables (factors found
only in certain societies at specific periods in history). An example of
a constant would be the physiological differences found between
the parent and child—the fact that each is at a different stage of
physical growth or decline but yet must accommodate him or herself to the other. This would be true of parenthood in any society,
and yet social factors might still be operative to some extent: Persons
age faster in most so-called primitive societies than in most modern
societies, and attitudes toward aging also vary from one culture to
another.

An example of a variable would be social change: not only its
rate but also its depth would vary from one society to another and
from one historical period to another within the same society.

In this book we are primarily concerned with the variables in
parenthood: the particular characteristics of our society that seem to
affect the role of father and mother.

To some extent parenthood in any society is probably traumatic
for both parent and child—at least this seems to be the point of
Lewis Feuer, who comments: "The conflict of generations is a universal theme in history."[45]

But as one harried modern father noted to us: "It's interesting to
learn that kids have baffled parents for millions of years. But I personally, today, in the here-and-now, still don't know what to do
about it!"

Indeed.

Chapter 2

Folklore about parenthood

Some years ago Thurman Arnold wrote a very interesting and provocative book called *The Folklore of Capitalism.*[1] In this study Arnold analyzed folk beliefs or myths about the American economy. His thesis was that capitalism in the United States had changed so drastically in the last century that hardly any of the traditional theories about it were relevant any more—and yet they were constantly being quoted by persons who opposed any change in the government's economic policies.

In later years John Kenneth Galbraith has taken up where Arnold left off and uses the term *conventional wisdom* to describe beliefs about American society that he regards as erroneous.[2]

The clinical psychologist Albert Ellis has also used this approach in analyzing American attitudes and beliefs about sex.[3]

In a previous book about the American courtship and marriage systems the first author made extensive use of the concept of folklore.[4]

The reception of the Arnold and Galbraith books leads one to believe that this type of analysis is interesting and worthwhile.

In this chapter an attempt will be made to analyze folk beliefs about parenthood. In any civilization there is always a large body of folk belief about anything very important. As the term *folklore* or *folk belief* is used here, it means widely held beliefs that are not supported by the facts. Usually, these beliefs tend to romanticize the

21

truth, although in some cases the reverse might be true. Reality might not be as bad as the folk belief would imply.

It is the writers' contention that persons living in modern civilizations are apt to think they do not believe in folklore, whereas in actual fact they do. Thus, they are apt to think their behavior is based on sound rational principles when in reality it is not.

The approach will be to state the folk belief and then to subject it and its implications to systematic analysis.

Rearing children is fun. No one can teach high school or college courses on the family without being impressed by this belief that rearing children is fun. It derives from the notion that "children are cute" (to be analyzed later). Young people are often heard to say: "Oh I just cannot wait to have children." The odd thing is that parents do not talk that way. This leads one to the conclusion that this belief reflects folklore and has no substantial basis in reality.

The truth is—as every parent knows—that rearing children is probably the hardest, and most thankless, job in the world. No intelligent father or mother would deny that it is *exciting* as well as interesting, but to call it fun is a serious error. The idea of something being fun implies that you can take it or leave it, whereas parents do not have this choice. Fathers and mothers must stay with the child and keep trying, whether it is fun, or whether they are enjoying it or not. Any comparison to bowling, listening to jazz records, or sex is strictly coincidental.

In the words of Dorothy Rodgers, the wife of the composer Richard Rodgers: "It's true, I think, as a wise friend told me, that parenthood is a one-way river: parents give and children take. The love of a parent for a child is often the most generous, giving and unselfish love there is."[5]

And, in the wry words of family therapist Frank Farrelly, the child's response is: "Gimmie! Lemmie! Iwanna!"[6]

We do not mean to deny that a great many parents enjoy their work and that they derive satisfaction from it. But to describe what parents do as fun is to miss the point. It would be like describing the sweat and tears involved in the artist's creation as fun. The life of Thomas Wolfe or that of almost any serious artist will convey the point.[7]

Brooke Hayward has an interesting way of helping us make our point: "One sleepless night when I was 13 or 14 . . . I finally accepted the idea that being a parent might be worse than being a child."[8]

Now that his military service is well in the past, the first author of this book can truthfully say that he enjoyed his years in the U.S. Naval Air Corps and that he would not have wanted to miss the experience. But it is also true that on almost any day of those three years he would have accepted his immediate discharge had it been offered. This feeling is very common to the millions of men who served in the armed forces during World War II (or any other war, for that matter). We think the sentiment also describes very accurately the feelings of millions of fathers and mothers.

The truth is somewhat as follows: Rearing children is hard work; it is often nerve-racking work; it involves tremendous responsibility; it takes all the ability one has (and more); and once you have begun you cannot quit when you feel like it. It would be helpful to young parents if they could be made to realize all of this before they enlist—or before they are drafted, as the case may be.

In pursuing the analogy between military service and parenthood, the writers have often heard parents refer to married couples who have no children as draft dodgers. The sentiment is similar to that which veterans of the armed forces have toward able-bodied men who somehow escaped military service in the last war (any last war will do). The veteran feels that military service is a rough experience but that it has to be endured for the sake of the country; his feeling toward men who did not have this experience is ambivalent. In a sense he resents their escaping what he had to go through, but in another sense he recognizes that there may have been valid reasons why they were not in the armed forces.

This does not mean, however, that most parents regret having had children any more than it means that veterans regret having served their country. Of course, we do not hear much from the men who were killed or maimed in the wars, and we also do not hear too much from parents who have suffered much the same fate rearing their children.

Kenneth Kenniston says it so well:

> . . . The parent today is usually a coordinator without voice or authority, a maestro trying to conduct an orchestra of players who have never met and who play from a multitude of different scores, each in notation the conductor cannot read. If parents are frustrated, it is no wonder: for although they have the responsibility for their children's

lives, they hardly ever have the voice, or the power to make others listen to them.[9]

Children are sweet and cute.   When young people see small children they are apt to remark: "Your children are so cute!" It is true, of course, that small children *are* cute (at times), but this hardly exhausts the subject—or the adjectives parents use to describe their children when they are *not* being cute. Think back on the other adjectives you have heard used commonly to describe children, some endearing, some impairing.

Several years ago the first author published the results of a study of young parents entitled "Parenthood as Crisis."[10] This report stated that parents in our society have a romantic complex about child rearing and that they tend to suffer from a process of disenchantment after they become parents. When this study was summarized in the *New York Times,* a flood of mail descended on the writer from parents, with the vast bulk of it agreeing with the findings of the study. The response to this paper led the writer to feel that he had struck a responsive chord in the collective bosom of American fathers and mothers.[11]

Children will turn out well if they have "good" parents.   Logically, this should be so, and one would certainly like to believe that it is so. For that matter, it probably is *usually* a correct statement—but not always. Almost everyone knows of at least one nice family with a black sheep in the fold. It seems to be a rare family, indeed, that has not had some tragic experience with at least one child (assuming the family consists of several children).

It would be comforting to think that parents can guarantee happiness and success (the twin gods of our civilization), but the sad truth is that they cannot. Children are so complex and so different, and out society is so complicated, that fathers and mothers simply do not have the quality control one finds in industrial production. Parents with skill and ability, of course, probably have a better batting average than those of us with more modest talents—but even the good parents do not bat a thousand.

Someone has observed that marriage is perhaps the only game of chance at which both players can lose.[12] It might be that rearing children should be added to this list.

It would be fascinating and interesting (and perhaps frightening) to know what the actual success and failure rate is in rearing children in modern America. The writers have seen no respectable research (including their own) which would answer this question, and in a certain sense it cannot be answered because the terms are so hard to define.[13] When has a parent been successful with any given child? At what age do we judge the product—adolescence, early adulthood, middle age, or the life span? Do we include material success, physical health, mental health, spiritual health, or what?

One strategy for answering these difficult questions bears repeating though. Nick Stinnett, Greg Sanders, John DeFrain, and Karen Strand carefully studied more than 300 families nationwide who perceived their marriage and parent-child relationships to be positive. These strong families volunteered to a request in newspapers across the country, and when asked what qualities made for a strong family commonly responded with the following:

1. Appreciation.
2. Communication.
3. Commitment.
4. Spending time together.
5. Religion.
6. Positive coping with stress and crisis.

To see what percentage of parents in the United States perceive they have strong parent-child relationships, in essence, that they are successful in parenting, researchers could compare a random sample of American parents with the 300 families in our strong family study. This would be a laborious task, but useful.[14]

In an extremely unscientific manner, the first writer has surveyed a few families, with very sobering results. Winston Churchill and his wife, for example, appear to have been successful with only two of their children, yet both of these parents were remarkably successful in the other areas of life.[15] Franklin D. and Eleanor Roosevelt, certainly two of the most loved and revered Americans of the modern era, seem to have been only moderately successful in rearing their children—and this appraisal comes from Democrats, not Republicans.[16]

It is true that such families have most unusual family stresses because of the heavy burden carried by the father and mother in discharging their many public responsibilities, but the writers have also studied some families at very modest social levels with somewhat similar results. We know many people who feel they have completely failed as parents. Others report partial failure: some of their children are okay, others are hopeless. But in all cases, we counsel caution; it is best to reserve judgment. Progress comes slowly in the world, and it may be a while before a child comes around. The second author's seventh-grade science teacher years ago was Henry Goebel, and dear old Mr. Goebel has the best advice of all.

Goebel retired a few years ago after teaching more than 40 years. He worked with literally thousands of youngsters and hundreds of their parents.

"Mr. Goebel, Mr. Goebel, we just don't know what to do with Johnny," anxious parents would say to the wise old educator.

"Wait a year," he would reply without flinching. Ninety percent of the problems would disappear in a year's time (or be replaced by new problems), and only 10 percent of the parents would dutifully report to Mr. Goebel for further advice.

"Mr. Goebel, Mr. Goebel, we waited a year like you said and we still don't know what to do with Johnny."

"Wait another," Henry Goebel would say with quiet determination.

Children improve marriage.   It would be nice to think so, but the research available does not support the belief. In his study of divorced women, Goode did not find that children had improved these marriages.[17] In a study of 852 middle- and upper-class parents, Rollins and Feldman found that only 18 percent of the husbands and wives reported higher levels of marital satisfaction after parenthood.[18] In an extensive review of the research on this belief, Charles Figley concludes: "A dramatic decrease in marital adjustment and marital communication occurs during the child-rearing period."[19] Norval Glenn and Sara McLanahan studied the effects of the presence of children on their parents' marital happiness with data from six U.S. national surveys. The researchers, in addition, looked at a number of important subpopulations of parents in these surveys: blacks and whites; males and females; highly educated people versus people with low levels of education; Catholics versus non-Catholics; women employed full time outside the home versus other women; and people who ideally wanted a lot of children versus people who wanted few children. The researchers found no evidence for positive average effects of children on the marriages of any of these subpopulations. "On the average children adversely

affect marital quality," the researchers concluded.[20] In his study of
fatherhood Leonard Benson decided that: "There is no evidence to
suggest that having children improves or enhances a couple's ability to handle marriage problems."[21] Jessie Bernard is quoted as having said: "Children rarely make for added happiness between husband and wife."[22] As S. M. Miller, the behavioral scientist, said:
". . . We had amazing naiveté about the impact of having children—a naivete, incidentally, that I see today having a similarly
devastating effect on many young parents. We just had no idea how
much time and emotion children captured, how they simply
changed a couple's lives. . . ."[23]

If you rear them right, they will stay right. This may have been
true in an earlier period of American history but it seems dubious
today. Forrest S. Tennant, a doctoral student in the School of Public
Health at UCLA, studied 5,000 American service men in Europe in
1971 in an attempt to determine whether being a Boy Scout, and
honor student, or an athlete in earlier years had any relationship to
later addiction to alcohol or drugs. He was disillusioned with his
findings. "I was hoping to come up with some recipes for parents,"
he said, "but it didn't turn out that way."[24] A lot of parents would
agree with him.

A mother said to the first author: "I am a devout Roman Catholic.
I took my four children to church every week for 15 years and not
one of them is a good Catholic today." In another interview a father
said: "My wife and I have never used alcohol and have never
served it in our home. We thought that if we set a good example, our
children wouldn't drink. Now, all four of them go to taverns and bars
and our oldest son has been diagnosed as an alcoholic. How do you
explain that?"

**The nature of the child being reared is really not very impor-
tant—good parents can manage any child.** Three psychiatrists,
after careful research, have concluded that this is a myth. In their
book, *Your Child Is a Person,* Stella Chess, Alexander Thomas, and
Herbert Birch report that the temperament of the particular child is
one of the crucial factors in successful or unsuccessful parental role
performance. It is interesting that the subtitle of this book is: "A
Psychological Approach to Parenthood without Guilt."[25]

Julius Segal and Herbert Yahraes argue that Wordsworth's observation that the child is father to the man should be a caution to

modern parents. In their article "Bringing Up Mother" they point out that babies, with their extremely different temperaments, often train parents as much as parents shape them. In fact, we'd love to see, for example, a study of the relationship between colic and child abuse. It is a grisly experience to hear an anguished parent's descriptions of the emotions which wrench one when an infant cries uncontrollably for three, four, even five hours at a time.[26]

Truly, think of all the other special children in the world and how their needs can change the lives of parents. Lynn Wikler, for example, does an excellent job outlining the "Chronic Stress of Families of Mentally Retarded Children." It is almost impossible to imagine what it must feel like to be faced with the probability that one will be involved in very basic level parenting tasks for the rest of his or her life.[27]

Myth:

Today's parents are not as good as those of yesterday. It is impossible to prove or disprove this sort of belief, of course, but it does seem to be prevalent. The truth is, as shown elsewhere in this study,[28] that standards applied to parents today have been raised, and it is also true that the laboratory in which parents have to operate (the modern world) has become infinitely more complex. All this tends to create the impression that parents as a group have deteriorated since the good old days of the 18th or 19th century. This sort of argument is usually clinched (at least to the satisfaction of the critic) by reference to the family of John Adams or Thomas Jefferson. Actually, nobody knows what most parents were like in the old days, but if we can compare them to what doctors and other practitioners of the era were like, it seems possible that they were not supermen or superwomen, but just plain fathers and mothers sweating out every child.

There is always a tendency to romanticize the past, and this seems to have done a very real disservice to modern parents.[29] Thumbing through books on life on the plains and prairies a century ago can be instructive. Invariably there will be a picture or two of a sod house in Kansas, Nebraska, or the Dakotas. The soddie will have a garden, mostly weeds, growing on the dirt roof; a cow may be up there on top munching away, too. The surroundings are unimaginably bleak. No trees or water; just dirt, dust, wind, and sun. The captions under the pictures are usually pretty predictable: "The Jones family on their farm in 1878: Jacob, his wife Emma, their 14 children, their cow Bessie, and a hired man." The children back in the days before planned parenthood are too numerous to name. Everyone in the picture is grim faced; each has "tombstones in his eyes." Winter is coming soon, and all 17 will be cooped up in the one-room dwelling for the better part of four or five months. Could anyone today sincerely believe that child abuse rates back then were less than now?

Childless couples are frustrated and unhappy. This may have been true in the 19th century or the early decades of the 20th century when fertility was more or less a cultural neurosis—but if it was true then, it is certainly not true now. Actually, the very early studies of marital satisfaction by Ernest Burgess and Leonard Cottrell, also by Burgess and Paul Wallin, failed to support this belief: some of the highest scores on the marital satisfaction scales used in these studies were made by childless couples.[30]

Parenthood in the 1980s is at last becoming a matter of choice—a man doesn't have to become a father today to prove his virility and a woman doesn't have to become a mother to prove her humanity. It seems to us that this is a step in the right direction.[31]

You shouldn't stop with just one. Folk wisdom dictates that only children are lonely and spoiled. Ellen Peck writes in *The Joy of the Only Child* that contrary to these beliefs, only children are brighter, get along better with their peers, and are less spoiled.[32]

Judith Blake examined family size and the quality of children. For the purposes of her research, she defined quality as educational attainment among adults and college plans among youngsters. She found that her research supports the so-called dilution model (in the average family, the more children means the lower quality of each child in terms of educational attainment and college plans). Further, she found that children do not suffer in this realm of quality from the lack of siblings, and that last-borns are not handicapped by a "teaching deficit."[33]

Sharryl Hawke and David Knox take a balanced view of the situation. They studied only children and their parents and found both advantages and disadvantages to such a family style. The advantages include less financial expense and emotional demands on the parents, and more possessions, opportunities, and parental attention for the children. The disadvantages include parents' feelings of giving too much attention and protection to the child, and the child's feelings of loneliness and need for more companionship.[34]

There are no bad children—only bad parents. This, in the opinion of the writers, is one of the most destructive bits of folklore relating to parenthood. As Max Lerner points out, parents have become the bad guys in modern America, while children and teachers and other custodians and child-shapers (such as the television station owners) have become the good guys.[35] And, just as on television, the bad guys always lose.

Actually, Orville Brim has analyzed a rather lengthy list of factors other than parents which affect the destinies of children.[36] These include genetic factors; siblings; members of the extended family, such as grandparents; schoolteachers; playmates; the youth peer group; and so on. He concludes that parents have been held unduly responsible for shaping the destiny of their offspring.

Lerner takes the position that parental critics tend to be "child worshippers"—the child can do no wrong, all children are potentially perfect (or near perfect), and parents should be able to rear *any* child successfully if they only knew enough and tried hard enough.[37]

The writers are inclined to the view that some children are doomed almost from the point of birth: Try as they will, their parents seem destined to fail in their efforts to solve the various problems that arise during the child-rearing process. In an earlier America this was conceptualized as fate, but in contemporary America there is no such thing as fate; fate is just another word for poor parental role performance. It seems to us that this is folklore or mythology. It is also very unfair to parents who have made valiant efforts to help their children attain a decent and productive life.

We believe that it is most illogical to view children as good while indicting their parents as bad. In our work with abusive or neglectful parents, we have yet to meet someone currently doing a poor job as a parent who did not as a child have parents who did a poor job rearing them. Rather than blame parents for their failures, we find it much more useful to help them learn new ways to success. One middle-aged black woman comes to mind here: "Two of the kids turned out pretty good," she summarized for us, after telling a long tale of a hard, hard life for her which began in the worked-out farmlands of southern Mississippi in the Depression and was ending up in a lower-class neighborhood in a northern city. She had endured poverty, racism, hunger, and lack of education. "And," she added, "two of the kids just aren't amounting to nothing."

Was it her fault? Did she fail as a parent? we asked intensely, leaning toward her.

"I don't know. Maybe. But I always tried. And always did the best I knew how."

That, to us, is not failure.

Parents are adults. This bit of folklore might depend on the definition of the word *adult*, but the fact is that more than 22 percent of teenage girls in the United States bear a child before their 20th birthday.[38]

One teenage mother said to us: "My husband and I are just kids. We're growing up with the baby." This experiment may turn out well, but it frightens most child-development specialists.

Children today really appreciate all the advantages their parents are able to give them. Oddly enough, the reverse seems to be true: Children today are less appreciative and not more so. Numerous observers of the American family have come to this conclusion.[39]

College students are very frank about this: They regard what they have received as their *right* and not as something to be thankful for.[40]

In a sense, this same sort of psychology is characteristic of all of us living in the modern world; we take for granted inside toilets, painless dentistry, and religious freedom and simply complain when the system fails to deliver what we have come to consider our birthright. Thus, parents derive very little satisfaction from giving children all the modern advantages—they only feel guilty when they *cannot* deliver the goods.

The hard work of rearing children is justified by the fact that the children will make a better world. This is a consoling thought, and one that most parents need desperately to believe, but there is very little evidence to sustain it. It has more to do with hope than reality. Whether one looks at crime or alcoholism rates or the prospects of peace in the modern world, the picture is not encouraging.

One can always hope, of course, that the new generation will be braver, wiser, and happier than their parents have been. It is dubious, however, that this will prove to be true.[41]

The sex education myth: children will not get into trouble if they have been told the facts of life. One mother said to us: "I do not see how such a thing (premarital pregnancy) could have happened to our daughter. She has known where babies come from since she was six years old."

This indicates how naïve some parents in our society are about the mystical power of sex education, which, at best, usually covers only the physiology of reproduction. Nothing is said about passion or seduction or the role of unconscious factors in heterosexual interaction. It seems to be assumed by such parents that sex is always a cold calculating act—as if Freud had never written a word to the contrary.[42]

The truth is that much (if not most) human sexual behavior is nonrational and only partly subject to continuous intellectual control. If this were not the case, illegitimate pregnancies in our society would be much fewer than they are and research data on adultery would be less massive.[43]

A great many human societies, such as the Latin cultures, have always assumed that sex was too powerful for most humans to control, and they therefore arranged that persons for whom sexual relations were taboo were never left alone together.[44] Our society is relatively unique in that we have adopted just the opposite policy— at least for single persons: They are permitted (and even expected) to spend hundreds of hours alone without ever having sex relations until they marry. Research tells us, of course, that considerable proportions of them do have sexual relations before marriage, but only relatively few ever get pregnant. Or if they get pregnant, they marry before the birth of the child.[45]

The writers believe in sex education and think it belongs in every school and college curriculum, also in every family. But one should not expect too much of sexual knowledge. Attitudes, values, passion, and a host of factors determine the sexual behavior of any person at any given time with a particular partner. It could well be that the art of seduction has as much to do with premarital sexual relations as sex education does. Certainly the subconscious and unconscious factors analyzed by Freudians have to be taken into account in understanding why people behave the way they do sexually.

Parenthood receives top priority in our society. This is a choice bit of folklore. Ask any employee if the company gives priority to his role as parent when they need a person in another branch in a different city. As a matter of fact, parenthood in American society has always had to defer to military and industrial needs, to say nothing about other community needs. Millions of fathers and mothers have to sandwich their parental role into niches between their other roles in the society.

The wife of a famous authority on the family once said to the first author: "My husband would have made a wonderful father, but he was never home when the children were young. He was always away making speeches on how people should solve their marital problems or rear their children. I took care of the children myself."

A divorced mother with three children put it this way: "My employer couldn't care less about my duties as a mother. The state requires me to be at work at 7:45 which means that I have to leave home an hour before the children go to school. Then I have to work until 4:30, so that the children are out of school over an hour before I get home. And when the schools are closed, I usually have to work because they won't give me time off. Don't tell me parenthood comes first in our society."

Love is enough to guarantee good parental performance. Bruno Bettelheim, one of the authorities on child rearing, says that love is not enough.[46] His main point is that love has to be guided by knowledge and insight and also tempered with self-control on the part of the parent.

It is quite possible, however, that the reverse proposition is true: that no amount of scientific or professional knowledge about child development will do parents (or their children) any good unless it is mixed with love for the child and acceptance of the parental role.

For example, the second author and his wife Nikki managed with their first daughter Amie's consent to get the child potty trained by age 31 months. Neither John nor Nikki at the time had any particular training in child rearing and picked up tips on a hit-or-miss basis. Seven years later, when second daughter Alyssa was born, the couple was loaded for bear: John was now armed with four years of experience in early childhood education and a Ph.D. in family studies, focusing on parent education and child development; Nikki had completed her training in early childhood education and had a bachelor's degree in human development. The DeFrains concentrated about $30,000 worth of education on the task of potty training Alyssa, and by age 28 months Alyssa succumbed.

In sum, it cost the DeFrains $30,000 to save changing diapers for three months. That's roughly $500 per diaper.

By the time daughter number three, Erica, came around, the DeFrains had completely given up. "Don't push the river," as the book title notes. Erica followed her big sister Alyssa around like a puppy most of the time. By the time Erica was 24 months old, four-year-old Alyssa had taught Erica how to use the toilet.

In a speech at the University of Iowa the first author argued that in his opinion most parents who fail as parents actually love their children—they fail in spite of their love.[47]

The one-parent family is pathogenic. No one would deny that it is helpful to have both a father and a mother in the home when children are growing up—this assumes, however, that the two parents are compatible and share the same philosophy of child rearing. In view of the rate of marital failure in our society, this statement is a large assumption.

But has it been proven that children cannot grow up properly in a one-parent family? In a careful review of hundreds of studies of children, Kadushin reached this conclusion: "The association between single-parent familyhood and psychosocial pathology is neither strong nor invariable."[48] Kadushin's main finding was that our society is not properly organized for the one-parent family—our social institutions were designed for the two-parent family system.

In a study of Head Start children, Aldous did not find significant differences in perception of adult male and female roles between the father-present and the father-absent children when race and social class variables were controlled.[49]

It does seem well established, however, that the chances of a child being in the so-called poverty group are significantly higher in our society when the father is absent.[50]

Parenthood ends when children leave home. It doesn't, of course. The out-of-sight, out-of-mind phenomenon does tend to help though; if you don't *know* that the kids are out late at night at a rock 'n' roll concert and that they're probably drinking or stoned, you can probably sleep better. Getting the young adults out of the nest certainly helps in this regard. But they still usually keep coming back: for money, to have their clothes washed, for advice and consolation, and so on. Parents are still giving more, and children are still receiving more for a long, long time after the nest empties.

To complicate matters, we have what some now are calling the reverse empty-nest syndrome. The children, after a stint in the real world, make a beeline for home. They come home after suffering a divorce; or they come home after college and spend several months hunting up a job while living off mom and dad again; or they get that job and get laid off and they're back again.

This leads to problems. The parents are getting adjusted to the freedom of childlessness. They can sleep through the night soundly, not half-expecting a call like one mother got:

"Mom?"

"Yeah, I guess it's me. But I can't tell for sure this late at night. What's the matter?"

"I got hit by a freight train."

"Oh. . . ."

It seems the young adult went through a railroad crossing a bit thoughtlessly and was broadsided by a 113-car coal train. Somehow he managed to climb free unscathed from his demolished clunker.

A popular writer was in Lincoln recently discussing the possibility of writing a book with the second author on the reverse empty nest. It seems she had just experienced it and was interested in exploring the issues with other parents. She happened to sit down with a very famous politician's wife during a conference and noted she was thinking of doing the book.

"Oh, Lord," the woman moaned. "Our boy just got a divorce and moved back home with us in Washington, and we're going crazy trying to cope!"

The empty-nest syndrome plagues many parents. Psychiatrists coined this delicious term to describe parents, usually mothers, who suffer from the debilitating sadness of losing the little birds to the world. It is certainly true that some parents despair over losing their young and wonder what they will now do besides rearing children to bring meaning into their lives. But researchers in family studies have modified this picture for us. As we mentioned earlier in this chapter, family life satisfaction does drop off rapidly with the advent of children. Researchers who follow parents longer into their middle and later years find that the satisfaction curve on the average rises after the children leave home. The pain of losing the young to the world for most parents apparently is more than adequately offset by the newfound freedom from responsibility. And as parents progress into the retirement years and become grandparents, satisfaction increases even more so. When our students study the results of these investigations they often wonder out loud if they should have children at all.[51]

Our reply: most people don't regret it in the long run. But don't go into this job starry-eyed.

And, finally, parents alone should rear the young. Actually, we believe the responsibility is far too great for two people or, increasingly, one person. If we do not have a legal mandate for community responsibility for children, we certainly have an ethical one.

We obviously are not advocating that all the children be shipped off immediately to a huge collective farm and daycare center somewhere out beyond the Salt Flats of Utah next to an MX missile site. But, in an important sense, we are all "our brothers' and sisters' keepers." It is healthy to have our children have contact with many other people: grandparents, friends, church people, and many more.

Margaret Mead put it so well shortly before she died. She argued that good care for children is unlikely to be given by adults "who find no meaning to life beyond the purchase of equity in a suburban house from which their children will move away, leaving their lives, once narrowly devoted to their own children alone, empty and meaningless."

If we are to change the situation, she argued, society will have to be restructured into communities in which the childless also have a responsibility for children and where parents see beyond the needs of their own biological or adopted children.

Today, she said,

> There is a proliferation of zoned, closed communities in which families with large numbers of children are excluded in various ways because, owing to the way in which school taxes are collected, poor families with children represent a burden to the childless affluent.
>
> The very necessary campaign in favor of zero population growth has carried with it—in many contexts—a rejection of parenthood and a rejection of children themselves; unwanted children have been classified as a kind of pollution.

All adults must take the responsibility for children, she argued.

> Children seen at a distance are at best only wards or stepchildren—provided for out of guilt or sentimentality requiring no genuine personal effort.

Only by involving adults, all adults—adults who have never had children and adults whose children have grown up—can we hope to combine reform in the care of specific groups of children—deaf children, crippled children, orphaned children, abandoned children— with a genuine attempt to rethink the ways our towns and cities are built and the way our lives are lived.[52]

So be it.

This completes our discussion of the folk beliefs surrounding parenthood in American society. The list could be expanded almost indefinitely but perhaps enough has been said to make the point.

Research on parenthood folklore

In 1972 Leslie Johnson of San Diego State College administered a questionnaire on myths (or folk beliefs) to 193 expectant parents (114 women and 79 men).[53] Three of the findings struck us as interesting: 68 percent of the respondents agreed with the statement: "Man has an inborn desire to have children"; 69 percent agreed with the statement: "Children are not born with problems, parents create them"; and 78 percent agreed with the statement: "If a parent prepares his child for the future, then the child will have the necessary resources to cope effectively with most eventualities." We submit that the respondents who agreed with these statements have been brainwashed—they are victims of folklore and mythology.

The social function of folklore about parenthood

It is a truism in sociology that one of the functional imperatives of any society (or social group) is that of replacement: the production and training of the people who will make tomorrow possible.[54] Along with defense of the group from attack, the replacement function is indispensable.

It follows that every society makes sure that reproduction (parenthood) will take place. Most societies, in addition, try to make sure that persons will only reproduce in some approved fashion—usually through some system of marriage. According to George Murdock, random reproduction is approved or permitted in very few human societies.[55]

When a societal function is relatively rigorous, as parenthood seems to be in our society, a rich ethos or romantic folklore evolves to assure that the role is not avoided by most adults. This can be seen in relationship to military service: The tremendous burden of bearing arms is made more palatable to people by the parades, the bands, the speeches about "serving your country," and the culture complex associated with patriotism. In the 1960s all of this was not enough to get many young men to volunteer to go to Vietnam, and the society has experienced a crisis as the result.

The main point here is that parenthood is so surrounded by myth and folklore that most parents do not actually know what they are getting into until they are already fathers and mothers. This creates many problems when the role proves to be more frustrating than they had expected. The lowered birth rate of the 1970s and 1980s seems to indicate that the mystique surrounding parenthood is not working as well as it did in earlier decades.

Summary and conclusion

In this chapter we have been considering some of the folk beliefs (or myths) that cluster about parenthood in our society. It is not difficult to understand why these beliefs should exist. They tend to sustain parents in what is at best a very difficult and often discouraging job; furthermore, they explain (or seek to explain) many of the mysteries that the experts have not been able to explain to the satisfaction of most parents. These beliefs in some instances represent tradition, while in other instances they represent so-called scientific fact.

Given the inadequate state of knowledge about parenthood and child rearing in our society, it is not surprising that otherwise intelligent fathers and mothers are found harboring folk beliefs and scientific fallacies about parenthood and child rearing. The fact remains, however, that some of these beliefs can be harmful at times and can damage the morale of conscientious parents. Some of the case studies in later chapters should illuminate this point.

Chapter 3

Parents and the behavioral sciences

Benjamin Spock, Dr. Spock to the countless millions who have followed his advice, is the acknowledged forerunner when it comes to influence as a professional focusing on child rearing. His book, *Baby and Child Care*, has gone through umpteen editions, and it is said that more copies of that volume have been sold than any other book, except the *Bible*. (The *Bible*, of course, doesn't count in this competition because it was co-authored.)

Anyway, Spock's words are a fitting beginning to our chapter on parents and the behavioral sciences:

> The first observation I have to make about child rearing in recent years is that a great many of our efforts as professionals to help parents have instead complicated the life of parents—especially the conscientious and highly sensitive parents. It has made them somewhat timid with their children—hesitant to be firm. They are a little scared of their children because they feel as parents they are being judged by their neighbors, relatives, and the world on how well they succeed. They are scared of doing the wrong thing. Many will say, "I'm so inexperienced that I'm afraid that I'll do wrong more often than I'll do right."[1]

In this chapter an attempt will be made to assess the impact of the behavioral sciences on American parents. The disciplines of sociology, psychology, psychiatry, and anthropology are included in the analysis.

The basic thesis presented is that parents have not really derived much help or encouragement from the behavioral sciences. On the contrary, it seems to the writers that fathers and mothers have been left feeling more confused, more guilty, and more inadequate by the incomplete and often contradictory findings of these disciplines.

The procedure will be to examine, first, the impact of sociology, psychology, and anthropology on parents, with a separate section on psychiatry after that. Some specific examples of inadequate behavioral science and its impact on parents will also be presented.

The impact of sociology, psychology, and anthropology on modern American parents

For more than half a century, beginning roughly in the 1920s, the social and behavioral sciences have become a major force in America. Literally thousands of sociologists, psychologists, psychiatrists, social workers, educators, child-development specialists, and anthropologists have been studying children and drawing conclusions about their parents. Their findings have appeared in a vast stream of books, magazine articles, professional journals, and newspaper stories.[2] One can hardly read a magazine or newspaper today without seeing at least one article on child rearing and/or parents. One study of a random sample of parents in a Texas community found that 96.9 percent of the parents surveyed did at least some child-care reading when their children were young and suggested that today's parents are consulting parent education materials more frequently than they did in earlier generations.[3] We know of no nationwide study of the use of child-care publications and materials, but the Texas survey suggests that such use is a widespread phenomenon. This is a relatively new development in human society, and one can hardly doubt that it has had considerable impact on fathers and mothers.

As behavioral scientists, the writers must of necessity believe, as most Americans believe, that this mass of research and observation will eventually be in the best interests of all of us—but, at the same time, it is hard to escape the conclusion that so far a major impact on parents has been to make them feel more confused and inadequate than ever.

In a recent talk the first author had with a pediatrician, the physician was deploring the mass of articles on children's diseases in the news media. "Every time the *Reader's Digest* comes out with a story on some new disease or wonder drug," he said, "my telephone rings for days. Every mother has diagnosed her child as having the disease, or as needing the new drug, and she merely wants me to confirm the diagnosis. I wish they would stop publishing that stuff."

The second author has come to a similar conclusion after several years of research on the effects of Sudden Infant Death Syndrome (SIDS) on parents.[4] SIDS or crib death is gaining wide attention recently. For no apparent reason, a healthy baby is found dead. Autopsy confirms that parents could have done nothing to save the child nor were they responsible for his or her death; SIDS remains a mystery to medical science. Since Biblical times, it has been a common belief that parents who slept with their infants could overlay them and smother the babies. Most people don't believe this anymore, fortunately, but dozens of research teams around the country are studying other causes for SIDS. Reporters for the media looking for news track down a researcher's latest tentative findings and instantly we have "hopeful news that a SIDS cure is imminent." This is all well and good, but we would like discretion exercised here. As one mother whose baby died told us: "Each time they come up with the SIDS 'cure of the month' I have to suffer once again through thoughts of whether or not it was my fault that she died. I have to examine in great detail what I did on that horrible day in light of these new 'facts.' It almost drives me crazy. . . ."

It is hazardous to release to the public partial bits of research that only a well-trained professional can evaluate properly. In the behavioral sciences, for example, the nature of the sample studied is crucial to professionals reading the material, but very few readers of the public press are able to evaluate sampling design. In questionnaire studies the nature of the questions asked is crucial, but newspaper people are not trained in these matters, and their readers even less so. The same sort of problem could be cited about any research method used in obtaining data about people.

In attempting to assess the impact of behavioral science on modern American parents, the writers have identified several concepts or developments since the 1920s which they feel have had an essentially negative influence on fathers and mothers.

Overemphasis on environmental factors in behavior. John
Watson's extreme version of environmentalism in psychology during the 1920s easily led to the conclusion that parents could do
anything with any child if the parents were only skillful enough.[5] It is
true that professional psychologists soon outgrew such simple theories of personality, but Watson and his followers had considerable
influence on the new profession of advertising—and mass advertising has influenced *all* Americans in some ways.

Sociologists embraced environmentalism in their theories of social interaction and personality. They discarded any belief in human instincts and evolved essentially a plastic personality model
that was largely the product of its social environment.

Underemphasis on man's organic nature. Sociologists, in particular, tended to ignore the fact that man is an animal and that all
of his behavior has some relationship to his organic nature. It is true
that the anthropologists were much more careful in this matter, but
this aspect of anthropology did not seem to influence sociologists to
any great extent.[6]

Edward O. Wilson, a biologist from Harvard, won a Pulitzer Prize
for his 1978 book *On Human Nature*, which focused on sociobiology,
the study of how genetic, biochemical, and social factors intertwine
in a complex mixture to produce behavior. Wilson argues that "the
human mind is not a tabula rasa, a clean slate on which experience
draws intricate pictures with lines and dots." Wilson believes that
the gap between biology and the social sciences is closing, and that
our focus of study should be sociobiology. "The question is no longer
whether human social behavior is genetically determined; it is to
what extent."[7]

The battle has raged ever since between sociobiologists and their
detractors about how much heredity, and how much environment
contributes.[8]

It is also true that psychologists stayed much closer to organic
factors in their research, an example being their interest in intellectual capacity in children and means of measuring it. But outside of
IQ tests and other measurements of motor skills, it is hard to see how
the knowledge of man's physical nature has entered into modern
clinical psychology as it filters down to parents in clinics or child
guidance centers.[9]

Sociologists have tended to assume a random distribution of organic factors in human populations, and hence they have felt that

these variables could be ignored in studying human behavior. Alex Inkeles has stated bluntly that he thinks this proposition needs to be reexamined by sociologists.[10]

Overemphasis on cultural factors. Sociologists and anthropologists, in particular, have tended to believe that almost any behavior at the human level can be explained by reference to culture patterns,[11] and yet in complex societies such as the United States there is almost endless variation in behavior within families, within social classes, within the sexes, within subcultures, and so on. It is not enough to explain the uniformities in behavior: The variations have to be accounted for also.

Oversimplified reasoning from the group to the individual. Parents are not confronted with a statistical aggregate, they are faced with a particular child or a small group of particular children. Any statistician will admit that when the size of any given cell is very small in quantitative research, the chances of error being present are very great. Thus, we can generalize about boys when we are analyzing thousands of cases, but any given boy may not be masculine at all—he may actually be more representative of the female sample than of the male sample.

It is very tricky reasoning from group behavior to individual behavior, but some writers do not worry about it very much.

It is also quite difficult to make the leap from statistical studies to application to individual cases. Richard Gelles, a well-known researcher with a decade of experience of survey research in the area of family violence explained in a beautiful article how hard it was for him to go from the researcher role to the clinician role. Gelles took a year off from his work at the University of Rhode Island to work "in the trenches" with abusive parents and their children at a hospital in Boston. In a refreshingly candid article, Gelles admits that he had to unlearn almost all of his research understandings of child abuse when he was working with it in a clinical setting. Gelles had spent a decade trying to measure the extent of violence in all the families in the United States. To use his own metaphor, Gelles was trying to see "the forest for the trees." But, ". . . to the clinicians, they can neither see nor even be bothered by the forest: they have a job to do for the tree!"[12] A parent's job is a clinical job, also. Most parents have little time to be interested in what the statistically average parent is up to. It may be some small comfort to know your troubles are only average, or normal troubles. But they still are troublesome, and a parent is bent on spending his or her time not on compiling aggregate statistics but fixing squeaky wheels.

Poor sampling. Kinsey was constantly belabored for his sampling deficiencies in his studies of American sexual behavior, yet there are relatively few studies of parents and their children that will stand close scrutiny of their sampling method or the conclusions that can be drawn from such a sample.[13] Social class bias is usually present, age factors are not held constant, religious affiliation is usually a problem, urban-rural composition is at variance with the general population, and so on. The universe studied may be very limited, but the conclusions drawn are often quite sweeping—especially so when the study is reported in the general press.

The research design can be criticized. Behavioral science even at its best is not flawless. Orville Brim, Harold Orlansky, and William Sewell and others writing in the 1950s and 60s found it possible to criticize almost every study of parents and children published during the earlier decades in the United States from the standpoint of research design.[14] Control groups were not usually used, samples were inadequate, questions were vague, interviews brief, and hypotheses not explicitly stated or else they were evolved after the data were collected and tabulated.

In 1971 James Walters and Nick Stinnett reviewed research on parent-child relationships and sensed a growing distrust among researchers for simplistic explanations concerning the direction of causality in explaining these relationships: "The era of viewing children solely as products of their parents' influence is past, for it is recognized that children themselves exert powerful influences upon parent-child relationships."[15] Almost without exception, Walters and Stinnett argued then, in the 1960s the direction of influence was considered to be from parent to child. Parents, in effect, raised children. And that was that. They criticized the theory upon which this research was based for failing to acknowledge changes in relational styles over the family life cycle, and differences among various ethnic groups. Also, in the majority of studies, Walters and Stinnett argued that relatively little was presented about the theory on which the research was based, and/or the theories failed to reflect the incredible complexity of the factors affecting relationships between parents and children. Furthermore, few studies in the

1960s included direct observations of parent-child behaviors, relying rather on questionnaire data. Seldom were responses of children compared to responses of parents for agreement (which could very easily be minimal). Reliability and validity of instruments was often questionable.

Walters and Lynda Henly Walters followed up the review of 1960s research in 1980 with a review of 1970s research on parent-child relationships.[16] They concluded that the 1970s were theoretically and methodologically a transitional period for research in this area. Some positive changes were being made. These included: improvement in computer technology and statistics; increased use of observational studies; increased use of multimethod research designs (looking at a problem in a number of different ways); increased use of longitudinal designs, in which the investigators go back occasionally to measure situations again; and recognition that deficit model research, which focuses on "negative," "undesirable" behaviors of children who come from homes in which some "deficiency" exists has certain drawbacks.

In a similar vein, Robert McCall argued that we currently "lack a science of natural developmental processes because few studies are concerned with development as it transpires in naturalistic environments and because we rarely actually collect or analyze truly developmental data." McCall argued that researchers seem to be enamored with experimental research rather than observation in a child's natural environment over a longer period of time. In fact, this love of experiments which are relatively simple and quick seems to dictate the course of study of child development rather than serve as only a tool. McCall said that the "wholesale denigration" of nearly all longitudinal methods is based on the notion that they are "hopelessly confounded or beyond the financial and time commitments" of the researchers. He added that inexperience in longitudinal study contributed to the lack of this type of research. He concluded that such attitudes are "extreme and unjustified."[17]

We, of course, are inclined to believe that a great deal of progress has been made in behavioral research in the past two decades; but, as researchers we know only too well how difficult it is to construct a study without major limitations. Most researchers have limited funds for their work; time is a constraint; access to a sample that is representative of the larger population is usually impossible; and data often is collected from brief questionnaires or interviews, rather than in-depth questioning or observation. It is, indeed, the rare study that cannot be challenged on one or more of these dimensions. This should be seen as less the fault of the researcher than simply the enormity of the challenge the researcher faces. But when studies are disseminated to the general public through the mass media, the flaws inherent in the research design are quite often not explained to the reader and gross misunderstanding can occur.

American fathers and husbands, historically, have been neglected. The writers have been appalled in reviewing the studies of American parents to see that in the 1950s and 60s only people like Brim and Otto Pollak seemed to worry about husbands and/or fathers.[18] Goode, for example, in one of the best empirical studies of divorce we have had, did not find it possible (or necessary?) to include any of the divorced men in his sample.[19] Daniel Miller and Guy Swanson, Robert Sears, and others, in quite elaborate studies of American parents, did not find it necessary to interview any fathers.[20] This past sin has been remedied to some degree, as we will demonstrate in Chapter 8.[21]

Social environment has been equated with parental influence. It is one thing to assume (or conclude) that personality is the net result of social interaction and exposure to cultural patterns, but it is quite another thing to assume that the social world of the child is the net result of the interaction *with parents*. It is true that in the early years the outside world is mediated by and through the family, but, as Marshall Clinard has pointed out, there are forces such as the youth peer group, siblings, and mass media.[22] Parental influence is not even synonymous with *family influence*, let alone *social environment*. For example, what order one is born into the family makes a great deal of difference on how one turns out, as any firstborn child will note (or any middleborn child, or any afterthought child, and so on).

The anthropologist Geoffrey Gorer has this observation about psychoanalytic theory: "In American psychoanalytic thinking the child is born faultless, a tabula rasa, and any defects which subsequently develop are the fault of . . . the ignorance or malice of its parents who mar what should otherwise be a perfect, or at least a perfectly adjusted, human being."[23]

The ultimate result of this sort of personality theory is to saddle fathers and mothers with complete responsibility for the shaping of their children.

The failure to account for accidental combinations of events that affect children and parents. In interviewing parents, the writers have been impressed with the fact that in some cases an odd combination of events seems to have determined what happened to a child or a parent. These might be conceptualized as "statistical freaks" that normally would not occur but occasionally do. For example, a child will meet a peer-group member at exactly the point in life when his father or mother is unable to give him close supervision, and then it happens that this particular peer is the one that could influence the child at this time in a negative way. A girl on the rebound from her parents could meet a nice boy in college, but to express her revolt becomes friendly with a young man who is able to influence her in almost any direction. It is easy, of course, to argue with the psychiatrists that there must have been some reason why she took up with this particular boy, but the fact is that all of us at some point in life have been so desperate for a relationship that we have accepted anybody who offered himself or herself—and sometimes we have met some very nice people that way. But other persons do not seem to have been so fortunate.

Jessie Bernard has noted that an accidental combination of events often upsets the predictions of social scientists.[24] We think this happens to parents and children also.

Critiques of behavioral and social science

In recent years there have been some trenchant attacks on the work of behavioral and social scientists in America and the Western world. William H. Whyte, Jr., in a book which had a large audience, lashed out with the following statement: "Scientism is the promise that with the same techniques that have worked in the physical sciences we can eventually create an exact science of man. In one form or another it has had a long and dismal record of achievement."[25]

A few years later Betty Friedan, in a book which sold several million copies, took up the cudgel: "Instead of destroying the old prejudices that restricted women's lives," she wrote, "social science in America merely gave them new authority. By a curious circular process, the insights of psychology and anthropology and sociology, which should have been powerful weapons to free women . . . canceled each other out, trapping women in dead center."[26]

In the 1970s an English sociologist, Andreski, launched another attack. In reviewing this book, *Time* magazine cites Andreski as believing that the work of social scientists is "boring, misleading, pseudoscientific, and trivial, and amounts to little more than ponderous restatements of the obvious masked by a smoke screen of jargon."[27]

The writers, as social scientists, do not necessarily agree with these critics, but in the field of child rearing and parenthood, there are at least two studies by competent persons which demonstrate that the "experts" have gone in cycles in their advice to parents. In 1950 Cecilia Stendler published a survey of articles on child rearing printed in popular women's magazines for the period 1890–1948. Her conclusion was that by the 1940s the experts were returning to child-rearing techniques that they had recommended in the 1890s.[28]

In 1953 Wolfenstein published a study of U.S. government bulletins on infant care. Read by millions of parents, these pamphlets reflected the best research available at that time. Wolfenstein found that the advice given parents changed from one decade to the next. Furthermore, the suggestions did not follow in a progressive pattern but went in cycles.[29]

Representative Barbara Mikulski (Dem.–Md.) may some day garner an award for possibly the most vitriolic attack on the social and behavioral sciences. The issues are even more hotly debated now in Congress as battles over shrinking budgets gain momentum. In Mikulski's words:

> Not one rummy has been taken off of Baltimore streets by this research. Not one drunken husband has been dissuaded from beating his wife or one drunken mother from beating her child. These research projects are like exotic, expensively mounted butterfly collections, hidden away in vaults and only exhumed from time to time to display to other collectors of the rare and unusual in mutual reaffirmation of their elite status.[30]

Charles Lindblom and David Cohen argued that the social sciences have never lived up to their promise. For one thing, social scientists look down their noses at other kinds of knowledge: knowledge garnered from the vast and important experiences that parents have had with their children, or the experience administrators have had operating programs.[31] But again we come back to the words of Dr. Spock, who wrote *Baby and Child Care* in a friendly manner and argued, "You know more than you think you do. Don't be overawed by the professionals and the scary things that your family and friends tell you." Spock noted that one of the reasons his book was so successful was because, in the words of one of many, many parents: "It sounds like you are talking to me, and as if you think I am a sensible person."

> I almost weep when I think that people can be pleased with as little as that. This is what people want—to be listened to and treated as sensible—not talked down to, not lectured to. It is one of the hardest things for professional people to avoid because we work so hard for so many years developing and acquiring expertise. After all the years of education and training, it is terribly hard not to become sort of condescending without ever meaning to be so. [32]

It is the writers' belief that American parents were persuaded to give up traditional child-rearing methods before a hard science of human growth and development had been achieved.

It is interesting to note that Bronfenbrenner seems to think that parents in the Soviet Union are doing better than parents in the United States, yet his survey of the scene in the Soviet Union was unable to discover any major research centers on child development or family life in their society. [33] If this is the case, what help has the massive research on the family in our society been to American parents? It is a good question. A curious question for professors with research orientations to pose, but a good one.

Psychiatric theory and parenthood

It probably is true that most American parents know very little about Sigmund Freud and his personality theory, but the fact remains that they have been influenced by Freudian theory whether they were aware of the gentleman from Vienna or not. This is true for two reasons: (1) American psychiatry and American social work have been heavily Freudian since World War I (though in the 1970s and 1980s family systems theory became a serious challenger to accepted dogma), and (2) Freudian ideas have been widely disseminated to the general public through the mass media. [34]

It also seems to be true that many of the books that have criticized American parents—such as the best seller by Edward Strecker after World War II[35]—have been written by psychiatrists whose training was essentially Freudian.

For these reasons it is essential that we take a good look at Freudian theory *from the parents' point of view*. This is not an evaluation of Freudian theory as it applies to marriage or psychotherapy: We are looking at it from the point of view of fathers and mothers. How adequately does it explain behavior, both that of the child and that of the parent? How helpful has it been to parents? How destructive? Has it been practical for most American parents?

Martin L. Gross, a New York researcher and author leveled a heavy broadside at psychiatry with the publication in 1978 of his book *The Psychological Society*. Gross, who spent eight years researching the book, charged that the psychiatrist's couch is a fashionable, expensive, and often worthless ritual that pervades all of American life. "We have become one great psychiatric clinic. Psychiatry has affected every aspect of our society: marriage, child raising, schools, justice. We're even analyzing each other." The result is a self-indulgent society, so insecure that those who can afford it rush into treatment at the first hint of stress. Psychiatry's greatest sin, Gross argued, is relieving the individual of responsibility. Blame is transferred from children to parents, and generations of parents have been programmed to accept the guilt. "The psychological revolution had as one of its basic tricks the belief that parents were to blame for virtually everything that happened to us."[36]

These are difficult questions, and the writers have no illusions about their ability to answer them adequately. But they are important questions that need to be asked, and perhaps a beginning can be made here.

There may well have been some positive influences from Freudian theory on parents, but it is the writers' belief that the net effect was negative.[37] The next few pages will attempt to support this argument.

It placed too much responsibility on parents.   Freudian theory was part of the broad theory of environmentalism, considered earlier. Along with Watsonian psychology and the personality theories of American sociologists, it held that the child was essentially the product of parental influence.[38] Freud probably placed greater emphasis on the role of siblings in personality development than did the sociologists and psychologists; but even there parents were the ultimate culprits, because they were supposed to create a family climate in which sibling relationships would be healthy or constructive.

It is the writers' contention that parents are only one set of factors that determine the outcome of the child's life[39] and that Freudian theory was one of the instruments used to enslave the modern parent. It may well be true that Freud himself did not intend that his concepts should be used in this way, but this does not mean that they were *not* used to that end. In the same vein, one can find that the teachings of Jesus have been used at various times in the United States to justify the enslavement of the black by the white race, yet we can hardly imagine that Jesus had this in mind when he was teaching his ethical system.[40]

Freud described the child as having "instinctual" drives and needs, and in this sense Freud viewed the human infant as being less passive than did the sociologists, the psychologists, and the cultural anthropologists. But Freud's instincts did not automatically produce any specific behavior—even the sexual instinct in Freudian theory is subject to endless conditioning and modification. Thus, the concept of *instinct* as used by Freud did not relieve parents of any responsibility because the end product was still undetermined at the point of birth. This was a somewhat different use of the concept of instinct than had been customary in biology and earlier psychology.[41]

Counterarguments have, of course, been mounting up over the years. Study these: "More and more professionals in the child-care field have begun to emphasize the importance of the child's own characteristics in influencing his development. As one result, the concept of parental responsibility is undergoing modification. It is no longer as fashionable as it was a decade ago to blame the mother for a child's behavioral and emotional difficulties," according to Stella Chess, Alexander Thomas, and Herbert Birch.[42]

Jerome Kagan argued that many people have assumed that the belief in "one's value" remains stable from early in life through adulthood. But of the millions of children who do not receive adequate amounts of love in early childhood, only a small proportion become pathological. Of the group who are pathological as adults, it is possible a large proportion were loved during early childhood. "At the moment, we do not know if there is a strong relation between early child treatment and later adult pathology, even though there may be a strong relation between the adolescent's belief that he is not valued and the frequency of his bouts of distress."[43]

Richard Q. Bell and Lawrence V. Harper broke new ground with the publication of their book, *Child Effects on Adults*, rather than the other way around.[44]

And Arlene Skolnick argued that parents are not Pygmalions with make-or-break power over a child's development. Even when studies do discover a connection between the behavior of parents and children, the direction of cause and effect are not necessarily clear. For example, a study correlating parents' severe punishment with children's aggressiveness is often taken to show that tough parents produce tough kids. It is quite possible that the opposite is true: tough kids make parents respond harshly.[45]

In Freudian theory parents are responsible for what happens to the child even after it becomes an adult. In psychoanalysis childhood never really ends: Adults only live out in a sort of dreamlike trance what happened to them in the first four or five years of life. They never really outgrow their childhood—they only relive it in different forms. Thus, parents are forever saddled with guilt and responsibility because mistakes made in the first few years are never really outgrown or outlived. They may be modified by expensive and long-term psychotherapy, but their influence is permanent.

As the writers read the history of parenthood in America, this was not always the case. Parents were expected to do the best they could with children, but at some point children became adults and were responsible for their own destiny. And if they believed in God even miracles could be wrought—without benefit of psychotherapy. There was also the notion that fate had something to do with what happened to people in this world as well as the next.

Freudian theory overemphasized the preschool years as determinants of adult personality. Some critics of Freud have labeled this "diaper determinism":[46] that nothing happens after the first few years which was not predetermined in the early years of life. Brim, however, cites several studies to the effect that people in modern society *do* change in behavior as they move into adult status—experiences in the nonfamily world (such as military service) have an impact that is not within the realm of parents to control. The peer group in urban society is powerful, as are occupational roles and marital relationships.[47]

It is true that the parent has the child *first*, but behavior is not always the result of first experiences. Sometimes the *last* event is crucial. By the same logic, one could lean toward the genetic theory of personality because the genes precede what the parents do. Yet, most of the behavioral scientists and psychiatrists have been willing to forget genetic factors, and as a rule have emphasized them little in their studies of personality.

The following quotation from Ernest Jones, the biographer of Freud, illustrates to what extremes the Freudians went in their emphasis on the child's first few years: "Freud has taught us that the essential foundations of character are laid down by the age of three and that later events can modify but not alter the traits then established."[48] This is somewhat devastating if you are a parent. Freud, of course, could never prove this theory of personality—it was merely a hypothesis he developed from the cases he saw in his clinical practice. Many scientists today, such as those in behavior modification, believe that since almost all human behavior is learned, it can be unlearned and relearned. These persons think that Freud was grossly incorrect in his personality theory.[49]

Jerome Kagan and Robert Klein observed children living in an isolated Indian village on Lake Atitlan in the highlands of northwest Guatemala and came to some startling conclusions in regard to the supposed irreversibility of infant deprivation. The researchers reported that during the first year of life, the infant spends most of his time in a small, dark, windowless hut. The mother rarely allows the baby to crawl on the dirt floor of the hut and believes that outside sun, air, and dust are harmful and to be avoided. The baby is rarely spoken to or played with; its toys consist of its clothing, the mother's body, oranges, ears of corn, and pieces of wood or clay. The mothers seemed to regard the babies like an American mother might view an expensive cashmere sweater: to be kept nearby, protected, but certainly not interacted with.

"We saw listless, silent, apathetic infants; passive, quiet, timid three-year-olds," the researchers noted. A few of the infants had such pale cheeks and vacant stares that they had the quality of "tiny ghosts." Deprivation had taken its toll; compared to American children of the same age, the Indian children were significantly delayed in development.

But as the children grew older they gradually were allowed outside into the world, and by age 11, the researchers noted that amazingly the children had developed into "active, gay, intellectually" competent beings. Many of the effects of infant and early childhood deprivation had disappeared, leading Kagan and Klein to conclude that, "Infant retardation seems to be partially reversible."[50]

Perhaps the most amusing, yet serious critique of Freudian critical periods theories is the work of Harry Harlow and his colleagues at the University of Wisconsin–Madison with so-called monkey psychiatrists. It seems that researchers are able to induce psychosis in monkeys by isolating infants at birth from social contact with other monkeys for the first six months of life. On emerging from isolation, monkeys typically have severe deficits: they display autistic, isolative behaviors; inappropriate aggression; an absence of sexual responsiveness; and for females who are artificially inseminated as mothers they are indifferent or brutal to their young. For a long time, researchers, extrapolating from critical periods theories, held that this psychotic state was irreversible.

Harlow and his colleagues successfully treated these psychotic monkeys by introducing "monkey psychiatrists" into their lives. The psychiatrists were younger monkeys, whose response to strange situations is often a frantic clinging to any big, warm body. When put in a cage with a psychotic older monkey, the tinier monkey psychiatrists immediately clung tightly to the psychotics. This, of course, caused great consternation for the psychotic who initially would vigorously try to shake off the alien. The infants, of course, would only hold on tighter. Within a week or two, the psychotic monkeys reciprocated with clinging behavior of their own. By one year after the experiment began, the psychotic monkeys were cured—indistinguishable in their behaviors from other normally raised monkeys.

"The role of gentle physical contact and model-serving exhibited by the therapists was likely of paramount importance for the isolate recovery. Many of these principles are not unfamiliar to human psychotherapists," the investigators concluded wryly. The data were "in direct contradiction to most traditional explanations of the effects of isolation rearing, such as the 'critical period' theories, and therefore we feel that a reexamination of existing theoretical positions regarding the basis for the effects of social isolation is in order."[51]

Freudian theory made psychosexual development too tentative and too hazardous.   It is hard to believe that the human race would have survived this long if reproduction were as tentative as some analysts have made it out to be—that is, that any boy or girl might become homosexual if the right stimuli were supplied (or not supplied) at the right moment. Brim has commented on this to the effect that it may be possible to make a girl out of a male infant but it seems to be a lot easier to make a boy out of him in most societies.[52]

In the Freudian system, there seems to be nothing *guaranteed* about the child's psychosexual development—it all depends on what the parents do, how they do it, when they do it, how often they do it—or what they do not do. There is no automatic unfolding of the male or female traits, as earlier generations apparently thought.

This seems to the writers to be too tenuous a picture of human growth and development. It would seem that *most* human beings would be seriously neurotic or even psychotic if their personalities were as plastic as the Freudians and other psychiatrists have theorized. In a very real sense, all child rearing is traumatic, not only for the child but also for the parents. Rosten puts it this way: "There is the myth," he writes, "that you can explain neurotic behavior by attributing it to an unhappy childhood. But all childhood is unhappy; all childhood is charged with uncertainty and fear, with conflict and frustration, with unbearable rage and unattainable desire. It makes little sense to talk about unhappy childhoods unless we ask why some people emerge from childhood with their productive capacities enriched, while others remain paralyzed by unresolved and infantile dilemmas."[53]

It seems likely that this fragile theory of human personality resulted from the limited sample observed by psychiatrists. They see only the children who have been damaged by their environment—they do not see the children who survived whatever trauma they experienced while growing up. Thus if a child becomes delinquent and it is known that his parents were divorced when the youngster was five years old, it is easy to assume that the divorce was a crucial factor in the child becoming delinquent. But in fact there are undoubtedly thousands of children who are not delinquent whose parents were also divorced while the children were young. What is the difference between these two groups of traumatized children? The research usually does not answer that question.

There is a revealing example of this sort of research problem in the literature on unmarried mothers. Several years ago Leontine Young published a book on unmarried mothers, in which she concluded that these girls had almost invariably come from homes in which the mother was dominant.[54] But a few years later, Clark Vincent matched a group of unmarried mothers with a group of girls who were not unmarried mothers, and he could not determine any significant difference in the family dynamics of the two groups.[55] He also could not isolate any particular personality pattern that would distinguish the unmarried mothers from the matched sample from the general population.

The art of sampling is relatively new in behavioral science and probably even newer in psychoanalysis and related psychiatric disciplines. Yet, almost anything can be proven and believed if the sample is sufficiently unrepresentative.[56]

It seems clear that this extremely tentative view of psychosexual development in children resulted in parents feeling more anxious and fearful—one could no longer rear children by tradition. Instead, parents were supposed to become "experts."

Freudian theory took the romance out of parenthood. Any parent who knows the Freudian conceptual system very well must approach his parental role with some foreboding, being convinced that, even with the best of luck, the most he can hope to produce is a "mild neurotic."

The complexity of human behavior

Human behavior seems clearly the result of the interaction of at least three basic sets of variables: the organism and its genetic components, the cultural norms of the social world in which the person lives,[57] and the psychodynamic (the unique experience of any given person). Another factor, which is seldom mentioned in books on personality but which parents talk about quite often, is the unpredictable and improbable combination of events. This is what earlier generations of fathers and mothers called luck or fate. It is literally true that the best efforts of parents can sometimes be nullified by some rare circumstance involving the combination of several events that would normally occur separately and that could be handled better in another sequence.

It is extremely difficult for any one discipline to deal adequately with all of these variables. As a result, each group tends to emphasize the factors it understands best. Since social, cultural, and interpersonal interactions can literally be *seen* (or felt), behavioral scientists tend to focus on these in their analysis. One prominent biochemist has observed that genetic factors have been "excommunicated" from the behavioral sciences for the last two generations.[58] He goes on to argue this is largely because human genetics are too complex for most social scientists to understand.

Parents suffer from their lack of knowledge of human genetics. They can understand one child and cannot figure out why another one is so different. Robert Ardrey says that except for identical twins, "the chance is one in a trillion that any two siblings will be genetically alike."[59]

All of this means that parents always have an inadequate understanding of their child and have to guess at factors they do not know about.

Some examples of inadequate science and its impact on parents

Parents and schizophrenia

In recent years parents have been held responsible if their children develop schizophrenia.[60] It is argued that this form of mental illness develops because of the "double bind" and other dysfunctional interaction patterns in the family. One mother said to the first author: "Our youngest son had to drop out of the university because he developed schizophrenia. The psychiatrist told us it was because of problems at home. But our three older children went through college without any particular problems—do you think we could have done that badly with the younger one?"

Actually, reputable scientists do not agree about the so-called causes of schizophrenia. Some of them believe that genetic factors play a major role in the etiology of this disease. A well-known sociologist makes this statement: "Although genetic studies of schizophrenia have not yielded consistent results . . . the results obtained have provided as much basis for the heredity theory as there is for any other.[61]

Parents with schizophrenic children will often read newspaper statements such as the following: "A noted psychiatrist and researcher said here Thursday that the tendency toward schizophrenia and related disorders is primarily inherited." The parent will note that the physician quoted is a professor of medicine at Harvard and the editor of a medical journal.[62]

In another newspaper report, two scientists will report that they have found that an enzyme deficiency is the key to schizophrenia. These two researchers have "discovered that an enzyme deficiency in the brains of schizophrenic patients appeared to upset the brain's metabolism, leading to abnormal production of chemicals that are known to have a mentally disturbing effect.[63]

Wilson, the sociobiologist, argues that "although the capacity to become schizophrenic may well be within all of us, there is no question that certain persons have distinctive genes predisposing them to the condition."[64]

Aldous Huxley, a brilliant philosopher and novelist, spent some time at the Menninger Clinic in Topeka, Kansas, studying mental illness. "I think it's pretty clear now that schizophrenia is an organic disease of chemical origin and probably one could find chemical means of coping with it," he concludes.[65]

". . . We do not know the etiology of schizophrenia," Dr. Dahlberg, associate clinical professor of psychiatry at New York University Medical Center concluded in the case of Julie Roy against Dr. Renatus Hartogs, her psychiatrist.[66]

What should parents believe if their child develops schizophrenia? Should they be saddled with guilt for the rest of their lives when the illness is so poorly understood? We do not think so.

Perhaps Mark Vonnegut, the son of the famous novelist Kurt Vonnegut, offers the best advice of all. Hospitalized three times for schizophrenia after graduating from Swarthmore, he said, "A more serious problem with most psychological theories and therapies is that they usually involve placing blame . . . your parents or someone else has screwed up. The fact is, there is no blame." In short, we are all guilty, and all innocent in the melodrama called life.[67]

Parents with homosexual sons and daughters

A striking example of behavioral science that has reversed itself within the last decade is the traditional theory about homosexuality. Until recently psychiatrists believed that certain types of family constellations produced sexual deviation—in other words, the parents were responsible.[68] One mother said to the first author: "Our youngest son was discharged from the Army as a sex deviate. I went to see a psychiatrist and he said it was my fault—that I was too close to my son. But our two older sons are heterosexual and I was close to them too."

In the 1970s, after a bitter struggle within the membership, the American Psychiatric Association voted to remove homosexuality as a form of mental illness from its handbook.[69] This created a split within the group which has not yet been repaired.

Some prominent homosexuals have gone out of their way to scoff at the idea that their sexual behavior was "caused" by their parents. One of these is Tennessee Williams, the playwright, who says that he chose homosexuality because he likes it better than heterosexuality.[70] Del Martin and Phyllis Lyon, in their book *Lesbian Woman*, plead with the reader not to blame parents when daughters become homosexuals—they agree with Williams that this lifestyle represents a choice and is not the result of parental influence.[71]

Laura Hobson, in her best-selling novel, *Consenting Adult*, has her young homosexual physician plead with his parents not to feel responsible for his behavior, that he chose this lifestyle.[72] In his study of the gay liberation movement in America, Laud Humphreys argues that the traditional theory of homosexuality is no longer valid.[73]

Does anyone know what really turns one person to homosexuality while another prefers the opposite sex? One well-known psychiatrist laughs at the idea that some particular family syndrome produces homosexuality. He says: "With perhaps 20 million American men who practice some form of homosexuality, it's inconceivable that all should have emerged from the same set of causes—the stereotype of the domineering, overprotective, feminizing mother and the weak or absent father." He goes on to say that in over 10,000 interviews with male homosexuals "I've heard . . . every combination and variation of parental history that you can imagine."[74]

Another report in the daily press concludes that biochemical factors are significant in the etiology of sexual deviation. A group of scientists at a well-known university makes this statement: "Preliminary results of a biochemical study of male homosexuals and heterosexuals have challenged the traditional view that all homosexuality is caused by social and psychological factors." They go on to point out that their research method is more sophisticated than that previously used in this type of study.[75]

Richard Green reported an exploratory study of 37 children who were being reared by female homosexuals or by parents who have changed sex (transsexuals). His findings are germane to our discussion here: 36 of the children reported childhood toys, games, clothing or peer group preferences that were typical for their sex; and the 13 older children reported erotic fantasies or overt sexual behaviors that were all heterosexually oriented. Green concludes: "I tentatively suggest that children being raised by transsexual or homosexual parents do not differ appreciably from children raised in more conventional settings. . . ." Homosexual parents don't seem to produce homosexual children; can we argue then, so facilely, that heterosexual parents are to be held accountable for producing homosexual children?[76]

Edward O. Wilson, the Harvard sociobiologist, reviewed the research on the causes of homosexuality. He came to a tentative conclusion, but cautioned that "all of this information amounts to little more than a set of clues." The clues are not decisive when put to the test of rigorous scientific methodology, and a good deal of additional research is necessary. "But the clues are enough to establish that the traditional Judeo-Christian view of homosexual behavior is inadequate and probably wrong." Homosexuality may have a genetic component in its causation; it may have evolutionary roots because it is important to social organization. Wilson notes that homosexual behavior is common in many other animals besides man, from insects to mammals. Homosexuality is a form of bonding, a cementing of relationships. This bonding has a survival value for many species and may be transmitted in part through the genes. He sums up, provocatively, that there is "a strong possibility that homosexuality is normal in a biological sense. . . . Homosexuals may be the genetic carriers of some of mankind's rare altruistic impulses."[77]

Possibly the most extensive research on the social and psychological causes of homosexuality comes from Alan Bell, Morgan Weinberg, and Sue Hammersmith, formerly with the Kinsey Institute at Indiana University. The researchers studied 979 homosexuals (gay and lesbian) in the San Francisco Bay Area and compared their findings with 477 heterosexuals. Max Lerner, a noted journalist, reviewed the book by the authors, *Sexual Preference: Its Development Among Men and Women*.[78] Lerner concluded that the book "Doesn't tell us for certain what causes homosexuality, but it does tell us what doesn't. Most of the theories thus far go out the window."

Lerner goes on to say that the theory of a strong attachment to either parent, especially the mother, does not work well; neither does role-failure theory, which posits that either parent fails to offer a strong role model of masculinity or femininity. Possessiveness theory, focusing on a strong possessive mother and a weak father does not work well. Nor does seduction theory, arguing that homosexuality is caused by an early seduction experience. The trouble with the theories, Lerner explains, is that these kinds of stories are heard in the histories of people who go onto become homosexual, but they are also heard in the histories of people who become heterosexual. The authors do not reject the theories as contributory factors in homosexuality's etiology; rather, they reject each of them as the single source of homosexuality.

One "massive factor," however, does show up in many histories. The authors call it "early gender nonconformity." Young boys who like girl games, and young girls who like boy games often go on to be homosexual. But is this a cause? Or an effect? The authors can't prove it from their research, but hypothesize that homosexuality is biologically caused, probably hormonally.

Lerner concludes that the researchers have given parents and families of homosexuals "some relief from the burden of guilt they have carried."[79]

Perhaps the most provocative answer to the question of why a person has a gay or lesbian orientation came to us from a young lesbian we know: "I guess it's because I had such warm, supportive, and loving parents!" she said with a twinkle in her eye. And then she launched into a long description of her family life which turned out to be very good evidence that she may have been right. It seems that her parents were both heterosexual, kind and loving individuals. She had an especially strong relationship with her father, who was adept at communicating openly and honestly with her. When she expressed her love for another woman to her father, he did not take offense but listened, helped her consider all the implications of her action, and then left it up to her to decide how she would live her life. "It was very, very hard for him," she said, "but he did it. And I love him for it."

Should parents blame themselves if their offspring turn to homosexuality? The writers think not.

Parents with hyperactive children

For several years psychiatrists James R. Morrison and Mark A. Stewart have been studying hyperactive children. In this syndrome children drive their parents and their school teachers up the wall: The children can't sit still, they talk too much, they have difficulty relating to their peers, and in general they are "problem children."[80]

In 1971 Morrison and Stewart published the results of a study of 59 hyperactive children matched with 41 control children and concluded that the hyperactive syndrome was socially transmitted from parents to children.[81] In 1973, however, Morrison and Stewart published a further study of 35 hyperactive children who had been adopted, and they came to quite a different conclusion: The behavior of these hyperactive children did not change when they were adopted and no evidence could be found that the behavior was being socially transmitted from parents to child. The researchers conclude: "These data are consistent with genetic transmission of the syndrome; a polygenic mode is postulated."[82] Morrison and Stewart realize that much more research will have to be done before the hyperactive syndrome is fully understood, but they are now skeptical that the behavior is the result of interaction between the child and its parents.[83]

Roger Freeman has argued that, "There is only one phrase for the state of the art and practice in the field of minimal brain dysfunction (MBD), hyperactivity (HA), and learning disability (LD) in children: a mess. There is no more polite term which would be realistic. The area is characterized by rarely challenged myths, ill-defined boundaries, and a strangely seductive attractiveness."[84] Along these lines, Marcel Kinsbourne and James Swanson noted that in many fields of medicine, speakers conventionally say that very little is known about a particular disease under discussion and that much more research is needed. But, "[I]n contrast, so much is known about hyperactivity that the information has become confusing."[85]

Helen Tryphonas, for example, states that there is increasing evidence for the notion that hyperactivity in children has a variety of causal factors: neurological complications following prenatal or perinatal trauma; maternal smoking during pregnancy; environmental pollutants, especially metals such as lead; fluorescent lights; family stress; genetic transmission; ingestion of artificial food additives such as colors and flavors; and allergies.[86]

The discussion in the research community is likely to continue for some time, we would guess, and until definitive answers are found (if ever), it would be wise to presume parents innocent until proven guilty. This advice, of course, goes for many problem areas.

Suicide, alcoholism, divorce, ad infinitum

The list of possible things that children do or become in life could go on into infinity. There are literally hundreds of offspring behaviors parents could search their souls over.

> He killed himself. He was so young, so successful. We thought he was happy. He had a girl friend and a good job, and money and a car. And now he's gone. He didn't even warn us. Not in the slightest. I can't help but think we were to blame somehow. Maybe I shouldn't have worked outside the home when he was a youngster. But we

were broke. I search and search and can't find what I could have done differently.

So now he's a hopeless drunk. He got into drinking when he went off to college. We have an occasional drink here at home, but we're not boozers. But he surely is: His wife took the children and left him, and he got fired from his job, and lost his driver's license. We tried to get him to stop going out with all his fraternity brothers back then, but how do you do that? How? We tried so hard. I still feel vaguely guilty. . . ."

His gambling got so bad. Off to the racetrack every day, spending the little money they had so quickly. I can understand why she got fed up and left. You know, I got a divorce when he was only 10. He cried and cried when his father left. But I couldn't go on with the man. He was a good family man, on the surface; respectable job, church-going. Yet he'd beat me almost every week. I couldn't go on. . . . I can't help but think that if I had stayed with his father, maybe he would see that you really have to try hard to make a marriage work. Maybe he'd be married still.

At some point, parents have to stop feeling guilty, though, and give themselves a break. We have heard countless parents tell us of their mistakes in life. And, it is good to catalog your downfalls on occasion so that you can improve upon your act when confronted with new challenges. But sooner or later we have to fly from our burden of guilt. Only a psychotic parent would wantonly hurt a child. The vast majority of us do the best we can. No more, no less. To unravel the Gordian knot of causes and effects in childrearing is probably an impossible task, anyway. And even if we were to un-ravel it, our course in the future would be no different: We'll still have to try again, not knowing for sure what the outcome will be.

Positive contributions of modern science to parents

Some features of modern science have certainly been of great help to fathers and mothers. An example would be modern medi-cine, with its arsenal of drugs and other treatment facilities. One can only imagine what parents went through in earlier centuries when a child became critically ill and the physician could be of little help.

In the field of mental retardation, modern science has been of great help to parents in being able to diagnose various forms of mental retardation and to offer alternate plans for care and treatment.

A new field is that of genetic counseling—helping couples determine whether it would be safe for them to go ahead with plans for parenthood.[87] Although too little is known about human genetics, at least the knowledge now available can be given parents by professionally trained genetic counselors.

In the area of family-relationship problems, many new treatment systems have been developed. Virginia Satir, Carl Whittaker, Murray Bowen, Salvador Minuchin, and others have evolved "total family" therapy systems, in which the patient is the whole family, not just one of its members. Essentially, this system hypothesizes a "sick family" rather than a disturbed individual.[88]

The behavior-modification group has also developed new treatment systems that are down to earth and relatively short term in the time required for treatment.[89]

Summary and conclusion

In this chapter we have attempted to analyze the impact of the behavioral sciences on the modern American parent. While the value of scientific research is granted, the results to date in the area of parenthood have not been too impressive. There is an infinite variety of parents and children in any modern pluralistic society such as America. It is not easy to generalize about them on the basis of limited research, inadequate samples, lack of control groups, and poor research design.

The better professionals recognize these limitations in the data and urge their application with some caution. But the less well trained professionals are not that modest in their consultations with parents. The most serious problem, however, in the opinion of the writers, develops when the research findings are written for popular consumption by the general public. Newspapers, magazines, and other forms of mass media in the United States are not noted for being reluctant to arouse public interest by sensational methods, and this tendency is compounded by the fact that journalists and other writers for the mass media have usually had no professional training that would equip them to recognize limitations in research method or design.[90] This places great responsibility on professional researchers in the family field to make sure that their findings cannot easily be misunderstood. This is not easy in the mass society.

Our intention in writing this critique of the behavioral sciences has not been to unfairly demean our profession, but, rather, to inject a dose of healthy skepticism into the reader's thinking about the findings of "science." For many people in the 20th century, the scientist has replaced the priest and shaman of earlier ages. Today we place an inordinate amount of faith in the printouts of our computers, just as in ancient times the religious hierarchy divined the entrails of sheep, we surmise, with ofttimes incorrect results.

Every so often the newspapers will come out with another curious story of a doctors' strike in some city or country around the world. And the reporter will quote one government statistician or another to the effect that since the doctors went on strike the death rate in that particular area went down.

We have yet to hear an adequate interpretation of these enticing statistics. And though we retain a healthy skepticism of physicians, we will continue to seek their advice and wisdom when illness threatens us. Likewise, we continuously advise people to get a professional assessment of their situation when they feel they have lost the way in life.

And, simultaneously, we caution that people exercise great caution in evaluating any professional advice they receive, because parenthood—like most every other aspect of life—is so incredibly complicated that even the best professional in the world is still only human.

Chapter 4

Role analysis of parenthood

William O. Douglas, a former member of the United States Supreme Court and one of the leaders of the conservation movement in our society before his death, made this statement about his own experience as a parent: "Few people I have known are competent to be parents. . . . The child who survives being brought up by its parents and emerges as an integrated person is an accident."[1] When it is remembered that Douglas knew some of the most capable people in American society, this comment becomes even more impressive.

Why is it that persons with remarkable ability often find parenthood so baffling? The writers believe the answer lies in the nature of the parental role—that it differs in several significant ways from other roles in our society. In this chapter the concept of role and the technique of role analysis will be used in an effort to dissect the unique features of the role of parent.

The use of role analysis

In recent years a body of knowledge known as role theory has come to be widely used by social scientists and some members of the various helping professions.[2] While there are different things that one can do with this approach, one of the most useful is that role analysis can be utilized to dissect small social systems so that we can see how each part is supposed to function and how it is related to the rest of the system. For example, in marriage counseling, one can analyze the role of wife in its various subroles, identify those producing problems, and proceed to find out the source of the problems. Is the husband complaining about his wife's failure as a sexual companion, or is it the housekeeping subrole that bothers him? Using this approach, such a complex interaction system as a marriage can be broken down into parts that can be analyzed separately.

Essentially, a role is a task that some person is supposed to perform.[3] Roles have to be defined, assigned, perceived, performed, and integrated with other role tasks. Every role carries with it a position in the interaction system that relates to status and prestige. In a well-organized family, the major roles have been identified, assigned, and performed with some degree of competence. Where this does not occur, the family may be said to be disorganized to a certain extent. Minor roles may be ignored or performed indifferently without producing too much difficulty, but major roles (such as care of young children) require constant and at least adequate role performance.

In the modern American family, male and female roles have been shifted and reorganized extensively since about 1920. Some families appear to be disorganized in that nobody seems to know who is supposed to do what. An analogy can be made here to bureaucratic theory: A business firm or an academic department may be said to be disorganized when major tasks have not been properly assigned or are not being performed adequately.

In this chapter we seek to apply role theory and role analysis to modern parents. We believe that this approach is helpful in understanding the problems that many American fathers and mothers appear to have.

The role is poorly defined, ambiguous, and not adequately delimited

It is impossible to interview modern parents without concluding that large numbers of them are confused, frustrated, and discouraged. They have been robbed of the traditional ways of rearing children without having an adequate substitute; they feel that they cannot achieve what they are expected to achieve; the standards for child rearing are too high; the authority of parents has been under-

mined by mass media, school officials, courts, social workers, and
the adolescent peer group.

When should children be punished? Is it legitimate to use physical punishment anymore? Has fear been outlawed as a tool to be
used by fathers and mothers when it seems appropriate? What is
meant by harsh child-rearing methods? Should fathers try to assume more authority with their children or less? Do parents have a
right to defy public authorities when they are convinced the authorities are wrong? What rights do parents actually have in contemporary America? Is it true that there are no bad children, only bad
parents? Is it true that the first few years determine what an adult
will be like 30 years later? Is it true that the violence so common on
television has no negative effect on children? Is it true that modern
parents are largely responsible for the increase in juvenile delinquency in the United States? Are parents responsible for the new
type of violence and sadism characteristic of juvenile crimes today?
Are parents the main cause of the increase in premarital sexual
relations reported by some studies? Is it true that mothers who work
outside of the home are virtually sentencing their children to juvenile delinquency or mental illness or both? Is the American mother
as bad as the best sellers say she is? Do psychiatrists know as much
about people as they think they do? Do parents ever have the right
to be different whether society or the child's peer group likes it or
not? And when does parenthood end anyway? If parents are responsible for "launching" their children into independence, when is
this supposed to begin? At age 16? 18? 21? What are parents supposed to do when children come back after an unsuccessful launching attempt, such as a divorce or job loss, or one of the many other
bruisings one can take in the world?

The writers submit that few, if any, of these questions can be
answered with any degree of certainty in contemporary America.
Parents have been made the bad guy in the drama of modern living
and have been blamed for the failures of all of the other basic social
institutions in our society—the school, the church, the government,
the mass media, the economic system, the armed forces, and so
forth.

No margin for error

In most areas of life there is some margin for error—even those of
us who have never had a serious automobile accident will admit

that at times we have been lucky, or that the other driver made it possible to avoid a serious collision.

We certainly feel in a profession such as teaching that some students will simply not learn—or at least they will learn very little. Yet if most (or even some) of the students learn, the average teacher or professor will find it not too hard to rationalize his or her failure to make the material meaningful to all of the students.

This same philosophical acceptance of some defeat is certainly found in medicine, law, the ministry, nursing, and social work. Nobody expects these professionals to save everybody who presents himself at their office. It is recognized and accepted that some people are "too sick" or "too maladjusted" to make effective use of the service provided. Parents, however, are expected to succeed with every child. This is disturbing to some parents. The writers have talked with many parents who have put it this way: "I am scared to death when I think that what happens to my children rests on my shoulders—it makes me feel so inadequate."

One factor has been the smaller family. It is one thing to fail with one or two children if you have five or six, but failure in the smaller family is more absolute. As an only child put it to us in a college class, "My parents only have one child and if I fail them all of their children will have failed them." She went on to say that this was a frightening spot to be in and that she hoped to have several children when she married.

The late John Kennedy said that one of the awesome burdens of being president in the nuclear age was that the chief executive could not afford to make an error in starting a war—hundreds of millions of people would be dead in a nuclear exchange before the error could be corrected. He pointed out that this was not the case in an earlier period of our history.[4]

It seems to us that the same thing has happened to parents: with the large family of the 18th and 19th centuries, an error with one child still left three or four other children that might turn out to be respectable representatives of the family. But the smaller family of the 20th century has left less room for error, and this has produced more anxiety and more guilt in parents.

Parents can't quit

One of the relatively unique features of the parental role is that you can't give it up with honor—fathers and mothers who desert their children in our society are viewed with great disfavor (and it is also a criminal offense if the child is a minor). This used to be true of the marital role in the 19th century, but today one can escape from an unhappy marriage without being disgraced. Americans can also get out of occupational roles that frustrate them or are too dull. But if you are a parent, even a very inadequate parent, you have to stay in the role and keep trying—even if you know you are failing. We think this is one of the most difficult aspects of the parental role.

One father said to the first author: "I don't like this kid of ours and he doesn't like me but what can I do about it? I'm his father and I have to do the best I can."

Children are locked in also: You can hardly say that "So and so used to be my father." They will always be your parents, for better or worse.

Responsibility without authority

In American industry one of the cardinal principles of management is that responsibility should be tied in with authority. In other words, a person in a position of responsibility should be given the authority to carry out his or her assignment. This is not true of modern parenthood.

In his history of the family in Western society, Carle Zimmerman of Harvard University points out that the father in Roman society during the golden era of the empire was absolute lord and master of his children as well as of his wife.[5] We will not dwell in this book on the delicate subject of the relationship of husbands and wives in contemporary America, but it would be a crude joke (or travesty) to suggest that the modern father is any lord or master over his children—indeed, he is lucky if they are not lord and master over him.[6]

It is easy, of course, to blame this condition on the contemporary American male, but the matter is not that simple. American society in almost every respect has become more feminine—even sports, to some observers[7]—and the reasons are not entirely clear. From the outside toilet in the dead of winter to the two-bathroom home is a long stretch, but Americans have made it in a little short of a century—and plumbers have done even better than that. Automobiles have been designed for women, saloons have given way to cocktail lounges, and so on. How would fathers escape such a massive assault on masculine dominance?

On a more sober note, clearly the rights of fathers and mothers over their children have been seriously proscribed in the past several decades. Parents in Wisconsin, for example, are no longer permitted to prepare their infants for burial in the event of death—yet their ancestors were allowed to do so.[8] And in states such as Minnesota, even university professors are not considered qualified to educate their children at home unless the state education department says so.[9] Parents who oppose medical procedures on the basis of religious faith have consistently had their pleas denied by the courts; parents who punish their children physically are often called into court to answer for their behavior. And, we are told that in only two states today does a child have to tell her parents that she is going to have an abortion.[10] There seems little doubt that parents today are as responsible as ever—and even more so—for their children but have much less authority over them. And what power has not been usurped by the formal society has been grabbed by the informal society of the child's peer group, especially at the adolescent level.

We do not wish to belabor the point. A good case can be made in defense of most or all of these proscriptions. But in our own families we have the distinct feeling that many agencies (including the church) are anxious to influence our children, but that none of them wishes to assume any final responsibility for them. That delightful bit is reserved for parents.

Judgment by professionals—not your peers

It is a basic principle in Anglo-Saxon law that persons charged with some offense are entitled to be judged by their peers, and especially so when the charge is serious. Parents in modern society, however, are seldom given this consideration: They are judged by professional practitioners. As a rule these professionals represent fields such as psychiatry, clinical psychology, social work, the teaching profession, or the law. In the opinion of the writers, this is one of the reasons why parent in contemporary America feel so threatened and insecure.

The first author's maternal grandmother reared 12 children, one of which did not turn out very well. This son ran away and was not heard from for several years. Grandmother was not judged by psychiatrists or professional social workers—her neighbors knew she was a good mother and they evaluated her parental performance. Today the situation is quite different.

Grandmother didn't even feel any guilt that one of her children had run away—her feeling was that if he was stupid enough to run away from a good home, he would have to pay the consequences. She was not a "bad" mother; he was a "bad" boy.

Some friends of ours had a son run away several years ago and they were told by a child guidance clinic that "Children don't run away from good homes." We think this is very debatable. Not so long ago a 14-year-old runaway told us: "I love Mom and Dad. I ran away from school because it's useless. And I ran to be free."

There is no traditional model for parents to follow in rearing their children

The old traditional model has been riddled by critical studies, yet no adequate new model has been developed. Instead we have had a series of fads and fashions in child rearing based on the research of the moment. Rose Kennedy, the mother of the late president, John F. Kennedy, has this to say about the advice given parents: "I am amused at reversals of scientific fashion among great and famous experts."[11] She says that she relied largely on tradition in rearing her large brood.

Perhaps the low point in American expertise on child rearing came in 1974 when Dr. Benjamin Spock, whose book on infant care went through 58 printings in various editions and sold over 15 million copies up to that point alone, apologized to the American parents who had used his book. Spock now feels that he helped produce a generation of "brats."[12]

Contemporary parents are expected to rear children who are not only different from the parents but better

Probably the title of this subsection makes the point as well as it can be made. Both Riesman and Lerner, as well as Brim, point out that it is not enough for modern parents to simply produce children who will replace them in the larger society, one reason being that the larger society is changing so rapidly that the old models will no longer suffice.[13]

This point is aptly demonstrated by the dilemma facing rural parents today: Rural society as the parents know it is disappearing from modern America—there is no place in rural America for the majority of the children growing up there. Modern agriculture is becoming a big business. The capital investment (literally hundreds of thousands of dollars), the managerial skills, and the technology required today to succeed in almost any phase of farm production are beyond the reach of most of the children growing up in rural communities.[14] This means that these rural fathers and mothers are rearing their children for a world the parents have never lived in: the urban world of commerce and industry, the world of the city and the suburb.

Arthur Pearl has developed the concept of "the credentialed society" to describe contemporary America.[15] He refers to the fact that even to drive a garbage truck today a person needs a high school diploma. This was not true in earlier periods of our history. In such a social system, there is no place in the economy for the school dropout: He is forever barred from gainful employment. This places great stress on parents to force their children to remain in school— even when the school situation is negative. Can we honestly say that school is good for everyone? With a straight face?

It is not enough to parents to produce carbon copies of themselves; they have to do what some of the new copying machines are supposed to do—turn out copies better than the originals.

It would seem that this is one of the reasons why contemporary parents feel so inadequate. They are not sure they are able to do what is required. And their children are not sure either.

To some extent, of course, American parents have always faced this problem, at least the immigrant groups did. But the country was expanding then, the frontier was still open, and individual ability rather than formal education was the main ingredient required for economic and personal success.

All parents will probably not be able to meet this challenge and some social institution other than the family will probably have to assume more of the burden. In the recent effort of the federal government to strengthen local school programs, especially in low-income areas, there is emerging a strategy of helping parents in these areas give their children a better chance.[16] Perhaps the function of the family in urban-industrial society will be delimited even more than it has been to date, with the government and the school becoming more dominant in the socialization of children and their preparation for adult life. Some of the programs designed to enrich the lives of preschool children from deprived families seem to represent this approach to the problem.

Parental responsibility is a one-way street in American society

Parents have endless and lifelong responsibilities for their children in our society but children don't have to reciprocate: They don't even have to help parents in old age unless they feel like it. This is in sharp contrast to many other societies. A graduate student from India told us: "If I do not take care of my parents when they are sick or old I would be disgraced in our village. I could never go home again." This man was sending $40 a month to his parents from a very modest scholarship—and he had a family of his own to support.

The popular writer, Dwight MacDonald, makes this comment: "Although there are many how-to books outlining the duties of adults toward children, I have come across none that reverse the field. It was different in the old days when etiquette books were as often aimed at children as their elders."[17]

The notion is certainly indelible in the minds of parents. A professional polling organization found that 67 percent of all parents in a random sample of U.S. parents believed that children "do not have an obligation to their parents regardless of what the parents have done for them." By birth, then, a child has certain inalienable rights. Fine. But no inalienable responsibilities? This is a curious belief.[18]

Parents have total responsibility for their children

In many social roles we are responsible for only one aspect of another human being. The writers, for example, as professors, are responsible for the student's intellectual development in a certain area, but the student's sex life or love life is not our responsibility. Parents, on the contrary, feel that whatever happens to their child is ultimately the responsibility of the father and mother. This is a frightening prospect. The wife of a famous man said to the first author: "When I brought our baby home from the hospital I was literally panic-stricken—what kind of a mother would I be? My husband was never home and I knew that the job was up to me. I was scared as hell and I still am." This woman decided to have only one child—the responsibility was too much for her.

Parenthood is a team effort

Most parents in our society operate as a team; the father and mother rear their children in cooperation. This may be a good system but problems arise when parents do not agree on child rearing. In a study of blue-collar parents, the first author found that the fathers were much more traditional in their philosophy of how to handle children and these men felt that their wives were spoiling their children.[19] One man said: "Our 13-year-old daughter thinks she is a queen—her mother does the dishes while the kid watches TV. I think it stinks."

When you remember the divorce rate in American society, plus separations and desertions, it seems likely that a lot of fathers and mothers are not getting along too well at any given moment and this must present problems for their cooperation as parents.

Each child is unique

Parents sometimes feel that since they understand one of their children they will understand the others as well. This may be true in some cases but it often is not true—one of the children will be so different from the others that the parents find themselves completely frustrated. One mother said: "We had no trouble at all with our son and we felt pretty smug. Then our daughter came along and after 16 years we still find her a complete mystery."

Genetically it is likely that siblings will be very different. An infinite number of gene combinations are possible and nobody knows what will come out when the genetic roulette wheel spins.

The impact of this is that what parents have learned in dealing with one child may not be relevant in trying to handle another child—in fact the earlier learning may even be a handicap in trying to understand the new son or daughter. And then, as one parent said: "When you have learned how to be a parent it is too late—the children are grown up and gone."

Most American parents have no training for this difficult role

It is usually assumed in our society that people have to be trained for difficult roles: Most business firms would not consider turning a sales clerk loose on the customers without some formal training; the armed forces would scarcely send a raw recruit into combat without extensive and intensive training; most states now require a course in driver education before high school students can acquire a driver's license. Even dog owners often go to school to learn how to handle their pet properly.

This is not true of most American parents. In his book, *Future Shock*, Toffler makes this observation: "Despite the increasing complexity of the task, parenthood remains the single preserve of the amateur."[20]

Higher standards of role performance are being applied to modern parents

It is true that Americans are constantly demanding better things—the one-bathroom house has given way to the two-bathroom house; the Model T automobile has been replaced by the latest creation from Detroit or Japan; a college degree now has the same meaning a high school diploma had in the 1920s. While these changes have been recognized in our standard of living, it is often not realized that marriages and child rearing are also being judged by new standards.

When the first author was a child, it was felt that children didn't need dental care, but now parents are expected to take the child to a dentist almost as soon as they get home from the maternity ward. And if the youngster's teeth need straightening, parents are expected to take care of this even though it will usually cost nearly $2,000.

Modern parents are expected to consult a psychiatrist if their child has emotional problems; if their son or daughter has an allergy, this should be diagnosed by a specialist; mental retardation is to be diagnosed early and the proper steps taken; eyes should be examined regularly; hearing problems should be identified early in life. . . .

It is the firm belief of the authors that in many different ways fathers and mothers today are being judged by higher standards of parental performance. If so, this could be a significant factor in parents feeling inadequate.

There is no gradual transition to the parental role

A medical student has several years to adjust to the idea of being a physician responsible for the lives of patients; a law student has several years to get used to the idea that someday he or she will be in court with the responsibility for the welfare of other human beings. With parenthood, however, the transition is sudden: One day you are not a parent and the next day you are a parent. It is true, of course, that for about nine months you are an expectant parent, but somehow this doesn't seem to prepare most people for fatherhood or motherhood.

In a study of parents who had planned to have a child, the majority of the fathers and mothers said they did not really understand what they were getting into.[21] These people did not regret having become parents, but they did report that the role was more demanding than they had realized.

In a classic paper Alice Rossi has identified several features of the parental role which may make the transition to it difficult: the fact that cultural pressures often persuade persons to have children who may not be well adapted to the role—or the cultural pressures result in people having more children than they can enjoy; the fact that many pregnancies are unplanned and perhaps not wanted; the fact that the parental role is irrevocable—it is difficult to quit being a parent once you have a child; and the fact that adequate guidelines for the parental role are lacking in our society.[22]

Some parents do not find their role difficult or frustrating, but whether these are in the majority or minority seems to be debatable.

We don't know what to make of the transition out of the parental role

You will remember Desmond Morris, the anthropologist, outlining humankind's evolutionary roots and dubbing us "the naked ape" in his book of the same name. His words on parenthood are most appropriate here: "The burden of parental care is heavier for the naked ape than for any other living species. Parental duties may be performed as *intensively* elsewhere, but never so *extensively*."[23]

Current economics and a strong undercurrent of faith in the power of a college education has prolonged the parental role in the past few decades. The young were often out of the home in mid-teens, after high school, or certainly the early 20s. Now college and graduate school can stretch these years out endlessly.[24]

Should a parent push the little birds out of the nest to fly on their own soon? Or would that be needlessly cruel? When is help actually helpful to a child? When is it a crutch which further atrophies the spirit? These are difficult questions to answer.

And even if the child has successfully left the nest and become an adult (by the developmental definition, one who is on his or her own), this newly attained adult is still a child in an important sense—for we all remain children as long as our parents are alive. "I'm 65 years old," John's mother notes. "But I'll be a child as long as grandma's around, and you, John, will be one as long as I'm around."

One poignant example we recall from literature is a scene in John Steinbeck's *The Grapes of Wrath*. The Joad family, spanning four generations, is about to leave Oklahoma for California in the Great Depression. The red farm lands of eastern Oklahoma are worn-out and blowing about in swirling, massive and deadly dust storms, and the Joads can stay no longer to watch their corn curl up and die in the hot July sun. A family vote has to be taken, but first everyone must express their opinions of what to do. Great-grandpa Joad, as eldest male, is looked to first for his words. Even though he is too old, too tired, and too confused to clearly make even the simplest of decisions, the family goes through the motions of hearing him out on the critical dilemma they face because that is his role as oldest male. He will carry his parental responsibilities, the family's symbolic father figure, to his grave a few days later on the road to the promised land of California.[25]

Role theory and parenthood

With the arrival of the first child, the married couple assumes a brand new role—that of father and mother. Even though most of them have looked forward to having a child, a significant proportion of them will find that they are poorly prepared for this new role, and some of them will even find that they are unable to function adequately as parents.

Some of the difficulty experienced by many new parents will be related to what Beatrice Wright calls "the discrepancy of expectations"—the role of parent will not be exactly as they imagined it to be.[26] For some of them, being a father or mother will be more satisfying than they had anticipated, while for others parenthood will be more frustrating than they could have imagined.

One source of difficulty related to the arrival of the first child is the fact that all through courtship and the childless years of marriage the young couple have functioned in a two-person group (dyad), but now with the beginning of parenthood they find themselves in a three-person group (triad). There is an old bit of folklore in our society which says that "Two is company but three is a crowd"—the point being that a triad is infinitely more complex than dyad, and that positive relationships among all members are much more difficult to maintain.[27]

In a three-person group there is always the possibility that the group will subdivide. Two persons will form a subgroup and leave the third person more or less stranded.[28] The young wife, for example, may be so enamored of her new role as mother that she begins to neglect her role as wife. If this happens, the husband-father may feel out of the charmed circle.

It is quite easy for an American mother to overload her parental role and become a mommy—a woman who always gives priority to her children over her husband. This is a problem of role balance—dividing one's time and energy among the various roles that make claims on fathers and mothers.

In family counseling, one gets the impression that role balance for the American husband is most often jeopardized by his occupation, his male peer group, or some hobby such as fishing or golf. When this happens, the wife feels neglected.

With the American wife, it seems that role balance is often upset by becoming a mother. The baby is so small and helpless, and its needs are so great, that the husband loses all of the priority he formerly enjoyed with his wife. Whether it is sex or social companionship, he may begin to feel neglected and be jealous of the new child.

Walter Toman has identified 64 basic types of conflict possible between a child and his or her parents.[29] It is true that children destroy some marriages, but the proportion is difficult (if not impossible) to determine. A simple way to approach the question is to ask parents themselves about it. The vast majority of parents will tell you that problems with children did not contribute to their divorce directly. Kathy Jordan found, for example, that 27 separated women came up with 56 separate causes why their marriage had ended; child-related problems were mentioned only twice out of these 56.[30] It is also true that children save some marriages, but here again the precise statistics are not available.

Arnold Green has argued that there are basic conflicts between the role of parent and other fundamental roles at the middle- and upper-class levels in our society.[31] The parent's drive for occupational mobility is often frustrated, Green thinks, by the presence of

children. Green believes that parents at these class levels develop a
deep ambivalence about their roles as mothers and fathers.[32]

Unfortunately, feelings of this nature are not uncovered in the
house-to-house surveys of parents so often published in professional
journals.[33] Being a parent is a sacred trust, one of life's deepest
experiences, and people do not readily admit the full range of their
parental feelngs. One mother said to us: "I love all of them and yet
on certain days I felt like killing each and every one of them." The
amazing thing about this statement is that this mother is actually a
very competent parent—she has reared five children with what
appears to be above-average results. Her feelings are very common
ones.

It may be that the stress of becoming a parent in our society is
related to the fact that parenthood (not marriage) actually represents the last step in the long process of becoming an adult in American society. This may seem obvious, but the writers have the distinct impression that many young Americans feel that marriage
itself is the last step into the adult world. This may indeed be the
case legally, but it certainly is not true psychologically or socially. If
this line of reasoning is sound, it would mean that the role of parent
would represent somewhat of a surprise to many young married
couples—they may think they are fully grown up when in fact they
have to prove it all over again when they become parents.

Parents who run away

It is common to read in the daily press about children (mostly
teenagers) who have run away from their parents. It is not often,
however, that one reads about parents who have run away from
their children. Desertion of children, of course, is well known to
social workers, but reference here is not to desertion but escape:
parents who are willing to go on helping their children but who no
longer wish to live with them.

In upper-class families, this situation has never produced any
problems—the annoying child was simply shipped off to somebody's boarding school. In the middle and lower classes, however,
matters have never been that simple.

In the following descriptions, a middle-class father and mother
felt that they could not go on living with their three semi-adult children. After much soul searching, the father accepted a position in
another country for several years—in other words, until the children
would be grown up and no longer living at home. The parents

offered financial aid for the children who stayed in college and paid room and board for a high school youngster who chose not to go away with his parents.

The mother explained the situation to the first author as follows: "My husband had an excellent offer to work in this other country. At first we felt it was impossible because the children were still at home. Then we realized that the older ones no longer shared our values or our way of life—they had all become hippies of one kind or another and cared very little for what we thought or felt. We offered the youngest one a chance to go with us and he turned down the offer. It seemed to us that we had done what we could for the children and that the time had come to think of ourselves. So we decided to go."

These parents were criticized in their community for "deserting" their children, but the father and mother seem to have very little (if any) guilt over their action. They say that the children seem not to have been affected one way or another by the absence of the parents.

One of the deficiencies in our social structure is that we have no way for parents and children to separate "with honor" when they are not getting along—with the exception of the upper-class boarding-school system mentioned earlier. The same problem exists in our marriage system: Husbands and wives cannot take a vacation from each other without gossip and criticism.

In any intense human relationship, such as that between parent and child, there are times when either the child or the parent (or both) needs to get away for a time to think things over. In some human societies, this appears to have been provided for. A graduate student of the first author's claims, for example, that in an American Indian community in which she did social work it was not uncommon for a youngster to live with somebody else for a year when the home situation became too tense. Margaret Mead describes a society in which the young semiadult males have bachelor houses in which they live.[34]

The situation in our society is especially acute at the high school level, when the child is so close to adult status and yet so far. Some homes are literally armed camps during this period, with parents and children scarcely speaking to each other. With many states now lowering the age of adult status to 18, it would seem that some means will have to be devised to give adolescents a more secure move toward manhood and womanhood.

When Rod Eirick and the second author launched a study of

single-parent fathers a few years ago, they had a stereotyped scene somehow falsely implanted in their brains. The image was of the liberated woman marching happily off to Yale law school to further her career in poverty law, while her smiling and wistful husband waved goodbye, knowing he would miss her but that his androgynous traits would carry him through the rigors of single-parent fatherhood unscathed.

The researchers actually had met a few families whose divorce scenario matched this one. But, in general, the picture was much, much different, and they were dead wrong. The real picture of how fathers end up with custody of the children after a divorce is more likely to be one of a runaway mother. She is running away from the stress of child rearing, the stress of marriage, the stress of money troubles, and work. She may have lost herself in alcohol, other drugs, or in an extramarital affair. Or she may have gone "crazy" to escape the stress, and ended up in a mental health center. The picture, often, is not particularly heartening or happy. Life, in short, has simply gotten the poor woman down. The father, not totally enthusiastic about his prospects, is often thus forced to assume the responsibilities of two parents.

There are, of course, other scenarios—especially that of the father who decides to fight for custody after originally leaving the children with the wife. Later, he decides she is doing a poor job with them, and he can do better.[35]

And yet, there remains a tremendous need for approved ways for parents to separate temporarily from their children. Respite care services are making a great impact on the well-being of troubled parents. Boarding school systems and military schools have been time-honored and socially acceptable ways of gaining some space from the young. There always has been old Uncle Jack on the ranch in Montana to send little Harold off to. Parents are often keenly attuned to other parents willing to trade days and weekends of freedom. A recent church auction we attended had two days of respite from children as one of the items up for bidding. Competition for the respite was brisk among the bidders.

Sharon Stitt made national headlines out of Seattle a few years ago when she opened up "The Parent Place Drop-In Center." Stitt, a single parent, advised that parents run away from home when child care gets them down. But don't head for the bus depot, head for Parent Place, a modest storefront in north Seattle. In addition to getting some distance away from the children, parents can participate in discussion sessions, counseling, and classes.

These very brief respites from the stress of child rearing can be most helpful, obviously. Parent Place in five years has come on strong, Stitt told us in a recent dialog. Between 60 and 80 clients show up a week for activities.[36]

There are numerous calls today for more energy-efficient use of public buildings, and closing up public schools during the summer months has always rankled some taxpayers. A few years ago, Graham Blaine, Jr., one-time head of psychiatric services at Harvard University Medical Services, came up with a solution that would save energy and preserve some parents' sanity. Blaine proposed that schools stay open 11 months of the year, six days a week, from 8 A.M. to 6 P.M. Children in custody of the school would range in age from 3 months until probably 18 (or younger if they're ready to leave).

Blaine argued that 15 to 20 percent of all adolescents are in deep trouble, trouble which overloaded families are incapable of handling. His ideas appeared in a book, *Are Parents Bad for Children?*

Blaine was, of course, soundly attacked from many fronts. It seems, however, that a 9 A.M. to 3 P.M. school may meet the majority of parents' needs, but it is quite possible that other parents need more support. After-school programs are springing up all over now, responding to the needs of dual-career families and single parents in need of extended care for their children. It seems inevitable that Blaine's ideas will slowly become reality, as school districts and other agencies tack program onto program onto program to fashion a more comprehensive approach over the years.[37]

The revolt against parenthood

Sometimes when I look at all my children, I say to myself, "Lillian, you should have stayed a virgin."[38]

Lillian Carter

I love children. I cannot imagine a life without them. But I am extremely realistic about children. I regard them for exactly what they are: A punishment from God.[39]

Erma Bombeck

. . . Any honest parent must describe the parental role very simply as that of civilizing the beast.[40]

Robert Ardrey

In the 1970s the birthrate in the United States showed a tendency to drop.[41] While it is still too early to interpret this trend accurately, it could be that the parental role has become so burdensome and so unrewarding that the new generation is thinking twice before joining the ranks. If seems clear that the woman's liberation movement has made its point that child rearing has been one of the main obstacles to women achieving social and economic equality.[42]

When Ann Landers, the popular columnist, asked her readers to write concerning their experience as parents, some 70 percent who responded said their experience has been negative.[43] This seemed to surprise Landers, who is hard to surprise these days. But a survey commissioned by *Newsday* in which a nationwide sample of 1,373 parents were interviewed, only 7 percent said they would not have children if they had it to do over again.[44] In an earlier study Daniel Miller and Guy Swanson found most of the mothers in their sample to be satisfied that they had been parents.[45]

The human species has been around for several million years and it seems unlikely that people will stop having children. But it does seem likely that parenthood in the United States is becoming more of a voluntary act—it is not the result of brainwashing or bad luck as often as it used to be. If this is true, we think it is a move in the right direction.

The child-free alternative

The National Alliance for Optional Parenthood in Washington, D.C. for the past decade has asked some provocative and useful questions of prospective parents:

1. Does having and raising a child fit the lifestyle I want? What do I want out of life for myself? What do I think is important? Could I handle a child and a job at the same time? Could I give up my freedom?

2. What's in it for me? Do I like doing things with children? Would I want a child to be "like me"? Will I prove I am a man (or a woman) by having a child? Do I expect my child to make my unhappy life happy?

3. Raising a child? What's there to know? Do I like children? Do I want to give a child the love needed? Is loving easy for me? Am I patient enough to deal with the noise and confusion and the 24-hour-a-day responsibility? What kind of time and space do I need for myself? What do I do when I get angry and upset? Would I take my feelings out on the child? What if I have a child and find out I made the wrong decision?

4. Have my partner and I really talked about becoming parents? Does my partner really want a child? Could we give a child a good home? Could we share our love for the child without jealousy? Do my partner and I understand each other's feelings on religion, work, family, child rearing, future goals? Do we feel pretty much the same way? Suppose one of us wants a child and the other doesn't? Who decides?[46]

Jean Veevers made a significant contribution to our understanding of voluntary childlessness by reviewing 22 empirical studies over the past several years which were concerned with various aspects of the deliberate avoidance of parenthood.

One critical issue in the study of voluntary childlessness is that of the beneficial or deleterious effects of having or not having children. Veevers broke these effects down into the following five categories:

1. Senescence. What are the long-term effects of childlessness? What will happen to people when they grow old and have no children? Will they die lonely, packed away in a nursing home as the stereotype goes? Veevers looked at two major studies in this area and concluded that though children are a sustaining force for many older persons, the data makes it apparent that many elderly childless persons are able to find alternative sources of support and companionship, or they manage effectively in relatively isolated situations.

2. Mental health. The majority of researchers conclude that the voluntary childless do not exhibit any more evidence of psychopathology or deviance from the norm than a control group of parents.

3. Occupational success. Veevers concludes that childlessness leaves individuals with an abundance of surplus time and energy that can be invested in the career or service area, for among persons of eminence, especially women of eminence, a disproportionate number are known to be childless.

4. Divorce. Does having children cement a marriage together? Are the childless prone to divorce? Veevers argues that the available data still do not allow for a definite conclusion at this time.

5. Marital morale and interaction. Even if we don't know what childlessness does to divorce rates, what quality marriage do husbands and wives have versus mothers and fathers? Veevers says that the data in this area are contradictory and inconclusive at this time.

Veevers notes that while voluntary childlessness will never become a dominant life style, it is increasingly gaining acceptability as one workable alternative, "ideally suited for some persons who would find the rigors of parenthood an undue and perhaps unnecessary burden and strain."[47]

Summary and conclusion

In this chapter the position has been taken that the parental role in contemporary America is poorly defined, not well delimited, and that most fathers and mothers have had inadequate preparation for the role.

It was also suggested that parental authority has been eroded in our society over a period of several decades, without any reduction in parental responsibility. This development apparently reflects the rights-of-children movement since World War I and has resulted in some confusion as to the rights of parents.

Another major point is that the parental role in our society is harder to withdraw from than other major roles. The best illustration of this is the new right of Americans to discontinue marriages that they no longer find congenial. There has been no comparable development for parents.

The chapter included some consideration of role theory as it relates to parenthood and noted the appearance of a new type of American parent: fathers and mothers who are still willing to help their children but who are no longer willing to live with them. Reference was made to what appears to be the beginnings of a revolt against parenthood in American society, and the child-free alternative was discussed.

Chapter 5

Parents and social class

In the past several decades, American social scientists have produced a mass of research on the behavior of the various socioeconomic levels in our society.[1] This material does not imply that all individuals or families at a given social level are identical in their beliefs and overt behavior, but simply that they tend to reflect a subculture or way of life evolved by the group over time. Some persons may be marginal members of their social class and reflect only partially its subculture. There may also be subcultures within subcultures: Dentists and physicians, for example, are both members of the upper-middle class in our society, but each also has unique group-behavior patterns related to the different nature of the occupations. Dentists have regular hours, to cite one difference, while most physicians do not.

It should be understood clearly that, while the terms *upper* and *lower* are used to designate positions in the American social class structure, these are not meant by social scientists to reflect value judgments—they designate, for the most part, power and prestige, not moral worth.

Some levels of the social class structure have been studied more intensively than others. The middle class, for example, tends to be overrepresented in much research, while the upper class is often missing entirely in many studies. In recent years special efforts have been made to reach low-income groups and to record their way of life.[2]

To the extent that American society is becoming a mass or homogenized society, the social class differences considered in this chapter may be diminishing, but at the moment this is a difficult matter to assess. Rural subculture, for example, may be disappearing, but at the same time other and new subcultures related to social class position may be evolving.[3] The reader needs to keep this in mind in considering the material presented in this chapter. Gerald Handel argues the dimension of social class "has emerged as the most enduringly significant large-scale influence on parenthood in the United States." He theorizes that other influences, such as religion and ethnic background, have been decreasing in impact but social class has not.[4]

Our analysis will begin with parents at the bottom of the social class structure—fathers and mothers rearing children at the poverty level.

Parents at the poverty level

The average American knows very little about persons at the poverty level.[5] Most college students have never met such a person or known such a family. In the affluent society, poor people are viewed as deviants—they really have no place in the society, and most of us do not know how we should view them. As Harrington pointed out long ago, most Americans would prefer not to see members of the poverty group and would like to forget that they exist.[6]

There is no universally accepted figure on the percentage of families living at the poverty level in American society. The problem is that authorities differ about what income a family needs to sustain a decent way of life in the contemporary United States. It would appear, however, that at least one fifth of all American parents are rearing their children at the poverty level.[7]

In 1978 a young economist at Stanford University made headlines nationwide by boldly declaring in his book *Welfare* that, "The 'war on poverty' that began in 1964 has been won. The growth of jobs and income in the private economy, combined with an explosive increase in government spending for welfare and income transfer programs, has virtually eliminated poverty in the United States." The author, Martin Anderson, was working with statistics at the time, not poor people. His argument, of course, caused considerable controversy, and he was hailed as a prophet by conservatives while vilified as the author of a cruel hoax by liberals. Anderson gained the attention of Ronald Reagan and became an adviser to the White House on domestic policy. But if the war on poverty is over, we would ask, why should the fight end with so many poor folks still around? Anderson's statistics strike us as a classic of wishful thinking, mixed with a liberal desire to sweep problems under rugs. And, they are a useful antidote to charges that Mrs. Reagan's purchase of $1,000 place settings for White House dinners is a mite extravagant.[8]

The poor have often been romanticized in our society. As James Rainwater points out in the paper cited earlier, the poor are viewed as being different biologically from the rest of us, or they are portrayed as happy and contented with their lot. Max Lerner comments on this: "One image that we shall have to discard . . . is the romantic image of the lower-lower-class family as stable, integrated, and happy, while the middle class is divorce ridden and neurotic."[9]

A mass of data can be cited to contradict the romantic folklore image of the lower-class family—we cite only a few representative studies. In his classic analysis of divorce in Detroit after World War II, William Goode found the divorce rate highest in the low-income groups, and higher among black poor people than among white people of the same income level.[10] In their study of mental illness and social class, Alfred Hollingshead and Frederick Redlich found psychosis rates higher in lower-class families than in the middle or upper class.[11] In his analysis of school dropouts, James Conant found much higher rates among the lower class.[12] Except for embezzlement, almost all forms of crime in modern America are highest in low-income groups.[13] Studies of physical disease find most ailments more frequent among low-income groups—this is especially true of such outmoded diseases as tuberculosis.[14] Surveys of dental care report over half of low-income children and adults suffer from serious dental neglect.[15] Alcoholism has always been common among low-income groups, but in contemporary America it may be almost as common among middle- and upper-income groups.[16] Kinsey found premarital sexual experience to be most common among the lower class (persons who had not gone beyond the eighth grade in school).[17] Rejection rates for the armed forces are almost three times as high in the poverty group as they are in the middle and upper classes.[18] Child abuse and neglect, including sexual abuse, is probably much higher in low-income groups of people.[19] Public welfare recipient rates are, of course, highest among the low-income families.[20]

A massive study by University of Michigan economists over a decade monitored the economic ups and downs of 5,000 randomly sampled American families and found that poverty is far less persistent but much more pervasive in American life than most people would have thought. The data from the study undermined the notion that poverty is a permanent, intractable condition for most poor people, trapping millions. Rather, it painted a more fluid picture of it, with people slipping in and out of poverty fairly often as time passes. Only one in five people considered poor in 1975, for example, was poor in every one of the nine years the people were interviewed by the researchers. On the other hand, almost a third of all the families monitored fell below the poverty line for at least one of the nine years. James N. Morgan, project director, argues that we need to distinguish between long- and short-term poverty. Different types of people need different types of programs. He adds that, "The problem is really a lot more serious than most are willing to recognize."

Probably the biggest factor underlying change in economic status is a change in family composition. Divorce, new children, and other domestic changes often result in dramatic shifts in economic well-being, particularly for women and children. A third of the women who were divorced and not remarried fell below the poverty line, even counting alimony, child support, and welfare payments; only 13 percent of the divorced men suffered the same fate. Those who remain "persistently poor over a long period of time were likely to live in households headed by a person over age 65, a person who has little formal education, or who is black, female, or disabled.[21]

Poverty involves a host of conditions that low-income parents have to cope with in rearing their children. Some of their specific disadvantages are summarized in the next section.

High birthrates

As a group, poverty parents have more than their share of children to rear. As Lee Rainwater and others have documented, low-income groups have less knowledge about family planning and less access to birth-control facilities than do middle- or upper-class parents.[22] This means that, in addition to their other handicaps, poverty parents are struggling with more children per parent than other social class groups in the society.

Slum neighborhoods

Studies have shown for a long time that certain behavior characterizes slum areas, regardless of what group happens to be living in the area at any given time. In their study, *Beyond the Melting Pot*, Nathan Glazer and Daniel Patrick Moynihan document the various behavior difficulties that have been endemic in certain slum areas of New York City, regardless of whether the area was inhabited by Italians, blacks, Irish, or Puerto Ricans.[23]

Parents at the poverty level have little choice about what neighborhood they live in. They must enter the urban community at what the sociologists used to call "the point of least resistance." It is undoubtedly true that some low-income parents are quite adept at getting the best out of their social environment—as Arthur Pearl and Frank Riessman argue[24]—but the fact remains that rearing children in a slum area is a challenge most parents would be happy to escape.

Inferior employment

Lower-class mothers are more likely to seek outside employment if it is available; and, if they find it, the working hours, the wages, and the conditions of employment are apt to be less than ideal. Low-income black mothers in Chicago, for example, according to St. Clair Drake and Horace Cayton in *Black Metropolis*, are likely to be domestic servants, commuting long distances to the suburbs and working long hours, six days a week, with little or no vacation time off.[25]

These mothers face almost insuperable problems in rearing their children properly, regardless of their devotion to them. The proper conditions for good parenthood are simply not available.[26] The three-generation or extended family system, with a grandmother or other relative in the home, has probably been the best defense these mothers have had for coping with their parental problems. But the three-generation or extended family system has never been very popular in urban America, and this tends to mitigate against these mothers using this coping device.

If the lower-class father is living with the family, his employment is also likely to be sporadic and not of the best nature. His wages are relatively low, his skills are limited, and his unemployment rate is generally high.[27]

A majority of the poor white families live in poverty-stricken rural areas, such as Appalachia, which offer very few, if any, public welfare or health services that might help these parents with their children.[28] The urban poor, bad as the ghetto is, have at least some public and private agencies to help them with some of their parental problems.[29]

One concludes that it is not only the low income that poses problems for lower-class parents; it is also the other conditions they have to contend with.

Inadequate education

These lower-class parents do not usually have a high school education. Many of them have not even completed the eighth grade. Some of them cannot read or write. All of this means that they face almost insuperable handicaps in trying to understand the world they and their children live in, to say nothing of trying to cope with that world.[30]

There is another dimension to this handicap: They find it difficult to retain the respect of their children, most of whom have more formal schooling than their parents, and this discrepancy is made more devastating by the fact that these children are living in a world in which a high school diploma is taken for granted, just as middle-class families often take a college degree for granted. But try out the label *illiterate* on yourself. It does not set well, does it?

It is certainly true, as Oscar Handlin and others have pointed out, that most of the earlier immigrant groups in America had this same sort of problem.[31] The second author's maternal grandparents, for example, came almost penniless to the United States from the Ukraine. Neither could speak English. Grandma Wolfe couldn't read or write in either German or Russian. Grandpa swept floors at a local saloon before the town went dry; the saloonkeeper taught him how to read English. Grandma Wolfe never did learn to read. But those immigrants and their children were living in a very different kind of world—a world in which poverty was taken for granted and formal education was unusual rather than typical. The world of the earlier immigrant and his or her children was also less dangerous and less complicated. There were fewer laws to violate, there was (apparently) less serious juvenile delinquency, and certainly the expectations applied to these immigrant parents were lower and less harsh than those applied today.

The fact is that these low-income parents need desperately to get their children through the school system, yet they themselves usually did not graduate and they lack knowledge of how the system works. Role models are powerful influences on a developing child; uneducated parents are hard-pressed to model a lifestyle alien to them. In a famous study, August Hollingshead demonstrated how middle- and upper-class parents manage to keep their children in school, regardless of the child's mental capacity or his social behavior.[32]

Poor health

With a few exceptions, such as heart attacks, there seems to be overwhelming evidence that the lower-class parent has more illness, both mental and physical, has less resistance to various diseases, has inferior medical and hospital care, and dies earlier than parents who hold a more favorable position in the class structure.[33]

Any person who has ever been a parent knows what it is like to try to take care of young children when the parent is not feeling well, and the situation is no different when trying to cope with an adolescent youngster under similar circumstances. In over 150 parent discussion groups conducted by the writers in the past several years, ill health was one of the items most often cited by fathers and mothers for not being able to live up to their own standards of parental performance.[34]

Some types of illness, such as tuberculosis, often result in the afflicted parent being out of the home for considerable periods of time. This might also be true of emotional disturbances.

For financial reasons, lower-class parents often go to work when ill, when other parents would stay home. Often they will be paid by the hour and lack benefit of sick leave. For the same reasons, they (and their children) often do not have medical attention when they should. These parents, because of their poor education and relatively low "social intelligence," are also preyed on by all sorts of medical quacks, such as patent-medicine vendors and other witch doctors. The money they do have to spend on medical care is often poorly spent.

Unstable marriages

One of the crucial factors for the parental team seems to be a stable marriage. If so, there appears to be evidence that marital instability rates are highest at the low-income levels. In one of the more impressive studies of divorce in our society, Goode concludes that divorce rates are inversely correlated with socioeconomic status—in other words, that divorce rates increase as income declines.[35] There also seems to be evidence that desertion rates are higher at the lower-class level.[36] To this list must be added the fact that the absent-father syndrome is more common at low-income levels.[37] All this adds up to the fact that poverty parents are more than normally plagued with marital problems as they struggle to rear their children.

Inadequate legal services

Numerous studies have demonstrated that low-income parents and their children do not receive their fair share of justice in America.[38] Children in the poverty group are more apt to be arrested for minor offenses in the community; when arrested they receive relatively poor legal defense; and when convicted the children of poverty families tend to receive more severe punishment; if they end up in jail, they can't see their kids very often because they can't afford to pay bus fare to and from the correctional center. Sometimes a whole year may pass without contact.

Low-income parents have less knowledge of the legal system and are unable to afford the legal services that would protect them and their children against unfair treatment in the courts. This is in sharp contrast to parents at the middle- or upper-class levels. Government legal services for the poor are under constant attack by conservative elements in the community, and budgets are so miniscule that programs sometimes have to put a moratorium on new clients because they can't take care of old clients.

Inadequate parenting education

We have been somewhat critical of professionals in the behavioral sciences in this book, but wish to point out that we still see a need for careful, well-planned, and well-executed programs for developing parenting skills. Poor parents are unable to pay much for the services they receive in this area, and so they often get what they pay for: Not much.

Recently we visited a positive parenting group meeting in a ghetto area. The scene was straight out of a Franz Kafka novel. About 60 parents and 75 screaming, runny-nosed children were packed in a sweltering gymnasium in a city recreation center. We talked, somehow, to the mass of people on the art of positive discipline techniques for child rearing. As the lecture proceeded, the shrieks of the children raised to a fever pitch. Most of the parents had the spaced-out, despairing, or oblivious look of the down-and-out. After the talk, we happened to sit down with a young woman of about 17; four preschoolers rolled and scrambled about her. Through glassy eyes she explained her recent efforts in discipline: "Robbie was beating up Sally, and I told him to stop. And he kept on doing it, and I told him to stop. And he kept on and he kept on." Her eyes began to focus keenly in the air on the scene which was vividly recreated in her mind. "So I took him upstairs into the bedroom . . . and I *really* told him to stop. And he did," she concluded in triumph. We shuddered to think what type of blunt instrument did the telling.

A young MSW about 25 was responsible for running this zoo and developing "positive parenting skills." An army of professionals with a jillion dollars might make a dent on the situation. Maybe. More likely, a group of dedicated volunteers could be marshalled by the community to make a real difference.

Blue-collar parents

This section focuses on the stable, employed blue-collar parents: factory workers, construction craftsmen, truck drivers, school custodians, and the like. These people are often referred to as *the working class*—a term which leaves much to be desired.[39]

Many years ago, in a classic study of Muncie, Indiana, Robert and Helen Lynd pointed out that one of the major differences between blue-collar workers and white-collar workers is that the former manipulate *things* whereas the latter manipulate *people*.[40] A good example would be the work of an automobile mechanic versus the work of a car salesperson. The Lynds felt that these two kinds of work tend to produce different types of behavior.

The average blue-collar parent in the United States has only a high school education, but in the white-collar middle-class world parents often have a college education. This poses some problems for blue-collar fathers and mothers, as we shall see later in this section.

The incomes of blue-collar parents in our society often exceed those of white-collar parents. In the writers' communities, for example, licensed plumbers can make $27,000 to $33,000 in a good year, whereas public school teachers in this area average $19,000 per year. It needs to be remembered, however, that income does not necessarily determine lifestyle.[41]

One great advantage that many blue-collar workers have over most white-collar employees is their protection by powerful trade unions. Seniority rights protect them against persons lower in the hierarchy; fringe benefits cover their medical expenses; and dismissal must be for very specific violations of work rules.

In spite of these advantages, however, blue-collar fathers and mothers have some very real problems in our society. These are analyzed in the next section.

Special problems of blue-collar parents

It was indicated earlier that there is considerable range of income, status, and security in the blue-collar world in contemporary America. The following discussion will have to be read with this in mind.

Some of the special problems of blue-collar parents include the following:

The number of blue-collar workers is declining. America is becoming increasingly a white-collar world. This is forcing the sons and daughters of blue-collar parents to move into white-collar occupations, which are increasing. For example, the steel workers' union has actually lost membership since World War II as the steel mills have been automated. The same situation prevails among printers, dock workers, and many other blue-collar work groups.[42] This means that the father may not be able to get his son into his union or into an apprenticeship; it also means that the blue-collar fathers and mothers are not as able to guide their children as the children move into a white-collar world. Such parents do not know as much about colleges, and they often do not push their children as hard in elementary or secondary school. It is simply harder for blue-collar parents to launch their children into the white-collar world than it was to help them get into a trade at the blue-collar level. Basically, such parents face the same problems farm parents face: Most farm children will not be able to find a niche in agriculture, yet both they and their parents have grown up in a rural world.

The percentage of mothers employed outside of the home tends to be somewhat higher at the blue-collar level. Ivan Nye and Lois Wladis Hoffman point out that this differential is not as pronounced as it was before World War II, but the fact remains that blue-collar mothers work outside of the home considerably more often than do mothers at some of the middle-class levels.[43] There is not much difference at the lower-middle-class level.

Blue-collar mothers have some compensating factors to offset their outside employment, however: They do not belong to as many voluntary organizations as do middle-class women and when they do belong they do not carry as much responsibility.

Blue-collar parents have some social distance problems with their children.   All American parents have this problem to some extent because of rapid change and the vast amount of social mobility in the United States. But blue-collar parents suffer more from this situation due to the fact that their children are being forced to move into the white-collar world. This is quite different from the lower class, where vertical social mobility is relatively rare.

There is a value stretch between blue-collar fathers and mothers.   In the first author's study of blue-collar parents a considerable difference was found between fathers and mothers in their child-rearing philosophy. The fathers tended to be traditional and authoritarian whereas the mothers were more inclined to be permissive and contemporary.[44] In a sense the men were adult-centered while the women were child-centered. These differences seemed to be related to the fact that the mothers worked in white-collar jobs and were exposed to middle-class values through magazines and television programs. Earlier studies by Nathan Hurvitz and Mirra Komarovsky found this same value stretch between blue-collar husbands and wives.[45]

Blue-collar parents are not reflected in mass media.   The vast majority of television programs, radio shows, magazine articles, and advertisements in our society focus on the white-collar world. An afternoon spent watching the traditional soap opera should confirm this for any reader. In the early 1970s CBS Television did develop a successful series featuring a blue-collar husband-father, but some labor leaders objected that the main male character, Archie Bunker, did not reflect credit on blue-collar workers.[46] In any event, blue-collar fathers and mothers, and their children, seldom see their world reflected in the mass media.

It is difficult to assess the net impact of this virtual exclusion from the mass media; but, in the past, minority groups in the United

States have complained that similar treatment of them has made it
more difficult to achieve a positive self-image. Another possible
effect is to make one unhappy with his world—if it is not worth
portraying on television or in the movies, is it worth perpetuating?

Blue-collar parents are becoming a minority group. In the
19th century, America was essentially a blue-collar society—the
millions of immigrants entered the social class system at the bottom
and it often took them two to three generations to work their way up
to the middle class.

This has now changed. The most rapidly expanding segments of
the economy are white collar, and blue-collar persons are becoming a minority group—just as farm parents have become. In the first
author's metropolitan community, the public school superintendent
has been quoted as saying, "We must stop counseling all high
school students to go to college and remind them that blue-collar
jobs are also rewarding and worthy of consideration."[47]

When all of the social leaders are white collar, when the mass-
media idols are white collar, how does a blue-collar father or
mother portray his or her way of life as something for a child to
emulate or admire? It is a good question.

Middle-class parents

Some social scientists have argued that parental stress is greatest
at the middle-class level.[48] Actually, there is a vast social distance
within the white-collar middle class: It is a long way from clerking in
a shopping center to being a surgeon, yet both are considered
members of the middle class.

In one sense it is always difficult to be in the middle—alternate
models of behavior exist above and below and you have to carve
out your own way of life. And yet, how many middle-class parents
would be willing to trade places with parents at the poverty level?

In this section, attention will be focused on two segments of the
middle class: parents at the bottom of the middle class (the so-called
lower-middle class) and parents at the top of the middle class (the
so-called upper-middle class). There is also a "middle" middle class
but the limited space prohibits discussion of them in this volume.

Lower-middle-class parents

The lower-middle class, the fastest growing social class in America, includes the person who checks out your groceries at the super-

market, the receptionist at the motel registration desk, the waiter or waitress in your favorite restaurant, and the government clerk who checks your income-tax return. There are literally millions of new jobs at this level in the "consumer society."[49]

These lower-middle-class people may not have unions to bargain for them or protect them; hence, they are frequently subject to low wages, long hours, and job insecurity. To the extent that they can be unionized, they represent one of the largest labor pools available to the mass trade unions.

Some observers of modern America, such as Max Lerner, regard the lower-middle class to be one of the least enviable positions in the contemporary social class system.[50] These people lack the pride of the old blue-collar aristocracy; they make less money; they have less skill to sell; and they lack job security. At the same time, they tend to identify with the more highly educated and prosperous white-collar groups above them.

Lower-middle-class parents are apt to face some very real problems. The wife and mother often works full time in an attempt to achieve the standard of consumption the family aspires to.[51] The marital failure rate at this socioeconomic level is relatively high.[52] These fathers and mothers tend to be ambitious for their children, pushing them toward college even though the parents themselves are not usually college graduates. If the children succeed in climbing the social class ladder, the family ties often suffer from vertical social class mobility.[53] The ability of the parents to guide their mobile children is limited by the fact that the parents have never lived in the social world the children are moving into. As socialization for the child's new position proceeds, some of the ideas and values inculcated by the parents have to be discarded. This sometimes hurts the parents or the child or both. And in the process, sibling relationships are often weakened also.

It is never easy to be at the bottom of a social class—the people above you have many advantages that you can see (and almost touch), and yet many of these patterns of life are beyond your reach. This produces a tendency for the lower-middle class to spend more than it should and to strive for a way of life that may not be realistic for them. It is a wise father and mother who can foresee the pitfalls in the lower-middle-class world.

In one lower-middle-class family studied by the first author, the husband and father was manager of a meat department in a small supermarket. In order to earn more money, he worked four evenings a week, or about 80 hours every seven days. He also moonlighted as a bartender on weekends. The couple had purchased a beautiful house with heavy mortgage payments and a high interest rate (the interest rate was high because they did not have enough savings to make an adequate downpayment on the house).

In addition to the new home, the couple was making payments on a new automobile, wall-to-wall carpeting, and a color television console ($800). When the husband could not make all of his monthly payments, the wife took a job at an all-night restaurant as a waitress. In addition to their excessive work schedules, this young couple (in their 30s) was attempting to rear four children.

Disaster was almost inevitable in this situation. One of the children became involved in a glue-sniffing incident, and when the juvenile court judge learned of the work patterns of the parents, he ordered them to spend a certain number of hours a week at home with their children. This, of course, made it impossible for the couple to sustain their standard of living—if it can be called "living." The crisis was finally resolved when the couple sold their expensive home and moved to a smaller community where the husband could earn an adequate living as a meat cutter.

It is not implied that this couple is typical of lower-middle-class parents. The case is presented to show what can happen when persons at this social class level become enamored of a way of life beyond their reach.

Upper-middle-class parents

Herbert Gans takes the position that the upper-middle class is perhaps the most comfortable position in the American social class system.[54] Most of these parents are physicians, lawyers, accountants, business executives, or owners of successful moderately small enterprises (stores, for example). Incomes are comfortable but not large enough to make the family conspicuous in the community. The vast majority of the fathers and mothers in the upper-middle class are college graduates, often with advanced degrees in some profession.[55]

With their income, these parents can choose the community in which to rear their children, can afford to send them to college, and, in general, can launch them into the competitive society.

In spite of their many advantages, parents at the upper-middle-class level have some very real problems:

These parents have usually won their socioeconomic position by personal effort and achievement. Physicians, for example, have gone to college and medical school for 10–15 years before completing their training. Business executives have often begun their careers at modest levels and have worked their way up through some large corporate structure to get where they are—a process that often involves a decade or more of perseverance after completing college.

All of this effort pays off in the sense that these fathers and mothers can give their children many advantages, but they *cannot* assure them of a position in the upper-middle class. The child has to win this position in the same way that the parents won it, through hard effort.

Here is an example: At the private college referred to earlier, the first author was adviser to a young man whose father was a gynecologist. It had always been the father's dream (shared by the son) that someday the boy would go through medical school and come home to join the father's medical practice. This dream became a nightmare when the son completed two years of a premedical program with a C average. At that point he was notified by the college's medical counselor that he would never gain admission to a medical school and that he should explore other careers.

Notice that there is simply no way for a physician or an attorney to get his son or daughter into his own profession unless the child has at least some minimum level of ability and perseverance. This problem is not faced by upper-class parents, who usually control enough wealth to guarantee a child's social position.

In the study cited earlier the first author did not find any drive for upward mobility in these college students from the upper-middle class—their concern, and that of their parents, was that they did not move *down* in the class structure.[56] As we shall see, this changed in the 1960s.

Upper-middle-class parents must also face their children's revolt. In this revolt, which began in the 1960s and became massive by the 1970s,[57] the sons and daughters renounced the way of life of their parents as being too materialistic and sought other values and other goals. Many of the upper-middle-class youngsters dropped out of college or refused to pursue long professional training programs. They dressed differently from their parents, used drugs other than alcohol for relaxation, and many of them experimented with sexual and marital patterns not approved by their parents. In sum, many of the children of upper-middle-class parents in the last several years have not found the way of life of their parents attractive.

Some of the difficulty in this parent-child gap is related to the fact that the children have relatively little faith in the future of human society as it is presently organized. They are not willing to struggle for 10–15 years to enter some profession, when they read almost daily in the press that the year 2000 may see the end of the world as we now know it. As one extremely popular youthful balladeer, Cat Stevens, intones:

> "I don't want to work away
> doing just what they all say,
> 'Work hard boy and you'll find
> one day you'll have a job like mine
> job like mine, a job like mine.
> Be wise, look ahead,
> use your eyes,' he said.
> 'Be straight, think right.'
> But I might die tonight!"[58]

Their parents were not faced with such a catastrophic view of the future—they felt that you could go to college for a decade or so and still have plenty of time to enjoy the rewards that would surely come when the training period was over. Their children, very often, are not convinced that this is the case. The children are also not convinced that the big house and the big cars are worth the rat race they involve.

There are those who argue that the generation gap has abated with inflation and recession in the late 1970s and early 1980s, causing a new fear and conservatism on the part of the young. We would concur that economics has had a great effect on attitudes, but that the cultural revolution of the 1960s made an indelible mark on those young people and many in later cohorts, just as the Great Depression forever chastened an earlier generation. It is not clear, as yet, how this dilemma of the upper-middle-class parent in the 1970s and 1980s will be resolved.

Upper-middle-class parents try to help the child attain self-realization. This is in place of internalizing external controls. These studies by Melvin Kohn and others,[59] conclude that blue-collar parents tend to emphasize conformity in their children whereas many middle-class parents seek to help the child discover his or her own goals and then to achieve them. This would appear to make the job of the middle-class parent more difficult.

Upper-class parents

It is difficult to write about these fathers and mothers because little research has been published about them. Paul Blumberg and P. W. Paul, for example, after studying material in the *New York Times* on 413 families who appeared to be upper class, conclude that "the upper class is perhaps the most untouched group in American life."[60] Most of the observations in this section will be from various popular books written about famous families.

On the surface it would seem that upper-class parents have all the advantages: They have money with which to hire people to help them with their children; they have power enough to assure their children a secure place in society regardless of the children's ability; they live in the best sections of the community; their children attend superior schools; medical care is of the highest quality available. In spite of these advantages, however, we shall see that upper-class parents have some very real problems in rearing their children. Some of these are:

Parents usually have other commitments that interfere with their parental role. Rose Kennedy, writing about her experience rearing her children, points out that her husband was absent the vast bulk of the time when the children were young. Joseph Kennedy was deeply involved in financial affairs that eventually created the family fortune, and he could spare very little time for his children.[61]

When Winston Churchill was a young child he saw his father for only an hour or so each week—in fact, he scarcely saw his mother either because both of his parents were very active in the social life of the English aristocracy. Winston was taken care of during his preschool years by an English nanny (a servant who specialized in caring for young children).[62]

A woman from the English upper class has observed: "The parents of Victorian times seem to have been amused by their offspring. Mothers might see their little ones once a day, the fathers once a year.[63]

The late English king, Edward VIII (the one who gave up his throne to marry an American divorcee), once wrote that as a child he was permitted to see his parents, the king and queen, one hour a day before their evening social engagements.[64]

The man who developed the medical uses of penicillin and who won a Nobel Prize for his efforts is reported to have scarcely seen his son during the first five years of the child's life because of the demands of his work.[65]

Eleanor Roosevelt talked about how difficult it was for her and her husband (who was elected president of the United States four times) to reserve time for their children.[66] Not only was the president immersed in public affairs, his wife was also a world leader and spent much of her time traveling on behalf of various humanitarian causes.

The recent biographies and autobiographies of upper-class families which reinforce the contention that the children are often neglected by parents and reared by nurses and governesses are too numerous to catalog in detail. They include: Adlai Stevenson, whose three sons almost worshipped him but whose career was so demanding that they saw him relatively little when they were growing up; Stevenson was governor of Illinois, ran for president twice, and was ambassador to the United Nations.[67] Nancy Mitford, a famous writer, who as a child was consigned to the care of outsiders, never did develop a positive relationship with her mother.[68] Dorothy Schiff, inheritor of a fortune who took over the *New York Post*, said, "The only time we had meals with our parents was Sunday lunch. . . . No parents were visible at supper, which John and I and our governess had in the breakfast room. . . . After our evening meals, we would join our parents for a short time in the library."[69] Sloan Wilson, author of *The Man in the Gray Flannel Suit*, who was brought up by a Scottish nursemaid named Annie, said: "My early youth was happy in an unconventional way, partly because both my parents were too busy to bother much with me."[70] Patty Hearst, the daughter of a wealthy newspaper family who was kidnapped by the Symbionese Liberation Army and held hostage, noted to her fiancé Stephen Weed that she didn't know her parents until she was 10.[71] Charles Revson, Jr., heir to the multimillion-dollar Revlon makeup products fortune, said he never really knew his father and was brought up by his nurse, Katie.[72] Christina Crawford wrote scathingly of her stepmother Joan Crawford in *Mommie Dearest*, charging that when upper-class parents can't handle their children they send them to boarding school.[73] Gloria

Morgan Vanderbilt, heir to a long line of wealthy financiers, concurred with this judgment.[74]

Those Fabulous Greeks,[75] an account of Aristotle Onassis who married Jacqueline Kennedy, adds to this picture; and *Their Turf*[76] is a curious book describing those enormously wealthy families whose lives center around their horses, who appear to play a greater part in the parents' lives than the children.

This is not necessarily intended as a criticism of upper-class parents. It simply means that they have often not had the time required to perform their parental role. Instead, they have had to employ nurses, governesses, and tutors to take care of their children. And once the children were old enough they have been sent to expensive boarding schools.

"The shadow of the ancestor" often haunts the children of illustrious parents. Father or grandfather or grandmother or somebody among the ancestors left a legacy of accomplishment that the children (or the grandchildren) cannot match. John D. Rockefeller, Jr., describes how he decided to leave the business world because he knew that in no way could he compete with the reputation of his father—the world's first billionaire. The son eventually achieved a significant and meaningful life in the field of philanthropy, establishing the Rockefeller Foundation.[77]

The children of Franklin and Eleanor Roosevelt faced this same problem of achieving some sort of self-identity: If you are a girl, what do you do with your life when your mother has been voted to be the outstanding woman of the world in her generation? And, if you are a boy, what do you do when your father has been elected president of the United States four times?[78]

Middle- and lower-class children have an advantage in that they have a chance to surpass the accomplishments of their parents. This is usually not possible at the upper-class level.

Wealthy parents have always had the problem of not spoiling their children. This is one reason why upper-class boarding schools have usually been known for their spartan characteristics—small rooms with little furniture, cold showers, modest food, early rising, and stern schoolmasters.[79]

Another related problem of upper-class parents is that of motivating their children to "do something" in this world, when the children already have everything that most people spend their lives struggling for.

Upper-class parents and their children face the problem of notoriety. There is a merciless glare of publicity that hovers over them from cradle to grave. One of the first author's students in recent years was the daughter of the state governor (her father was also one of the wealthiest men in the state). This girl talked at length about newspaper photographers and reporters following her car, some of them hoping for material that could be used against her father politically. She described a minor automobile accident that made headlines all over the state when the reporter wrote that the governor's daughter had the accident "while returning from a wild cocktail party." The girl claimed that she had actually been attending a very mild social event at her sorority house.

One nice advantage that upper-class parents have is that they don't have to drive their children to achieve "success." The family has already achieved its place in this world—the only problem is not to lose it. An upper-class mother said to the first author: "Our oldest son went into the family business and has done quite well. He is now vice president of the company. But our younger son wanted no part of the business and has become a sort of ski bum—he lives in Aspen most of the time. We don't care what he does as long as he is happy and doesn't get into trouble."[80] Notice that this is quite a different situation from upper-middle-class parents whose children have to repeat the parents' struggle if they are to remain at the same social level.

A Chicago psychoanalyst, Roy R. Grinker, Jr., made headlines not too long ago by charging that children of the super-rich often grow up to be "emotional zombies," lacking any real feelings. "These individuals are not ordinarily thought to be a group in need, and very little has been written about them," Grinker said, but argued that the problems they face are startlingly similar to the problems of poor children.

Among the symptoms of those in treatment, he sees chronic mild depression, emptiness, boredom, superficiality, low self-awareness, lack of empathy, and intense pursuit of pleasure and excitement. They also believe they can only be happy with children like themselves, have little interest in work, superficial goals and ideals or none at all, and believe that travel and spending money extravagantly will solve their problems.

"These are deprived children: They have had no valuing, interested parents. What the family has gained in money it has lost in feeling and at times even common sense. . . ."[81]

Summary and conclusion

In this chapter attention has been centered on parents at five different levels of American society: parents at the poverty level; blue-collar parents; lower- and upper-middle-class parents; and parents at the top of the social class system.

The reader should remember that there are endless variations within these social class levels. The attempt here was to extract some general patterns that would often (but not always) be found at the different social class positions.

Chapter 6

Minority-group parents

What would it be like to have a child come home from school saying that he or she had been called a "nigger"? How should a parent react in such a situation? Do you teach the child to be "careful" in such circumstances or to punch the name-caller in the face? Black parents in America have had to face this kind of problem for a long time.

How should Jewish parents react when their child is called a "kike"? What should native American parents (American Indians) do when their child is labeled a "savage" in movies shown on television? How do you explain racial and religious prejudice and discrimination to a child?

These are the kinds of problems minority parents in the United States have had to struggle with ever since the republic was founded, and even before. The parents may be able to handle unfair treatment, but what should they teach their children? If you encourage the child to "adjust" to discrimination and injustice, will conditions ever improve? But if you teach the child to "fight the system" what will happen to the youngster? In some families one parent may want the son or daughter to protest unfair treatment whereas the other parent may think this is unwise. Very often the younger generation wants to struggle to change the system while the parents feel that the best strategy is to accept conditions as they are. Very real family problems can develop from these situations.

In this chapter we will be exploring the special problems of minority parents: black fathers and mothers, American Indian parents, Puerto Ricans living in the United States, Mexican-American parents, Jewish parents, Chinese-American parents, and also Japanese-American parents. Many homosexual parents also feel they are a minority in American society, and so their unique challenges will be discussed. There are other minority groups in our complex society but these are the major ones.[1]

It is the writers' contention that all American parents have a difficult role but that the difficulties are increased if the father or mother is a member of a minority group. This chapter is intended to explore and analyze the special problems of these parents. But first let us look at the concept of minority group.

The concept of minority group

The main thing about minority-group status is that it always involves prejudice and discrimination.[2] Whether the parent is a Jew, a Roman Catholic, an American Indian, a Puerto Rican American, an Afro-American—no matter what minority group a person belongs to—prejudice and discrimination are always involved.

Statistically, a minority group may actually constitute a majority of the population, as blacks do in many counties of the South and in Washington, D.C.

In terms of power, the minority group is always at a disadvantage. The dominant group controls the economic system, the political system, the police force, and so forth.

The basic image of the minority group which is projected by the dominant group is often one of inferiority, worthlessness, and potential violence.

And lastly, the dominant group often always feels morally superior. It is not that they have ever mistreated the minority group. On the contrary, they feel that they have always been good to the minority group and cannot understand why these people are not grateful.

With this brief background, let us now turn to the analysis of specific problems faced by parents in the major minority groups in the United States.

Black parents in America

In a major review of the research on the American black family, Robert Staples emerges with a great deal of skepticism as to what is really known about this family system.[3] Staples writes: "In an overall assessment of theories and research on black family life, their value is diminished by the weak methodology employed; the superficial analysis that ensues from the use of poor research design; biased and small samples; and inadequate research instruments."

Staples takes the position that even black sociologists have misread the black family because they have used white middle-class family norms in looking at the black family. Most of the generalizations about the black family in America—that it is dominated by women, for example—are myths in the opinion of Staples. Marie Peters tends to support Staples in this analysis.[4] Peters put together an excellent summary of the strengths of black families as mentioned by several investigators:[5]

1. Strong kinship bonds. Black families appear more willing than white families to take in relatives (grandparents, children) into their households.
2. Strong work orientation. Dual-job families are common among blacks.
3. Adaptability of family roles. Robert Hill has argued that role flexibility in black families is a most effective coping mechanism.[6] Working mothers are not a threat to their husbands' egos; their contributions have been a matter of necessity. The typical black family is not a matriarchy or a patriarchy, but egalitarian in style. (Harriette McAdoo suggested, in this vein, that black families may have a longer tradition of egalitarian marriages than white families, who are relatively new to the dual-job realm.[7])
4. Strong achievement motivation. Black parents want their children to get an education, even go to college.
5. Strong religious orientation. Emotional, spiritual, and intellectual satisfaction has come to black families from the black churches. Many black men and women with ordinary or menial jobs have achieved self-actualization through church work.

Black parents must cope with racism. In view of this, it is difficult to decide what special problems black parents do face in the United States in the 1980s. One can be sure, however, that racism has not disappeared from the land and this problem in itself is massive. While racism has many facets, it involves psychological, economic, political, legal, and moral dimensions.[8] A black child cannot grow up in our society and escape racism in some form—and parents must somehow cope with the problem when the child encounters it.

Black parents have often had to rear their children in conditions of poverty. Black children are more than three times as likely to be growing up in poverty as white children.[9] The poverty syndrome in our society includes a number of factors including inadequate housing, deteriorated neighborhoods, poor police protection, inferior schools, below standard health services, high unemployment rates, above average crime rates, low educational level of parents, exploitation by merchants, plus prejudice and discrimination.[10] One can see that any parent who can rear children successfully under such conditions is indeed a heroic person. Andrew Billingsley argues that black parents in America have done quite well in view of the circumstances under which they have had to operate.[11]

Black parents have to deal with an unusual generation gap. All American parents have to struggle with a generation gap between themselves and their children, but it seems to the writers that several factors make this problem more acute for black parents. Many black parents of today were born and reared in the Deep South (often in rural areas) while their children are living and growing up in the urban North.[12] These two social worlds are far apart and somehow black parents have to bridge the gap.

Furthermore, the average black parents have had relatively little formal education whereas many of their children are attending high school and even college.[13] Many of these children are moving into the middle class and away from the blue-collar world of their parents.

Finally, many black parents grew up before the civil rights struggles and they had become used to traditional white-black relationships. When their children decided to revolt against racism, even using violence when necessary, some black parents were unable to accept this behavior in their sons and daughters.[14]

Not all of these generation-gap problems were unique to black parents—upper-middle-class white parents found it difficult in the

1960s to watch their offspring battling with the police over the war in Vietnam[15]—but it seems to us that some of these problems were more intense in black families in recent years.

The problem of self-identity and cultural identity. Much of the African cultural heritage of black Americans was lost during the period of slavery. In the modern era black men and women have been trying to recapture this lost heritage.[16] What part of Africa did we come from? What were my ancestors like? Black parents not only have this problem of identity for themselves but they also have to try to help their children with the problem. It is not an easy task.

"Black people are out of style." Those are the melancholy words of Vernon Jordan, former head of the National Urban League, wounded a few years ago by a sniper. The Reagan administration has decided that balancing the national budget is more important than maintaining present funding levels for many social programs which are beneficial to blacks. He has taken his budget-cutting scalpel to welfare, CETA jobs, food stamps, and medicaid, while increasing the military budget. The Reagan administration, of course, argues that by bolstering the economy blacks will benefit with increasing numbers of jobs in the private sector. But black leaders remain skeptical out of habit and experience that business will rush into the breach if the federal government eases its pressure to hire blacks on the one hand and cuts back job-training programs on the other. As Marvin Dunn, a black Miami psychologist says, "The private sector does not need welfare mothers." Reagan, according to a Gallup poll, has the lowest confidence rating among blacks of any recent president. In 1980 the average black family income stood at $15,806, compared to $24,939 for whites. Black unemployment today runs about three times as great as white unemployment; blacks are often relegated to low-paying and menial jobs. Unemployment among black teenagers is an astronomical 50.7 percent, compared to a 15.6 percent rate for white teens. Jesse Jackson, a Chicago civil rights activist, says, "We cannot turn to the judiciary, the executive, or the legislature. Washington has turned its back on us." Jackson notes that "This is a four-act play, and we're just in the first half of the first act. We're not even in the intermission yet, and people are already looking around to see if this is the program they paid for." His words were prophetic. Not long after, a September 1981 march on Washington by a collection of dissident groups including blacks, labor, feminists, students, and many others drew 260,000 to the nation's capital to protest Reagan's budget cuts. The great throngs assembled in Washington in response to the Vietnam war a decade earlier rarely numbered that many people.[17]

In concluding this discussion of the problems of black parents in the United States, it needs to be remembered that the black family is now found at all social-class levels of our society—upper class, middle class, blue-collar working class, and low-income lower class. Some of the problems of black parents will be found at all social-class levels while others will be unique to a specific class position.

American Indian parents

As a group, American Indian parents probably face the most difficult situation of any parents in the United States: 80 percent of Indian families are reported to be on public welfare; the income of Indian males is half of that of adult white males; unemployment of reservation Indians is triple that of blacks and quintuple that of whites; infant mortality rates run 50 percent higher than non-Indians; school dropout rates are high; illiteracy is common; the death rate from cirrhosis of the liver is triple that of the general populace, as alcoholism may plague 40 percent of some reservation populations; general health status is rated very poor; and life expectancy is below that of both white and black Americans.[18]

Conditions vary, of course, from one tribe to another, but even the relatively well-to-do tribes, such as the Menominee of Wisconsin and the Navaho of the Southwest, are reported to be suffering from hunger and severe poverty.[19]

The American Indian has never been accepted as an equal by other Americans. He was not even granted full citizenship until 1924—seven years after Puerto Ricans were given their citizenship and over a half century after the blacks in America had been granted citizenship.

Tragically, the American Indian found, as did the Afro-American, that legal rights and actual rights are far from being the same thing.

The following problems would seem to face Indian fathers and mothers as they try to accept their parental responsibilities in modern America.

Language problems. The children often learn a language at home that is not used at school or in the larger society. As William

Brophy and Sophie Aberle point out, the Indian views the world in ways quite foreign to most Americans, and this greatly complicates the adjustment of the Indian child in the public school system.[20]

Language problems have always plagued new arrivals in America, except for the English-speaking settlers of the colonial area. But most of these other groups learned English (or American) rather rapidly because they had to in order to survive in the open society. The Indian, however, the first to arrive on these shores thousands of years before Leif Ericson or Columbus, was not forced to learn the language of the invaders because he was shunted off to isolated reservations, where he continued to use his own language. This may have helped to preserve some small part of his cultural heritage, but it also complicated his dealings with the outside world.

The reservation system.   Roughly two thirds of all American Indians were still living on reservations in the late 1970s.[21] The other one third have migrated to metropolitan centers.

The reservation system accomplished its original purpose: It put Indians away, where the rest of Americans would not have to interact with them and, in effect, could forget about them.

From the Indian's point of view the reservation system has been a disaster: It did not really preserve Indian cultures; it did not produce viable Indian communities; and, at the same time, it prevented the Indian from participating in the larger American society.[22]

Culture conflict.   Among the hundreds of Indian tribes in the United States, there are innumerable conflicts between the historic culture of the tribes and that of the larger society.[23] These include not only language but also marriage and family systems, child-rearing practices, property ownership, religious faith, and so on.

Parents face the difficult task of living in one world and rearing their children for another world. The more the child learns about his tribal culture, the stranger the outside world appears to be. Some minority groups in the United States, such as the Jews, seem to be able to preserve their own subculture while competing successfully in the larger society. To date few American Indians have been able to do this.

Poverty.   The amount of poverty among American Indians is almost beyond belief. In some counties in the United States, some 80 percent of all Indian families are eligible for public welfare. It has been estimated that the Indian has a poverty rate approximately four times higher than that of the general population in American society.[24]

It is not only the inconvenience and the embarrassment of not having money—it is also the self-degradation. As Michael Harrington makes clear, the day of the "honest and deserving poor" has long since departed in the United States.[25] Poverty today has a moral tone it did not have in an earlier America. Only the hippies, it seems, can live at the poverty level in our society and feel superior, but it is partly because they came from affluent homes. It is extremely difficult to laugh at money, especially if you have never had much of it.

Poverty affects all phases of Indian life, such as housing, food, medical and dental care, education, and clothes.[26] Welfare programs help Indian parents meet some of these needs, but only at a bare subsistence level.

Self-image. Psychotherapists tell us that a negative self-image is one of the traits found in the emotionally disturbed person in our society.[27] In view of the Indian's position in modern America, it would be odd if he or she did not have a self-image that was destructive.

The late Senator Robert Kennedy, in 1968 reported that in one Indian tribe in Idaho the suicide rate was 100 times the national average.[28]

The American black community is in the process of rediscovering its African heritage and is using this to help restore self-respect and a sense of identity. It would seem that the American Indian needs very much to do this also.

Excessive fertility. In the 1960s the birthrate for American Indians was double that of the general population. It is difficult to update these statistics precisely, but we can say that the birthrate for Indians today, both rural and urban, is still higher than for both rural and urban whites.[29] It is difficult to see how Indian parents can hope to solve their problems at this fertility level. Perhaps new contraceptive methods and new attitudes toward planned parenthood will help to solve this problem.

Smallness of group. It is difficult to obtain accurate figures on the total number of Indians in the United States. One reason is the difficulty of defining who is an American Indian.[30] In the 1960s the U.S. Bureau of Indian Affairs calculated that there were

500,000–600,000 Indians on and off of the reservations, but by the 1980 census the number of persons listing themselves as Indians had jumped to approximately 1.4 million.[31] One theory about the increase is that Indians are beginning to recover pride in their cultural heritage and are now willing to identify themselves as being of Indian descent.

Being six tenths of 1 percent of our population, Indians find that most other Americans have never known a real live Indian; ideas about them are formed from television programs and Hollywood movies.[32] This, of course, produces gross distortion of what Indians are like. Most college students, for example, have never had a high school or college friend from the Indian community.

The smallness of their population also places Indians in a power deficit: There literally are not enough Indians for the rest of the population to be afraid of. There are also not enough Indian votes in most states to be a decisive factor in political elections. This type of problem can only be solved by Indians forming a political alliance with other minority groups. In the past this has proven to be very difficult.[33]

Dale Van Every points out that historically Indians have found it very difficult to work effectively as a group—because there are several hundred distinct tribes with different languages, diverse cultures, and separated by thousands of miles.[34] In recent years valiant efforts have been made to unite the American Indians, but that has proven to be a difficult task.[35]

Mexican-American parents

The 1980 U.S. Census counted 14.6 million persons in the country of Spanish origin (out of a total population of 211.9 million). A few called themselves Puerto Rican, but the vast majority were of Mexican descent. These people, often referred to as Chicanos, are concentrated in the Southwest and West, lands which they once owned and feel that were stolen from them by the Europeans. Some are very bitter about their lost land.[36]

Mexican-American parents have many problems: They, like some blacks, often work as migratory farm laborers, which means not only low pay and no job security, but also moving from one community to another. These are most difficult circumstances for parents to function in. Furthermore, migratory farm workers are usually viewed as "outsiders" in whatever community they happen to be living in at the moment.

In addition, Mexican-American parents and their children usually face a language barrier, and this has been a severe problem for these children in the American school system.

Along with other minority groups, Mexican-Americans have been stereotyped by the majority group as being lazy and untrustworthy. Thus they have had to struggle against prejudice and discrimination in addition to their other problems.[37]

Some of the young Chicanos feel that aggressive action is required to improve the lot of Mexican-Americans in the United States—a tactic that not all parents approve of.

Many observers feel that Chicanos have managed to preserve a strong family system in spite of the many problems they have had to face in our society. There is, however, a good deal of controversy in social science circles as to the nature of the Chicano family. Alfredo Mirandé does an excellent job of outlining these alternate views. On the one hand, the traditional social science view holds that the Chicano family is rigid, cold, and unstable. The sympathetic view holds the family to be warm, nurturing, and cohesive. Both sides are in agreement on a number of characteristics though: (1) that the Chicano family is characterized by male dominance; (2) rigid sex-age grading so that older people order younger people around, and men order women; (3) well-defined patterns of help and mutual aid among family members; and (4) a strong commitment to family and subordination of individual needs to family demands.

Mirandé argued that both views are stereotypes. The former is a stereotype developed by predominately Anglo investigators; the latter, more sympathetic view, was developed by predominately Chicano investigators. Both overemphasize male dominance in the Chicano family. He propounds a more balanced view. "A review of recent research studies suggests that the dominant pattern of decision-making and action-taking in the Chicano family is not male-dominated and authoritarian but egalitarian. Husband and wife share not only in decision making but in the performance of household tasks and child care; sharp sex role segregation appears to be the exception rather than the rule among Chicano couples."

The Chicano family, according to Mirandé, has been subjected to many of the same forces the Anglo-American family has had to contend with, including increasing urbanization, industrialization, and acculturation. Middle-class urban Chicanos appear to be more equalitarian now; the influence of the church seems to be on the decline; and the importance of the *compadrazgo* (god-parent) system is waning. These changes are not a rejection of traditional Chicano values in an effort to Americanize, but, rather, a modification of their own strong sexual and familial values in order to better deal with emerging social forces.[38]

Vicky and Ron Cromwell studied male dominance in decision-making and conflict-resolution in white, black, and Mexican-American families and came to a similar conclusion. They found that to label black families as matriarchal would be to fall into a stereotypic trap; likewise, Chicano families in their study were not found to be partriarchal.[39] Glenn Hawkes and Minna Taylor found, in the same vein, that the case for male dominance in Chicano families has been greatly overstated.[40]

Puerto Rican parents

The Puerto Ricans in the United States are unique in the sense that they entered the society as *citizens* (citizenship was conferred on all Puerto Ricans in 1917).[41] Minority groups such as the Chinese and the Japanese had difficulty getting into the United States because of anti-Asian immigration laws, but the Puerto Ricans, being citizens, could enter and leave as they wished.

Puerto Rican parents had two advantages when they migrated to the mainland: Not only were they citizens upon arrival but they were also accepted as *whites*, thus avoiding the racial caste barrier that has always faced black parents and American Indian parents.[42]

It is difficult to know exactly how many Puerto Ricans are in the United States at any given time due to the tendency for families to return to Puerto Rico when economic conditions deteriorate in the United States. In the 1960s Oscar Lewis estimated about 1 million were living on the mainland, with perhaps 600,000 of these being in New York City.[43] The 1970 census estimated that 1.4 million persons of Puerto Rican birth or heritage lived on the mainland. The 1980 census did not break down the "Spanish origin" category any further to differentiate Mexican-Americans, Puerto Ricans, or Cubans, so we do not have more current figures. Some argue that census estimates are far too low.[44]

The concentration of Puerto Ricans in a few urban centers has produced two effects: (1) a feeling in the areas of concentration that the Puerto Ricans were invading the country and (2) almost complete ignorance in the rest of the country of what a Puerto Rican is like.[45] This sort of situation tends to produce not only fear but also widespread ignorance and misinformation.

Language. With a native language derived from Spanish, Puerto Rican parents face their first handicap. They cannot help their children learn English (or American) because they do not speak the language themselves. This puts the children at a serious disadvantage in the school system and perhaps in the labor market.

The language barrier also creates problems for the father or mother. They have difficulty communicating with the school officials, the public welfare workers, the police, and so on. Language problems have always plagued immigrant parents in America, and the Puerto Ricans are no exception.

Matriarchal family system. Oscar Lewis reports that among low-income Puerto Rican families, the mother is the stable, dominant parent.[46]

There is nothing inherently wrong with a mother-centered family system, but with the father absent and the mother employed outside of the home this family system can be extremely vulnerable. Rearing children is a tremendous challenge for two people, let alone one. This possibility is accentuated in the United States by the absence of the extended kin network found in Puerto Rico itself.[47]

Among middle- or upper-class Puerto Ricans, of course, the family system is patriarchal; but these are relatively rare in the United States. In light of what is happening in white, black, and Mexican-American families, it is reasonable to conclude that the Puerto Rican family may also be evolving in response to changing social forces, including the feminist movement. We could, however, find no very recent studies of the Puerto Rican family which have examined this possibility.

Poverty. Puerto Rican families in the United States are often at or near the poverty level.[48] Unemployment may run six times as high as unemployment for the nation as a whole.[49] This is nothing new to most of these parents because they were also poor in Puerto Rico—that was the main reason for migrating to America.

But being poor in your native land, surrounded by friends and relatives, is quite different from being poor in Spanish Harlem in New York City or in the slum areas of Chicago.

It hardly needs to be repeated here that poverty symbolizes a host of related problems for parents, such as poor housing, inadequate schools, deteriorated neighborhoods, marginal jobs, worse than average health, and skimpy police protection. Parents who can cope successfully with this list of problems deserve some sort of medal.

Excessive fertility. Most minority groups in the United States have higher than average birthrates. Puerto Ricans, being Roman Catholics, have a special problem in that their church does not approve of most modern methods of contraception. Clarence Senior, however, in his study, reports that only about 25 percent of Puerto Ricans in the United States are active in the church and that their religious affiliation has little to do with family planning.[50]

In a study of a Puerto Rican action group, Lloyd Rogler found that it was extremely difficult for these Spanish-speaking Americans to understand or cope with urban social welfare agencies.[51] This seems to be a problem which most minority parents face, regardless of their language facility.

American Jewish parents

Religion. Regardless of what other cultural differences they may have, most of the minority groups in America are nominally Christians. The society was founded and populated largely by Protestants and Catholics, and these groups have shaped the basic institutions and are largely responsible for its tone.[52] Jews, no matter what their degree of orthodoxy, are thus a distinct religious minority. At one time or another, Jews have been persecuted in almost every nation in Western society.

It is easy to underestimate the depth and strength of anti-Semitism in the contemporary world, but those who do have forgotten too soon the atrocities of World War II.[53]

Jewish parents are not naïve about their tenuous position in a civilization founded by the followers of Jesus. Most of their ancestors

suffered at one time or another at the hands of Christians who pro-
fess nothing but love for their fellow man.

The problem, then, for American Jewish parents is to somehow
help their children preserve their own cultural heritage without
seeming to feel odd in the society. One Jewish father said to the first
author: "At times I am inclined to doubt that it is worth the trouble
(and the potential danger) of preserving our Jewish subculture—I
am tempted to join the Methodist church and not even have my boy
circumcised."

It takes a nice balance and a gentle touch for American Jewish
parents to help their children become not only good Americans but
also good Jews. It is the perennial plight of the small religious minority that faces Jewish parents in our society.

Racism. The average American thinks of Jews as a separate
race in the same way that Afro-Americans are considered to be a
distinct race. Social scientists have argued for decades that Jews are
a cultural group, not a separate and distinct race, but this message
seems not to have filtered down to the average citizen.

Thus, in a very real sense, Jews in our society have suffered from
racism as have the blacks and the American Indians.

All sorts of negative qualities have been attributed to Jews by
racists, and Jewish parents have the problem of helping their children understand the nature of those Americans who hold such beliefs.

It is no accident that the Ku Klux Klan in the United States has
always been bitterly anti-Semitic. This is part of the racist attack on
minority groups. And a band of American Nazis stirred the country
when it announced plans to march in full regalia through the streets
of Skokie, Illinois, Chicago's most heavily Jewish suburb. Forty thousand Jews lived in Skokie at the time of the planned 1978 march;
fully 10 percent of them were survivors of the Holocaust.[54]

The problems of success. American blacks, as well as American Indians, have usually been accused of being lazy or lacking in
ambition. Jews in our society are criticized for being just the opposite. They are condemned for being too aggressive, too clannish,
and so forth.

In a sense, the ability of the American Jew to compete in our
society has been used against him. Although as a group they have

one of the highest standards of living in the United States today, many Americans forget that the average Jewish immigrant entered our society at the bottom and that his or her affluence today often represents several generations of effort.[55]

Miscellaneous problems. Jewish children, as other minority-group children, never know when they will run into prejudice and discrimination. When this happens, the child is confused and hurt. Parents have to help their children understand such treatment and respond appropriately.

The problem of interfaith marriage is a constant one for American Jewish parents. In some communities, their children can simply not find suitable marriage partners of their own faith. One Jewish college girl put this to the first author in these words: "I come from the Deep South. My father owns a beautiful clothing store in this town of 35,000 and we are the only Jewish family in that town. I was sent up here to meet 'a nice Jewish boy' and you know what happened? I fell in love with a Protestant boy whose parents don't have a dime. We are engaged and my mother is about to have a stroke."

Parents cannot help but think that these interfaith marriages contribute to the rising divorce rate among Jews, which one New York rabbi described as being "shocking." Until the mid-60s, divorce was such an unusual occurrence among Orthodox Jews that it was considered something of a scandal. But today even among the Orthodox the divorce rate has reached an estimated 10 percent; among Jews generally, it has climbed to a "catastrophic" 40 percent. "This is the most formidable threat to the Jewish survival facing us today," Rabbi Dr. Walter S. Wurzburger said.[56]

These are real problems for any small minority, and parents have to be flexible and imaginative to cope with them.

The American Jewish community is by no means united or homogeneous. There are wide variations in religious orthodoxy as well as vast differences in social class position. This heterogeneity within a relatively small minority poses its own problems for Jewish parents.

Other minority-group parents

It is an interesting and puzzling fact that Chinese and Japanese parents have done quite well in the United States in the face of extreme prejudice and discrimination.[57] These people did not enter the society as slaves, as the Afro-Americans did, but as Asiatics they suffered from the same racist attitudes that have plagued American blacks and American Indians. As late as World War II, the Japanese-Americans were confined to what were essentially concentration camps, no matter what the government called them. The controversy still rages today as to whether or not these people should be somehow compensated for the loss of their homes, land, and freedom four decades ago.

Parents who are homosexuals

The American Psychiatric Association in 1974 officially deleted homosexuality from its lexicon of mental disturbances.[58] Though the AMA's decision sparked a controversy that will continue to be debated for a long time, it is a good measure of how at least one major group of professionals feels about the subject. And, it is a rationale for including a discussion of parents who are homosexuals in this chapter on minority parents.

There is some provocative research on this topic, and we would like to simply outline a few of these studies. Lesbian mothers have received more attention than gay fathers, as far as we could tell, so we'll begin with them:

Bonnie Mucklow and Gladys Phelan studied 34 lesbian and 47 traditional mothers in the Denver-Fort Collins area in an effort to measure maternal attitudes toward child rearing and self-concept. Their conclusion: "It seems probable that lesbian and traditional mothers are more similar than different in maternal attitudes and self-concept." The researchers showed the parents a set of color slides of children's various behaviors and asked them to respond to a number of questions which would indicate adult-centered, task-centered, and child-centered attitudes. Also, a 300-item personality test looking at self-confidence, dominance, and nurturance was administered to the groups.[59]

Mildred Pagelow reported problems and coping patterns of 23 heterosexual single mothers as compared to 20 lesbian single mothers in Southern California. She concluded that though both groups reported "oppression in the areas of freedom of association, employment, housing, and child custody, the degree of perceived oppression is greater for lesbian mothers." In a court battle over child custody, judges often award children to the father when a mother proclaims her sexual orientation as being lesbian. Recently, some lesbian mothers "of otherwise demonstrated respectability" have been granted conditional custody (the condition being that they do not cohabit with an unrelated adult female). Both heterosexual and lesbian mothers recounted problems in finding adequate housing for themselves and their children, often being refused because they were single-parent families. Lesbians had the additional problem of often being evicted by the landlord if their sexual orientation somehow came out. Single parents are rarely awarded alimony; child support is often nonexistent or irregular. So, women are often forced into the work force. Pagelow cited the extensive literature on employment problems of female workers, including limited opportunities, lack of advancement, restriction to sex-typed occupations, and seasonal employment. Being lesbian brings an added risk: the constant fear of job termination. The lesbians tended to share housing with other adults more often, own their own homes, and to operate their own businesses more often than the heterosexual mothers.[60]

Karen Lewis complemented these findings with her study of 21 children of lesbian parents in Greater Boston, aged 9 to 26. Few of the children were living in satisfactory circumstances prior to learning about their mother's lesbianism. Intense marital discord before the mother's sexual orientation was revealed to the children made life in these families difficult, and the children agreed afterwards that the breakup of their parents' marriage was far more traumatic than finding out about their mother's lesbianism. The researcher found the children to be accepting of their mother's lifestyle, and almost without exception "the children were proud of their mother for challenging society's rules and for standing up for what she believed." Lewis concluded that the lesbians made adequate parents, "for sexual preference does not matter as much as the love, caring, and maturity of the adults and their effort to help their children become self-reliant and self-assured."[61]

Brian Miller studied 40 gay fathers and 14 of their children in large and small Canadian and American cities. He examined common beliefs about gay fathers and presented his countering data:

1. That homosexual men have children to hide their homosexuality. This does not appear to be true, for most of the men in his study did not identify themselves as homosexuals until after they had children.
2. That gay fathers molest their children. None of the gay fathers reported having every molested their sons; and only one father

reported that once an inebriated guest made oblique overtures to the father's teenaged son. The father intervened to stop the fellow.

3. That gay fathers cause their sons to be gay. The 40 gay fathers had 48 daughters and 42 sons. Twenty-seven daughters and 21 sons were old enough for the parents to assess their sexual orientation. The fathers reported that one of the sons and three of the daughters were gay. "There does not appear to be a disproportionate amount of homosexuality among the children of gay fathers." The gay argument is rather compelling: Straight parents failed to make me straight, so how could a gay parent make a child gay?

4. That community harassment of gay parents is detrimental to the development of their children. Miller found that gay fathers took pains to not have their children exposed to homophobic harassment.

All of the men Miller interviewed feared that coming out of the closet to their children would be a painful experience. They thought the children would be repulsed and hate the father for the years of deceit he had inflicted on their mother. But, of the men who admitted their homosexuality to their children, all found the experience to be more positive than they had anticipated. The father's honesty was appreciated and coming out relieved tensions in the family.[62]

Bruce Voeller, executive director of the National Gay Task Force, notes that in his experience the majority of gay fathers and lesbian mothers are still married, and their spouses do not know they are homosexual. He explains that they come from all walks of life—senior officials in the government, teachers, blue-collar people, and social workers. They feel locked in and have a responsibility to their children and wives or husbands, but carry guilt at leading a double life.[63]

Summary and conclusion

In this chapter an attempt was made to identify problems that are relatively unique to minority-group parents. Some of these problems, such as prejudice and discrimination, complicate the child-rearing process for all minority fathers and mothers, whereas others, such as poverty, are found only among certain minority groups.

While racist attitudes and practices have afflicted all minority groups in the United States, blacks and American Indians have probably been the major victims.

About one sixth of all American parents are members of one minority group or another.[64] In view of the difficulties under which these fathers and mothers must function it seems to the writers that they have been heroic in their determination and their achievements.

Chapter 7

The American mother

This chapter will focus on the role of mothers in American society. Fathers will also have their own chapter. Since World War II, American mothers have been the victims of some very vicious attacks. We wish to look at these attacks and judge their validity. After some historical perspective, the chapter will close with a discussion of the revolt against motherhood which began in the 1960s and continues into the 1980s and a look at the simultaneous search of many women for a new balance between women's roles in the home and outside in the community.

Historical background

Following World War II, American mothers were subjected to an attack so vicious that one wonders why they were willing to go on bearing and rearing children. A famous psychiatrist, Edward Strecker, accused them of almost causing the United States to lose World War II by emasculating their sons.[1] A popular writer, Philip Wylie, wrote an even more devastating book called *A Generation of Vipers*, in which he charged American mothers with the psychological castration of their sons.[2] His reference to *vipers* refers to the child-rearing practices of the American mother by which she sucks the life blood out of her male children. This is strong language, and

127

one might dismiss it as being merely the bitter reminiscences of an unhappy man except for the fact that the book became a runaway best seller—some 400,000 copies of the book were sold within the first few years of publication. It is difficult to imagine a book of this nature selling well unless it met with a responsive chord in the minds and hearts of its readers. It would be interesting to know who bought the book—mothers? fathers? sons? daughters? Unfortunately, we do not know.[3]

In commenting on the Strecker book, Geoffrey Gorer, the English anthropologist, has this to say:

> According to this book, Mom, the clinging, possessive mother, not only causes psychoneurosis, she is the main cause of every unpleasant phenomenon, from schizophrenia, through lynching to National Socialism and Japanese Emperor Worship! . . . reading it, one would almost think that Americans were produced by parthenogenesis, so vestigial is the role given to the father in forming his children's character.[4]

Although Gorer's own critique of the American mother was more moderate and more humane than that of Strecker or Wylie, it is interesting that he labeled this chapter, "Mother-Land."[5]

In 1965 Robert Ardrey, the anthropologist, joined in on the attack on the American mother. He says: "She is the unhappiest female that the primate world has ever seen, and the most treasured objective in her heart of hearts is the psychological castration of husbands and sons."[6] Ardrey goes on to argue that the American mother "has everything" but that she is trying to escape the roles that human evolution prescribes for her. This last statement did not win any friends for Ardrey in the women's movement.

Vicious as these attacks are, they are all by men, and one is tempted to dismiss them as the anguished cry of males who did not like their particular mothers. But in the 1960s the attack was joined by at least two women—Betty Friedan and Alice Rossi. Friedan wrote a best seller in which she argued that the American mother had been trapped into motherhood, with disastrous results for her children, her husband, society, and herself.[7] In essence, this book launched the contemporary women's movement in the United States.

In 1964 Rossi wrote a paper with an antimom tone that reminds one of the masculine attacks on the American mother. Rossi states: "It is a short-sighted view indeed to consider the immature wife, dominating mother, or interfering mother-in-law as a less serious problem to the larger society than the male homosexual, psychoneurotic soldier, or ineffectual worker, for it is the failure of the mother which perpetuates the cycle from one generation to the next, affecting sons and daughters alike."[8] This statement leads one to think that America could solve most of its problems if we could just get rid of mothers.

In one study of Appalachia, mothers were blamed for what happens to children in the area—certainly one of the most amazing findings of any study of that distressed region.[9]

Erik Erikson took the position that most of the portraits of the American mom are really caricatures: They take certain features of the maternal role and exaggerate them out of proportion.[10]

The American mother since World War I

In the attacks on the American mother cited earlier, it appears that mothers were being regarded as if they were an independent variable—that they either operate outside of the larger society or cause that society to be the way it is.

A family system cannot be evaluated apart from the society in which it functions. If American mothers are as devastating as their critics would have us believe, then it is difficult to see how the nation has survived. Max Lerner is making this point when he writes: "If the American family is sick, then the class system must also be sick, and the whole economy, the democratic idea, the passion for equality, the striving for happiness, and the belief that there can be free choice and a future of hope . . . the point is that the American family is part of the totality and reflects its virtues as well as weaknesses."[11]

Erikson takes a reasonable position when he argues that American parents have to be given some credit for the accomplishments of American society in the last several decades. He writes: "It seems senseless to blame the American family for the failures, but to deny it credit for gigantic human achievement."[12]

We have the impression that somehow the American mother has been made "the bad guy" in the contemporary family. If so, this is a dramatic reversal of the situation in the 19th century when the father was the tyrant and the producer of neuroses in children. How did this change come about?[13]

It seems to us that the energy behind the attack on the American mother is related to the emancipation of women, which began in the United States during World War I and continued during the 1920s.[14] This was a period of massive social change—or revolution—in our society. The great wave of immigration from Europe was dwindling to a trickle; millions of farmers and their children were moving into cities; the new jobs were industrial jobs; and women were invading not only the world of politics but other pockets of American society more or less closed to them before—colleges and universities, all sorts of community activities, industry and business, and even that male sanctuary, the saloon (known as a speakeasy during Prohibition). Out of all of this social explosion not only a new American woman emerged, but also a new American male and a new American family.

The new American male will be discussed in another chapter. Here we wish to concentrate on the new American woman and the new family system.

As we see it, the American father either abdicated or was pushed out of his position as head of the family during the process of female emancipation. The extension of public education to women, the development of adequate contraceptive devices which gave women some control over their bodies, and sexual desegregation in the workplace all were key factors influencing the change.

In a metaphorical sense father was kicked upstairs, as they say in industry and was made chairman of the board.[15] As such he did not lose all of his power—he still had to be consulted on important decisions—but his wife emerged as the executive director or manager of the enterprise which is called the family. The extent of this shift of responsibility can be seen in the wife and mother's new role or position as director of the family budget. If there was any one symbol of the Victorian father's power and glory it was his complete control of family finances. In many Western societies prior to the modern era, married women (mothers) could not even own property in their own names; if they worked, their income belonged to their husband; and most of them were regarded as being too emotional to handle money.[16] Only big, strong men could do that.

Today, in modern America, the wife-mother is responsible for over 80 percent of the family's consumer expenditures—almost a complete revolution from the pre-1920 era.[17]

It is not clear whether the American father abdicated from his throne or was the victim of a palace revolution, but when the shoot-ing and shouting of the 1920s and the 1930s were all over, the little woman had emerged as the power behind the throne, so to speak. At this point we are not concerned with an evaluation of this trans-formation but are merely trying to understand what happened.

By the beginning of World War II, the American mother had become the bad guy in our family system. As the executive and administrator of the family, she assumed more and more responsi-bility, made more and more decisions, and aroused more and more hostility.

This change can be seen in the psychiatric literature from 1890 to 1960.[18] In the early days of psychoanalytic theory, it was the strong, patriarchal father who was the bad guy in the family system of Europe, the system inherited by the United States. It was the father that children feared; he made the crucial decisions; he handed out punishment; he dispensed money. Any hostility that was available could readily be focused on the old man. One can see this pattern in the play about his own family written by Eugene O'Neill.[19] The mother is sweet, loving, and forgiving, while the father is stern and forbidding.

In contemporary American psychoanalytic literature, the typical father is seen as a passive dependent type—not very strong and not very sure of himself.[20] On television he looks even worse—pathetic and confused.

It is difficult to hate the current stereotypical American father; he merits your sympathy and understanding. It is the American mother who draws the hostility; she is the one who hands out money and says yes or no.

When any group of human beings in a society battles its way out of an inferior social position, hostility is always generated. This can be seen clearly in the current struggle of the American blacks for equality; white backlash is very apparent. It appears that a consid-erable amount of male backlash against women is still to be seen in American society.[21] Some men take the position, "OK, they wanted to wear the pants, now let them see what it is like." It is difficult to determine how widespread such an attitude is among American men, but it is certainly not rare.

The foregoing analysis leaves many questions unanswered—some of which will be taken up in the chapter on the American father—but it seems to us that something of this nature must have taken place to explain the venom and the popularity of books such as Strecker's and Wylie's.

How does one explain the attacks on American mothers by women such as Friedan and Rossi? In some ways they represented the type of person who looks back at a social revolution and is bitter because its basic goals were not achieved. Friedan and Rossi were *disenchanted* with the plight of American women; they fought for their freedom, won it, and then did not know what to do with it. This is the point of view of Midge Decter who argued that women such as Friedan had freedom of choice in their lifestyles but did not know what to do with the freedom.

Friedan recently came out with a new book, *The Second Stage*, which demonstrates that her thinking has evolved considerably in light of changing social forces. The feminist frontier of the 1980s, she argues, is the family. This notion is guaranteed to anger many feminists, but Friedan believes that for most women nurturing, child bearing, and warm family relationships are important. Her book will be discussed in greater detail at the end of this chapter.[22]

It seems that urbanization is related to many of the basic changes in the modern American family, and it undoubtedly played a part in the shift of power from the American father to the American mother. Although, theoretically, the urban father had more time to spend with his children than the farm father had—because of the eight-hour day and the five-day week—the fact remains that the urban father's job was *away* from the home while the farmer's was not.

In the early days of the move to the city, before metropolitan areas became so dominant, city fathers could often go home for lunch, but this pattern rapidly disappeared as cities became larger.

It is our hypothesis that the assumption of power by the American mother took place between 1920 and 1940, an era that produced feminine equality but had not yet drawn women into jobs and the myriad of community roles they sustain today. This was actually the heyday of the full-time mother that Rossi writes about—a woman who no longer had a farm to distract her and had not yet gone to work outside of the home. With her husband away at work all day, this mother had ample time and opportunity to pervade the lives of her children.

It is our belief that this picture no longer fits the American mother—either she works outside of the home, engages in community activities, or serves as companion to her husband when he wants her to. In any event, she lives a rather busy, hectic life. One might say that the doting mother in American society has been replaced by the distraught mother.

Other socioeconomic changes were also involved in this shift of power. A woman who had as much education as her husband and had won legal and political equality was no longer content to be a second-class parent at home. She wanted as much to say about money and children as her husband. If she held an outside job, not common for mothers in the 1920s or the 1930s, this was another reason for demanding equality in the home. And as the divorce rate increased, mothers increasingly served as both mother and father.

Insofar as there ever was a possessive or smothering type of American mother, the lower birthrate of the 1920s and the 1930s might have been a factor—as families become smaller, each child becomes statistically more precious.

The economic catastrophe of the 1930s, blandly referred to as the Depression, apparently reduced the prestige and power of the American father, judging by the research of Ruth Cavan and others.[23] This, then, must have strengthened the position of the mother. Even in recent years the charge has been made that the nationwide AFDC child-welfare program has favored mothers over fathers in low-income families.[24]

The last socioeconomic force to be cited here is war. During the several decades under discussion here, America fought two world wars. Millions of husbands and fathers were away from their wives and families for periods of two to five years. It seems only logical (and necessary) that while the men were away, the women took over and did things that had to be done, not only in the home but in the community and larger society also.[25] And when wars end, things never entirely return to their prewar state. The U.S. divorce rate was almost as high right after World War II as it is today; the men came home expecting an old life that had changed dramatically while they were in the military. Women found that it was difficult to relinquish their newfound "Rosie the Riveter" independence to the returning veterans.

We have now completed our attempt, inadequate as it may be, to explain the reasons for the bitter attacks on the American mother. Next we turn to an examination of some of the evidence used in these attacks.

The nature of the data used in the attack

A considerable proportion of the data used to condemn the modern mother has been taken from the clinical files of psychiatrists and psychiatric clinics. Strecker, for example, a psychiatrist, used data collected on men discharged from the army for psychiatric reasons during World War II.[26]

In an attack by Ferdinand Lundberg and Marynia Farnham, the data were drawn from the files of a woman psychiatrist in private practice.[27] In a chapter on the American woman as mother, entitled "Mother and Child: The Slaughter of the Innocents," the following statement is made: "The spawning ground of most neurosis in Western civilization is the home. The basis for it is laid in childhood, although it emerges strongly later, usually from late adolescence until middle age, provoked by circumstances and conditions encountered in life. And as we have pointed out, the principal agent in laying the groundwork for it is the mother."[28]

On the surface, there is nothing wrong with using psychiatric case material in analyzing American society. But unless the person doing the analysis has had good research training, a number of dangerous pitfalls, including the following will seriously damage the value of the findings.

The sample. It should be remembered that psychiatric case material is drawn from a very limited and biased sample. The general population that copes with its problems is automatically excluded from the clinic or private practice sample. Furthermore, such samples are heavily biased in their social class composition, as August Hollingshead and Frederick Redlich have demonstrated.[29]

The crucial error committed by the users of psychiatric data is to generalize from the clinic or private-practice population to the general population in the society. A classic example of this would be Lundberg and Farnham.[30]

The failure to use a control group. In social science research design, a control group serves to check on our findings. Are the variables used to explain the behavior actually responsible for the behavior? If the Strecker book[31] for example, had utilized proper research design, a sample of soldiers who were *not* discharged from the Army for psychiatric reasons would have been matched with the cases Strecker was using. In this way it might have been determined whether there was a significant difference in maternal patterns between the men who broke down psychologically in the army and those who did not. Without such a control group, we really do not know what factors produced the psychiatric casualties.[32]

This may not impress the reader untrained in research methodology, but some amazing results have been obtained when psychiatric data have been subjected to control-group analysis. In a study of unmarried mothers, for example, Clark Vincent matched a group of girls who were *not* unmarried mothers with a group who were, in order to test the findings of an earlier study that had concluded that the unmarried mothers had suffered from a maternal syndrome that was relatively abnormal or unique.[33] The analysis of the control group revealed that these so-called normal girls reported a relationship with their mothers that was not significantly different from that reported by the unmarried mothers.[34]

Failure to seek for other explanations of the behavior. If you are convinced that the American mother is what is wrong with our society, then you do not need to look for other possible explanations of the problems under consideration. It seems that most of the critics of the mother in our society are guilty of this error. They simply do not grant the fact that forces other than mothers influence children and that it is extremely difficult to rear a relatively untroubled child in a troubled world. The American value system itself—hardly created by mothers—may be one of the major factors producing personality disorganization in the United States.[35] Our highly competitive economic system subjects youth and parents alike to great stress. Conflicts in our culture related to sexual ethics, racial relations, or science versus religion, probably have some relationship to schizophrenia, the most common psychosis in our society.[36] But, except for writers such as Lerner, Riesman, Erikson, or Brim, one seldom sees these other factors considered by the critics of the American mother.[37] Brim was struck by this anomaly when he wrote his classic analysis of the family education movement in the United States. He writes: "As a social scientist, one is struck by the fact that parent education seems to operate as if the parent existed in a social vacuum."[38] One certainly has this impression when reading the attacks on the American mother.

Failure to look for contrary data. A basic principle of the scientific method is that every effort should be made to identify and assess data that might contradict your tentative conclusions. Even a single case that does not fit the theory may require a totally new approach to the analysis. Such niceties of the scientific method do not bother the critics of the American mother. They simply ignore data that might contradict conclusions they have already reached. This may make exciting reading, but it is hardly science.

Failure to look at the total picture.   Guided by Freudian theory which elevated the importance of the critical early years in the development of children, many researchers have grossly neglected a more all-encompassing lifespan perspective. If one believes the theory which traces the important developmental events to the early years of life, then one will look closely for any evidence which shows that a child's troubles, for example, began in those years. Since mothers have most of the responsibilities for children at that time, they quickly get the finger pointed at them. But, as we have already suggested, a growing body of research and theory questions the validity of critical periods thinking.

In *Constancy and Change in Human Development*, editors Orville Brim and Jerome Kagan assembled a compelling set of scholarly papers which show that:

> . . . There are important growth changes across the life span from birth to death, many individuals retain a great capacity for change, and the consequences of the events of early childhood are continually transformed by later experiences, making the course of human development more open than many have believed.[39]

Brim and Kagan argue that though it is a natural human tendency among both laypersons and developmental psychologists to want to search for continuous threads in people's lives, the evidence belies the notion that there is some optimum, critical time early in the individual's life that influences his or her course so changelessly across the lifespan. The editors argue that this is a refreshing and hopeful perspective, for if we believe that experiences, say, in the first three years of life create lasting characteristics, then we could easily adopt a harshly conservative social philosophy which views any attempts at helping people later in their lives as essentially futile.

What does all this have to say, then, about mothers' responsibility for the development of their children? In short, though mothers play a major part in how their children turn out later on in life, this is only one influence among a vast number. Mothers are especially influential in the early years (and there is growing evidence regarding the importance of the father in child development). But as the child gets older, influence from inside the family tends to lessen as outside influences grow in importance. And as outside influences grow in importance, the child changes in ways the family is not necessarily to be held responsible for. There is, then, evidence of both continuity *and* change in human development; some threads can be traced back to a certain degree, but at the same time new experiences and influences on the child are continually coming in from the greater society in which the child lives.

This concludes our analysis of the evidence used against the American mother. If we were on a jury trying this case we would have to vote "not guilty." Most of the indictment is based on circumstantial evidence that will not bear careful scrutiny, in our opinion.

We now turn to a role analysis of the American mother with the hope that this will give the reader insight into some of the dilemmas faced by mothers in our society.

Role analysis of the American mother

It is our thesis that one of the problems of the American mother is that she is overcommitted; she has more responsibilities than she can meet. Far from being the full-time mother that Rossi writes about,[40] the American mother has expanded almost all of her roles since the end of World War I. Some observers even claim that today's mother puts in longer hours than her grandmother did.[41]

Modern appliances have, of course, lightened the burden of housecleaning and laundry, but as one woman said: "That machine does not take the diapers off of the baby and rinse them out. Nor does it put the diapers away or put them back on the baby. The machine *only washes* them." And as modern appliances have proliferated, our housekeeping standards have inflated. Perfection and the quest for it probably keep homemakers as busy today as they were years ago.

In the next few pages we wish to show how the role commitments of today's mother in our society have been expanded.

The role of wife. Being a wife today is not the same as being a wife in 1900. In the area of sex alone, today's wife is supposed to be a sexual *companion* for her husband; she is not supposed to just submit to him as the Victorian wife did. She is supposed to share her husband's enthusiasm for sex. This is part of the total partnership that contemporary American marriage is dedicated to. With the knowledge that many women are capable of multiple orgasms, compared with most men's more exhaustible prowess, wives are now implicitly expected to add sexual olympics to their repertoire.

In many other ways, her role as companion to her husband has been expanded—bowling, golf, fishing, hunting, smoking, drinking—the modern wife's place is not "in the home" but out in the world with her husband.[42]

It is true that this "togetherness" pattern is often not found at lower-class levels, as Herbert Gans and others have pointed out; but insofar as America is becoming increasingly a white-collar society, the ideal of husband-wife togetherness would seem to be spreading.[43]

To the extent that the modern American wife-mother commits herself to being a companion to her husband she has expanded her role as wife.

The role of mother. We argued in an earlier chapter that modern American parents are operating under higher standards.[44] Mothers today are expected to be informed about new medical findings, such as new vaccines, and to make sure that their children receive them; they are supposed to be alert to new community programs for children, such as those available at the YMCA or some other community service agency, and to get their children interested and enrolled. Schools, PTAs, Girl Scouts, Boy Scouts, Little League baseball—all of these child-centered organizations expect (and even demand) more from today's mothers than even before in our society.

Of course, today's mother will not be criticized by her neighbors or her family if she buys a child's birthday cake at the supermarket—she has an advantage here over the mothers of yesterday. But it seems that she has paid dearly in time and serenity for such conveniences.

Expansion of the home-management role. In taking over the family budget and the job of purchasing agent, the American mother got herself into more work than she bargained for. The first author's mother had her groceries delivered to her home daily, but today's woman has to go to the supermarket and bring the family groceries home herself. And if she wishes to shop economically she has to visit more than one store to take advantage of specials. *McCalls Magazine*[45] surveyed 35,000 of its predominately middle-class women readers and concluded that, "The belief that women are incapable of managing money is as phony as a three-dollar bill." In 7 out of 10 of these American households, the woman said she was the financial overseer.

Mothers today shop for the men in the family as well as for their daughters and themselves. It is not uncommon today to see an American mother mowing the lawn with the power mower and even painting the house; community college courses in "Powder Puff Automotive Mechanics" abound for good reason. But in an earlier America, at least in the cities, this was man's work.

Expansion of the community role. In an interesting book called *The Gentle Legions*, Richard Carter[46] has described the massive effort of American wives and mothers to raise funds for the voluntary health organizations. These efforts have often been lampooned by comedians, but as Carter says, the triumph over polio was no joke.[47] The $160 million raised for these health organizations by American women is no joke either; and no mean feat. The authors know one woman who is currently chasing three children and working on four "crusades." She moaned: "And now the cancer society called and wants me to be a team leader for a fifth. How many diseases are there in the world, anyway?"[48]

Reuben Hill of the Family Study Center at the University of Minnesota points out that the American mother has taken on the "community liaison" role in our family system.[49] She is the major line of communication and contact with the schools, the welfare agencies, the youth organizations, the church, and the various health services.

This community role of the American mother is often taken lightly by her critics, but as one minister said: "Without the mothers this community would collapse." He may have been thinking only of his own church, but we feel that he had a more generally relevant point.

Expansion of her breadwinner role. It is amazing that American mothers are still being labeled "full-time" mothers when they are working outside of the home in larger and larger numbers. From 1948 to 1980, for example, the number of mothers with outside jobs who had children in school increased from 26 to 58 percent.

And 42 percent of mothers with preschool children work outside the home.[50] It is difficult to see how these women can be called full-time mothers. They remind one of a group of ants scurrying about in an attempt to meet all of their commitments.

Being caught in "the superwoman squeeze," as the saying goes, is nothing new for American women—nor, for that matter, new for women in other industrial nations. Hedrick Smith in his magnificent book, *The Russians*, writes: "under socialism, women are liberated. They have the opportunity to work all day, and then go home, do the shopping, do the cooking, keep house and take care of the children." Smith notes that a much larger percentage of Russian married women and mothers are in the labor force than in the United States, but that Russian men don't help out at home. The Soviet government has been unable to provide convenient shopping centers similar to those in the United States, so women there typically spend two or more hours a day just trying to buy food for the family. Most of this time is spent standing in endless, interminable lines.[51]

With the expansion of the breadwinner role has come a good, liberal dose of conservative guilt, sprinkled on by society and mothers' own acute sense of their personal failings when put in a no-win double-bind between work and family. *Time* Magazine recently asked the question: "Six million mothers with children under six are working, but how are they caring for their 7 million kids?" Conservatives, such as anti-ERA spokesperson Phyllis Schlafly, are quick to answer that the mothers can't be doing a very good job. "There's no real substitute for the care of a real mother," she intones, totally neglecting fathers and adding to the uneasiness already felt by many mothers of preschoolers who attend daycare centers because the family needs mom's income.[52] Claire Etaugh did an excellent review of research evidence and popular views of the effects of nonmaternal care on children and found that child-care books and popular magazine articles have tended to downgrade professional care of young children over the past 20 years, but researchers have come to a different conclusion: "That high-quality nonmaternal care does not appear to have adverse effects on the young child's maternal attachment, intellectual development, or social-emotional behavior." Etaugh found evidence that a shift has occurred recently, and more favorable attitudes toward working mothers and professional care of the young are appearing.[53]

Margaret Poloma, Brian Pendleton, and T. Neal Garland recently followed up on an earlier study of dual-career families, and found that though their marriages had effects on how the careers developed, the greatest challenges came with the advent of children. Many of the respondents in the study noted that, ideally, the combination of professional career, marriage, and motherhood is certainly appealing, but that in reality it may take a "superwoman" type to be able to manage such a life. The researchers conclude that the structure of the American family makes it "virtually impossible for married career women with children to have career lines like those of their male counterparts."[54]

Suzanne Model takes a similarly negative view:

> Little relief is in sight. Labor force participation among all women continues to grow. But, married women who work for the second income so common in our inflationary economy are likely to accept a smaller salary, the more so the more successful the husband. Unknowingly, such women have reinforced their second-class status at home. They remain in a weak bargaining position with respect to their husbands. Their caretaking chores at home simultaneously legitimize their weak labor market position. Prospects for disrupting this vicious circle are not very bright.[55]

As we shall see in the following chapter on the American father, the male parent has certain disadvantages inherent in his position in the family and the working world, also. Model and other researchers who look at household tasks are adept at pointing out how difficult the tasks are which a mother faces, and how little help she can expect from the average father. But a trap researchers can easily fall into is looking only at male participation in "traditionally female tasks." A father may spend little time cooking, cleaning, washing, ironing, but may do a great deal to maintain the family car(s), the house, and the yard. By failing to take all the various arenas of work in a family into account, one may come up with a picture that erroneously paints the male as a king and the female as a slave. This certainly is the case in some families, we know; in most others, we believe, it is not true at all.

Expansion of her decision-making power in the family vis à vis her husband. As the American mother moves increasingly into the work force outside the home, a concomitant increase in her family power has been detected. A study by the University of

Michigan Survey Research Center found that the number of women who think husbands should make the major family decisions dropped from 66 percent in 1962 to only 28 percent in 1980. Researcher Arland Thornton says, "This doesn't imply that women now think they should be the ones to have the final word. Instead, I think it means that these women think there should be a sharing of responsibility."[56] To us, this study indicates a revolution in beliefs in less than two decades.

Many husbands, of course, will fight against their wives' attempts to gain more power in the family. These husbands can easily find allies: conservative relatives, friends, and neighbors; colleagues at work; and pastors of conservative churches. We believe that part of the reason that the divorce rate has increased so dramatically in recent years is that many women have found they can survive financially without their husbands' support, and they simply don't have to put up with his autocratic ways.

In all these changes, sparks are guaranteed to fly; divorces will inevitably occur; but the more adaptable people will see new opportunities for growth and change, and one result will be happier marriages and families.

In a similar vein, Colette Dowling, author of *The Cinderella Complex*, talks about "the feminization of poverty." She notes that with the increasing divorce rate and subsequent failure of many fathers to keep up on their child-support payments, many women and their children are thrown into poverty after relative abundance in marriage. Dowling notes that women have often felt that they had a choice of building a career or building a family. She feels, however, that they have no choice in this matter, because of the tenuous nature of marriage.

> Women should not think of themselves as having a choice between working for an income or staying home for 20 or 30 years. We are suffering by seeing it only as an option. We must look at our lives as income generating lives . . . perhaps women will take brief sabbaticals for child rearing when their children are very young, but then we shouldn't say, rather vaguely, 'Well, I think I'll stay home for a few years while the children are young.' . . . Young women should have very specific plans for how long they will stay home, what they will do to maintain skills, how they will maintain business contacts, etc.
>
> Otherwise, it's like playing Russian roulette, expecting someone else to come along and take over those responsibilities. This is not fair to men or women.[57]

In defense of the American mother

We believe that a good defense can be presented for the contemporary American mother. Some of that defense has been or will be discussed in detail in other chapters and need not be considered at length here.

In our opinion the record of the American mother in recent decades needs to be judged against the following background.

The depression of the 1930s. America has seldom experienced a catastrophe more devastating to individuals and families than the economic disaster of the 1930s.[58] In a society dedicated to making and spending money, few things are more disturbing than unemployment. The studies of Ruth Cavan, Mirra Komarovsky, and Robert Angell reveal some of the demoralizing effects of the Depression on family life.[59]

The magnitude of the Depression is often forgotten—15 to 20 million people were unemployed at one time or another in the 1930s.

The first author was a social worker visiting families on relief during the period 1934–36. In this capacity he had the opportunity to enter homes and interview hundreds of families suffering from unemployment. It was perfectly obvious to anyone but those unwilling to look or listen that the lives of these men, women, and children were being twisted out of shape by years of unemployment and economic deprivation.

Some of these children were the ones that Strecker found discharged from the Army for psychiatric reasons a decade later. Is it any wonder? Who was so naïve as to think that a social disaster such as the Depression would not exact its toll in human lives?

The first author witnessed firsthand the heroic efforts by mothers in the 1930s to hold their families together. But one seldom reads about these mothers—instead we hear about those who failed. Failure is much more visible in our society and, to many observers, infinitely more interesting.

The increase in marital instability. It seems reasonable to suppose that a good marriage is a very basic factor in successful parenthood. But it is quite difficult to achieve a sound marriage in American society. From the mid-1970s to the present, the divorce rate has hovered around one divorce for every two marriages.[60] If we add the unhappy marriages that are not dissolved to the number of divorces, the marital failure rate becomes alarming.[61]

Murray Straus, Richard Gelles, and Suzanne Steinmetz shocked many Americans recently when they released the results of their nationwide study of violence in families. After studying a representative sample of 2,143 families, they conclude:

> Drive down any street in America. More than one household in six has been the scene of a spouse striking his or her partner last year. Three American homes in five (which have children living at home) have reverberated with the sounds of parents hitting their children. Where there is more than one child in the home, three in five are the scenes of violence between siblings. Overall, every other house in America is the scene of family violence at least once a year.

Consider the entire length of a marriage in this country, the researchers go on, and the result is that the chances are almost one out of three that a husband or wife will hit each other some time. Almost three out of four children are hit at some time by their parents.[62]

The prognosis for change in a violent spouse is not good. Husbands, being on the average larger than wives, usually do greater damage to their spouses in a fight. And we have had numerous dialogues with specialists in domestic abuse and the counseling of battered women who are quite pessimistic when asked if a violent man will change.

"I see woman after woman after woman after woman," a tired social worker told us, "and I can tell them their story even before they begin telling it to me." She went on to explain that one of the commonalities of the women's stories is that they have been beaten over a long period of time, and like wives of alcoholics, they have held out long and fervent hope for change that never comes. "I let these women talk themselves out, and then try to help them see that he is not going to change unless some drastic action is taken. She'll simply have to leave him. He may seek help after that; most likely, he won't. But she's got to think of herself and the children and get out of the situation.

"But so often they won't. The women won't change. They've been beaten down and told they were dirt for so long that they can't change; they've come to believe that it's their fault for being beaten up. It's all so crazy," the tired social worker concluded, putting her head in her hands.

When marriages fail in the United States, custody of minor children is given to the mother in over 90 percent of the cases. This means, very often, that the mother is performing not only her maternal role but that of the father as well. More will be said about this in Chapter 9.

In 11.7 percent of American families in the last decade, no father was present—the mother was head of the family.[63] One can readily see tht it is not easy for any parent, no matter how capable, to rear children alone. This is often forgotten when critics are leveling their attacks against the American mother.

The failure of the American father.   Most of the data on personal disorganization indicate that the American male has more problems than the American female.[64] If one looks at data on crime, alcoholism, drug addiction, violence, suicide, automobile accidents, extramarital sex, desertion, and so on, the male rates are significantly higher than those for the female. In reviewing the record of the two sexes, Ashley Montagu has concluded that females are superior to males at the human level.[65] While material of this nature is subject to various interpretations, the fact remains that men in modern America pose more problems for public authorities than women do.

One can argue that this male-female differential in social adjustment reflects dysfunctional child-rearing methods, as the psychiatrists do; that it reflects genetic differences between the two sexes, as the ethologists do; or that it reflects greater cultural strain on the male, as sociologists usually do.[66]

More will be said about the American father in a separate chapter, but it does seem clear that he has failed quite often as a parent in our society in recent decades.

The women's movement in the United States.   The social historian, William O'Neill, points out that the women's movement in our society is not new—it really began during World War I and continued through the 1920s.[67] Today's American woman is a totally different breed from her female ancestors of the 19th century. It should be obvious that any group struggling with a social revolution has many demands on its time and energy. It is simply not possible to be at home with your children all of the time if you are involved in various community activities and also holding an outside job—a pattern that describes many contemporary American mothers. We do not mean to imply that the Victorian mother was a superior parent; she was simply a different kind of parent.

One female college student said to the first author: "I was glad when my mother resumed her work as a teacher. Before that she was just a mom. Now I realized that she had a profession and was an important person in our community. I felt proud of her." It needs to be remembered that the Victorian mother was often very narrow in her interests and not in touch with the outside world.

No matter how one views the feminine revolution it has to be taken into account in looking at the contemporary American mother.

The record of American mothers in recent decades is itself open to debate. The critics of the American mother would have us believe that we *lost* World War II. The fact is that most Americans performed well during the war and that the nation since then has gone on to become one of the most powerful in the history of the human race. While the United States has innumerable domestic and international problems, to say that American parents are failing to produce competent adults is to ignore the accomplishments of this society in the past few decades.

Miscellaneous observations in defense of the American mother. In the Strecker and Wylie books, the major criticism of the American mother concerns her rearing of her sons. It is an interesting fact that upper-class families in the United States, also in England, have never trusted mothers to rear sons—these have been sent away to boarding schools to be disciplined by stern male teachers and headmasters.[68] This may represent sound thinking, but most American mothers have had no choice in the matter; they have had to rear their sons for better or worse.

In many of the criticisms of the mother in our society, it is implied that she is too easy on her children—that she smothers them with attention and caters to their every whim. But what about the traditional Jewish mother? She is usually represented as sentimental and gratifying, yet Jewish children in the United States have compiled an enviable record.[69] The Italian mother resembles the Jewish mother in many respects, and yet her children also seem to have done reasonably well in the relatively short time they have been in this country.[70]

Sylvia Porter came up with probably the most provocative argument in defense of the American housewife/mother not too long ago when she reasoned that a housewife is worth a million dollars. At least. Porter, a well-known journalist specializing in financial matters, noted that a New York jury had awarded a husband $375,000 when his wife died in the collision of two jets over the Canary Islands. The husband had sued for $1 million for the multitude of services the wife performed in the family.

To some people this may have seemed ludicrous, but Porter went on to note that the average American housewife who stays home and is paid $000.00 a week for taking care of husband and children spends a minimum of 12 to 14 hours a day, 7 days a week working.

Her unpaid services can be classified in 12 different job categories: nursemaid, housekeeper, cook, dishwasher, laundress, food buyer, chauffeur, gardener, maintenance man, seamstress, dietician, and practical nurse. Taking the standard pay rates for each of these professionals and multiplying it times the 99.6 hours that the average housewife works each week, it all comes to roughly $25,500 adjusted for recent inflation.

But since it is nonpaid work, it does not show up in the Gross National Product (GNP). A housewife, in an important sense, thus does not exist. Porter adds:

> You, this U.S. housewife, may start your hard working day as early as 5 A.M., to get the kids off to school, and your husband off to work. If you're lucky, you may finish 12 to 14 hours later. You have no guarantee of a vacation at any time; you receive little if any appreciation from your own family or others.

An unjust and wildly discriminatory situation, she concludes.[71]

The revolt against motherhood

Starting in the 1960s, a revolt against motherhood developed in the United States. The opening shot in this revolt was fired by Betty Friedan when she published her very popular book, *The Feminine Mystique*, in 1963. Her thesis was that the price of motherhood was too high in contemporary America—that women's lives were being twisted and distorted by a role that forced mothers to become martyrs to their children. Judging by the sales of the book, this argument did not fall on deaf ears.

Friedan's remedies included the following:

1. Not all women should marry; marriage as a way of life has been vastly oversold to modern women.
2. Not all women should have children. The idea that motherhood

is the essence of life is ridiculed by Friedan—she argued that this is part of the mystique that confuses modern women.

3. Women who do have children should have fewer children. Friedan pointed out that the world is already overpopulated and that reproduction should represent a deliberate choice, not some outmoded cultural compulsion.

4. Sex and motherhood should be separated in the sense that women (and men) should have access to better contraceptive methods, and abortion should be readily available to women who become pregnant but do not wish to become mothers.

5. American women should fight for social change that would make motherhood compatible with a free and creative life for all women.

Traditionalists were shocked and angered by Friedan's attack on motherhood, but many middle-class women (college graduates) and the younger generation found it most enlightening.

Actually, after World War II, American women were victimized by a number of myths (what Friedan labels *mystique*). The marriage rate went so high that a girl regarded herself as a reject if she had not roped and corralled a man by the age of 25. As Friedan points out, this is nonsense.

Even this was not enough: If she did not bear three or four children (in the 1940s and the 1950s), her contemporaries considered her almost sterile—and she regarded herself in this light also.

Finally, she could not pursue a career while her children were of preschool age because this would make the children neurotic and would saddle the mother with guilt for the rest of her life.

In the 1970s and 1980s this revolt against motherhood seemed to become more aggressive, if one can judge from some of the titles of popular books: *Mother's Day Is Over*, *The Baby Trap*, *The Case against Having Children*, and *Pronatalism: The Myth of Mom & Apple Pie*.[72]

It is impossible to say how many women agreed with Marilyn French's view of motherhood when her book *The Women' Room* came out recently, but it quickly became a bestseller. And the vision of pregnancy and parenthood therein is bleak:

> I don't know what it is like to be pregnant voluntarily. I assume it's a very different experience from that of the women I know. Maybe it's joyful—something shared between the woman and her man. But for the women I know, pregnancy was terrible. Not because it's so

painful—it isn't, only uncomfortable. But because it wipes you
out, it erases you. You aren't you anymore, you have to forget
you. . . . You have been turned, by some tiny pinprick in a con-
dom, into a walking, talking vehicle, and when this has happened
against your will, it is appalling. . . .

It is this sense of not being a self that makes the eyes of pregnant
women so often look vacant. They can't let themselves think about it
because it is intolerable and there is nothing they can do about it.
Even if they let themselves think about afterward, it is depressing.
After all, pregnancy is only the beginning. Once it is over, you have
really had it: the baby will be there and it will be yours and it will
demand of you for the rest of your life. The rest of your life: your whole
life stretches out in front of you in that great belly of yours propped on
cushions.[73]

In more restrained discussions by Jessie Bernard and Jane
Howard the case against compulsive motherhood is well stated:
American women, for a long time, have been brainwashed into
having children whether they wanted them or not; and their motherhood burden has deprived them of choices that might have been
better for them.[74] This was certainly true during the baby-boom
years following World War II.

Howard is convinced that the feminine revolution is here to stay.
She writes: "Women won't ever be the same. I have hardly found
one of late, of any age or station, who has not to some degree been
affected by the new wave, an inescapable wave, of feminism. Even
those who loathe it, and there are many, can hardly deny it.[75]

If Howard is right, motherhood in the United States is entering a
new era. What began as a mild revolt by women in the 1920s has
become a social revolution in the 1960s, 1970s, and 1980s. Where
and how it will end nobody knows.

Young people today do not think it wholesome that one's entire
life be centered around parenthood—or anything else for that matter. One university student put it this way to the first author: "I
wouldn't want to think that my parents dedicated their lives to me—
the idea scares the hell out of me. My mother always worked (she
taught school) and I'm glad she did. Kids should be just *part* of life—
not all of it."

Our guess is that most mothers will endeavor to strike some sort of
balance between family and community involvement. This search
for the best of both worlds will take into account the notion that
activity in both arenas brings good news as well as bad.

James Wright studied six large national opinion pools and concluded that work outside the home and full-time housewifery "have
benefits and costs attached to them," and that the two groups of
women do not differ significantly in life satisfaction.[76] Similarly,
when Nick Stinnett, Greg Sanders, and the second author looked at
hundreds of strong families around the country, about half had
working mothers and half had full-time homemakers.[77] Indeed, no
clearcut patterns emerge.

Betty Friedan argues that the feminist frontier for the 1980s will be
the family. "Today the problem that has no name is how to juggle
work, love, home and children," she notes. As men's and women's
roles converge even closer, feminist rage will continue to diminish.
More and more people are coming to realize that we are all in the
same boat. Friedan writes that the first feminist wave died in the
1920s when its leaders never addressed the issue of the family; the
same thing will happen again if feminists do not work to bring about
changes to support dual-job and dual-career families—including
flextime, daycare, and job sharing.

Erica Jong hailed Friedan's work as "courageous." In her review
of *The Second Stage*, Jong adds:

> I have always agreed with Friedan that many feminists were beating
> their heads against a wall by trying to deny the importance to most
> women of nurturing, child bearing and warm familial relationships.
> Denying women's needs will get us nowhere—but deeper into the
> trouble we are now in.[78]

Summary and conclusion

In this chapter some of the attacks on the American mother published in the last few decades have been examined. It was argued
that the attacks have been based on biased and inadequate data.

The rise of the mother to a position of power in the American
family was traced and it was suggested that this new power was
one of the factors involved in the attacks on mothers.

The complex role of mother in our society was analyzed and it
was suggested that this role has been expanded in recent American
history. The chapter closed with a look at the women's movement in
the United States and its impact on motherhood. In the next chapter
we continue our discussion of family roles with a look at fathers.

Chapter 8

The American father

In this chapter, the role of the American father will be examined in some detail. In the previous chapter it was seen that the American mother has been subjected to numerous attacks in recent decades, and the debate over her role has raged back and forth incessantly. In contrast, the American father was almost ignored by behavioral scientists and writers from the end of World War II until the early-1970s. With the advent of the women's movement, fathers have increasingly and inevitably become of interest. Although the examination of the father's role is in its infancy when compared to the microscopic attention mothers have been subjected to, his importance in the family is finally being recognized. The woman's movement, in short, may be the greatest thing that ever happened to fatherhood, and, concurrently, his most difficult challenge.

The role of the father is closely linked with the role of husband, and it will be seen that this has been one of the major problems of the American father in recent decades—his marital problems often interfere wih his paternal performance.

The neglect of the American father in family literature

Starting in the 1950s, numerous studies were made of the American mother, but literature on the American father was relatively sparse. Charles Ferguson did a historical study on the male in Western society;[1] Elaine Kendall has a satirical treatment of the male in American society;[2] Myron Brenton wrote an analysis of the identity crisis of the contemporary male;[3] Margaret Mead conducted a cross-cultural study of male and female roles;[4] ethologists such as Desmond Morris have published studies of male roles in the primate world;[5] and Leonard Benson did a scholarly analysis of the scattered research on the human father.[6]

It is in the field studies of American parents, however, that the omission of fathers in the 1950s and 1960s was most glaring. Robert Sears, for example, in interviewing 379 "parents," did not find it necessary to include one father.[7] Daniel Miller and Guy Swanson had 582 mothers in their sample but no fathers.[8] Robert Blood and Donald Wolfe talked with 909 mothers but excluded fathers from the sample.[9] In a study of divorced parents, William Goode located 425 mothers but did not attempt to locate any fathers.[10]

In reviewing the research on unmarried parents, Clark Vincent discovered that for every study of unmarried fathers there were 25 studies of unmarried mothers.[11]

The *Handbook of Socialization Theory and Research* has only five specific references to fathers in 1,140 pages of text.[12] In a survey of family research, B. J. Ruano and his associates found that of 444 papers published from 1963 through 1968 only 11 utilized data from husbands and/or fathers.[13]

In a study of child guidance clinic case records, Otto Pollak discovered that fathers were almost completely ignored by clinicians working with child behavior problems.[14]

In her study, Kendall found approximately 15,000 books on women in the New York City Public Library compared with about 1,000 books on men.[15]

In reviewing the research on divorced fathers and their children, Pauline Bart was amazed to find that these men had not been studied.[16] She wrote: "No one has studied divorced men and their children. Why not?" (The oversight has since been corrected, of course, but it was allowed to stand far too long.)

The second author reviewed 53 popular parenting manuals on the market in 1974 and concluded that the vast majority of authors neglected to seriously discuss the father's role in child rearing. Only Benjamin Spock in *Raising Your Child in a Difficult Time*[17] and Joseph Church in *Understanding Your Child from Birth to Three*[18] at that time openly questioned the value and basis for assuming differences between the behaviors of mothers and fathers. All other authors either failed to discuss the issues or implicitly or explicitly accepted the traditional role of father as the dominant breadwinner and mother as the nurturant caretaker. "They neglected to discuss any alternatives, which, the investigator concludes, indicates a sexist bias in their writings."[19]

A striking exception to this neglect of men and fathers, historically, was the work of Melvin Kohn, who used fathers rather than mothers in his comparison of American and Italian parents.[20]

This exclusion of fathers from the literature on parenthood seemed to rest on two assumptions: (1) that mothers can report accurately what fathers think and feel and (2) that fathers are unimportant in the child-rearing process. Are these assumptions valid? In a study of foster parents, David Fanshel discovered that foster fathers emerged with quite a different profile when they were actually interviewed rather than described by foster mothers.[21] John Seeley and associates, in an elaborate study of suburban parents, concluded that interviews with fathers yielded significantly different versions of child rearing from those obtained from mothers.[22] In a study of divorce, John O'Brien found that divorced men give a different view of the divorce process from that given by women.[23] In a study of domestic court reconciliation cases, Jeanne Mueller concluded that it was not possible to obtain an accurate account of the reconciliation process by interviewing only the wife.[24] Mueller's study suggests "a serious bias in samples which have included only wives or ex-wives as respondents." In a study of birth-control and abortion practices, Adrian de Winter concluded that family-planning programs that exclude the husband and father from interviews make a serious error.[25] The writers contend that the burden of proof should be on the shoulders of those who exclude the American father from research samples.

Positive signs on the horizon

Fathers are represented more adequately in recent research published in two major journals on the family, and we presume this trend has occurred widely among the professions. Rick Straker surveyed the *Journal of Marriage and the Family* and *Family Relations:*

Journal of Applied Family and Child Studies, both publications of the National Council on Family Relations. He looked at each volume of both journals from 1976 through 1981, judging whether each article on parenthood was concerned with studying only mothers, only fathers, or both mothers and fathers. Straker's figures are useful to look at:

In the *Journal of Marriage and the Family*, he found that 9 articles looked at mothers only; 2 articles at fathers only; and 15 articles looked at both in their study.

In *Family Relations* (formerly *The Family Coordinator*), Straker found 6 articles studying mothers only; 24 articles on fathers only; and 24 articles on both mothers and fathers.[26]

In a similar vein, Julie Claybaugh and Elnore McCoy looked at popular books on how to rear children published from 1974 to 1981. She used a similar methodology to the second author in his earlier research on sexism in parenting manuals.[27] Books were categorized in one of two ways: those that had a serious discussion of the father as a nurturant being; and those that neglected to bring up this issue. As you will recall, in his earlier research, the second author found only 2 books out of 53 that looked seriously and in-depth at the father's role as a nurturant caregiver to children. In Claybaugh's follow-up study in 1981, the results were quite different. She studied 29 books on child rearing that came out in the seven-year period and found that 10 took a serious look at the father's role in child care and 19 did not. The topic is much more common in the writings than before. Claybaugh concludes that, "More and more authors are realizing that the father is not just a breadwinner."[28]

Role analysis of the father in modern America

The parental role has, historically, been a peripheral role for the American male. Historically, in our society, the parental role has been central in the lives of women and peripheral or marginal in the lives of men. This may not be fair or even wise in the light of modern knowledge but it has been true nevertheless. And even though American society is changing and fathers are beginning to play a more important part in the lives of their children, it seems clear that even today the role of mother is hard to escape if you are a woman. Even such a modern person as Jacqueline Onassis, the widow of the late John F. Kennedy, has been quoted as saying: "If you fail with your children, then I don't think anything else matters very much."[29]

For the American father, the situation has been quite different— his occupational role has usually taken precedence over his parental role. His image of himself and his status in the community have been based on his work performance and not on his ability as a father.[30] This means that in the priority system of the male, children rank below work. To the extent that this is true, potential conflicts are set up between the father and his wife. She thinks decisions should be made on the basis of the welfare of the children, whereas the husband thinks that his job and his career come first.

A physician's wife said to the first author: "I think that our children and our marriage should be the most important things in our lives, but my husband (a surgeon) always puts his patients and his work at the hospital before me and the kids. I get sick of it."

The American father has to relate to a new type of American mother.   In earlier periods of American history, the father could usually assume that his wife (the mother) would assume most of the responsibility for any children the couple might have. This is changing very rapidly. More and more women in the United States are insisting that their husbands share the job of child rearing. The writers happen to think this is a trend in the right direction, but many American men feel otherwise. In a study of middle-aged blue-collar men who frequent a particular tavern the first author found that most of the men were by no means ready to accept equal responsibility for the care of children—even when their wives were employed outside of the home.[31] Gene Marine and Warren Farrell reported similar attitudes in American men.[32]

There is some evidence that attitudes may be changing, especially with the younger generation of men who grew up in more feminist times. The second author's study of younger blue-collar husbands in Madison, Wisconsin, found that the average male was doing about 30 percent of the child care in the family (average age of children was in the preschool years) and said they wouldn't mind doing even more of the child rearing if their jobs weren't so constraining.[33] Alan Booth studied a large sample of metropolitan husbands and asked the question: "Does wives' employment cause stress for husbands?" Booth's answer: ". . . Wife's employment has little effect on the marital discord and stress experienced by the husband. If anything, a husband whose wife is employed enjoys a happier marriage and is under less stress than a man married to a housewife."[34] The stresses and strains caused by the crunch of revivified feminism against the rock of chauvinism in the late 1960s and early 1970s may be lessening.

The father's parental role in the United States is peculiarly tied to the success or failure of the pair-bond between himself and his wife. In a great many human societies, a father can still be a good father even if his marriage leaves much to be desired; mistresses or women of some category other than wife are made available to him, and he can still reside in his home with his wife and children.[35] This is usually not the case in our society. In contemporary America men are expected to be faithful to their wives or else leave the home and marry the other woman.

All of this means that if anything happens to the marriage of the American male, he may find himself separated from his children and partially cut off from them—and this may happen in spite of his honest desire to be a good father. In other words, it is difficult in our society to be a good father if you are not also a good husband. According to Oscar Lewis, this has not been the case in societies such as Mexico.[36]

Other complications result if the marriage fails. Sooner or later the husband will find other feminine companionship, often with a woman who has children of her own, so that the man is now committed to two sets of children: his own offspring and those of his new love. In order to attract and hold a divorced woman or a widow with children, the male has to show a substantial interest in her children and their welfare—and in the process may neglect his own children. Thus, he may actually be doing a good job as a parent with one set of children, not necessarily his own.

The novelist Herbert Gold has a sketch in which a man is attempting to explain to a young daughter why he will not be living with her and her mother any more (they are getting a divorce). "I still love you," the father tries to explain, "but I no longer love your mother." He goes on to try to make it clear to the child that he still wants to be a *father* but not her mother's *husband*. This is too complex for the little girl, and after a long silence she says: "I'm getting sick of big words like love."[37]

The human male lacks the biological bonding to his offspring that the mother has. This is a difficult matter to write about because most human behavior is learned, but the fact is that humans are members of the primate family (the great apes) and these fathers have played a relatively minor role in the rearing of infants. Man's closest relatives, biologically, are the gorillas and chimpanzees, and while these males are relatively homebound they do not usually take care of the young.[38]

Humans are also classified as mammals (as are cats and dogs) and the male mammal is a notorious dropout as a father.[39] With only a few exceptions, such as the beaver and the wolf, the mammalian father is seldom seen once the fun of procreation is over. Elaine Morgan has this to say about mammals and fatherhood: "In the great majority of these cases daddy's role is purely genetic; his interaction with any individual mummy is apt to be casual and fleeting, and his individual reaction to his young offspring minimal or nonexistent."[40]

Kingsley Davis has this to say about human fathers: "The weak link in the family group is the father-child bond. There is no necessary association and no easy means of identification between these two as there is between mother and child."[41] Desmond Morris makes the same point.[42]

Compared to most primate and mammalian fathers the human father is a paragon of virtue. But it requires elaborate socialization and well-designed cultural norms to keep him by the cradle.

By the preceding, the writers do not mean to imply that human females have some sort of maternal instinct—the previous chapter should have made that clear. Most female behavior at the human level is learned behavior, but the fact remains that the human mother gets pregnant and the male does not. This means that for the better part of a year the mother carries the infant inside her body and the male does not. It also means that when the baby is born the mother has to be present and the father does not.

Added to this biological difference is the fact that in the past American girls have been socialized for motherhood more systematically than the boys have for fatherhood—the girls start life with dolls and baby buggies while the boys begin life with baseballs and footballs.[43]

In addition to differential socialization for parenthood, the cultural norms for mothers in our society have been more severe than they have for fathers: A mother who neglects or deserts a child has been blamed more than a father who does the same thing. Thus we have had a double standard about parenthood just as we have had about sex.

All of this adds up to the fact that it has been more difficult to integrate the American father into the child-rearing process than it has been to integrate the American mother.

An upsurge of interest in fathers, particularly fathers with infants, has shed some new light on the old arguments that are appropriate to add here.

Michael and Jamie Lamb reviewed several studies which invalidated the common assumption that fathers play little part in the social and personality development of infants and conclude that fathers are particularly important in the development of sons.[44] In another review of research, Michael Lamb notes that pregnancy and childbirth "are exciting events for both parents and that fathers are active in interaction with their newborn infants, both when their wives are present and when they are absent."[45]

Ross Parke and Douglas Sawin argue similarly that the father's role in infancy is currently undergoing a reevaluation. "Evidence from cross-cultural, historical, comparative and biological sources indicates that the father is capable of playing an active role in infant development," they note.[46] Though mothers spent more time with the babies, fathers and mothers did not differ in their care taking competence as measured by sensitivity to infant cues in feeding situations, the researchers concluded after a series of observational studies. Parke and Sawin summarize that, "Fathers are alive, well, and playing an active and important role in infancy—a role that is likely to increase in the future."[47]

Some problems of the American father

In recent years a great many books have been published about the very real problems of the American woman. In some ways this has tended to give the impression that the American male is in pretty good shape. The writers are not convinced that this is the case. Some of the more obvious problems of the American father are discussed in this section.

Economic problems. In the 1970s and 1980s, several million American fathers have been unemployed at one time or another.[48] Many others have been employed only part of the time. Others earn less than it requires to support a family. Even with more wives working outside of the home than ever before, a vast number of American men are under economic pressure.

The strategy of the mass media in our society is to keep several years ahead of the consumer. Just when we have decided that a certain type of home refrigerator is all we need, the advertisers begin pushing a new and bigger model that we are supposed to aim for. This was seen in the 1960s in the tremendous drive to outdate the black and white television receivers and replace them with color sets. One father said to us: "Our black and white set works just fine, but the wife and kids have been after me for six months to trade it in on a color set." He finally made the trade at Christmas time and found that his old set was worth only $50 on a trade. The new color set cost approximately $500. This man worked in a factory and his take-home pay at the time did not average over $400 a month. He says that he manages to get by only because his wife works also.

For the 20 or 30 percent of fathers on the bottom of the economic system, the financial problems are more stark: They are faced with not being able to provide food, clothing, or housing for their families. They are also faced with the knowledge that in a society in which most people are reasonably well off, they are not. This is the meaning of "relative deprivation"—it is not only what you do not have, it is also what the people around you do have.[49] In other words, it is quite different being hungry in India where millions are on the verge of starvation than it is being hungry in the United States where most people overeat.

The writers believe that *most* American fathers suffer from economic problems of one kind or another. We even interviewed a young physician earning $45,000 a year who said that his financial pressures were almost too much for him. Only those who have sweated out economic problems know how they can affect family life: the quality of the husband-wife relationship, the feeling of the children for their parents, and the attitude of the father and mother toward being parents. A man's self-image in our society is deeply affected by this ability to provide for his family. Many times the self-image is not too positive.

Sexual problems.   In the 1940s Alfred Kinsey and his research group estimated that almost half of American husbands were involved sexually with another woman at some time during their marriage.[50] More recent research indicates that at least half of younger married men would at some time become involved in extramarital intercourse (and possibly a third of their wives would, too).[51] In the 1960s Masters and Johnson found that American men suffer from a number of sexual problems in addition to adultery.[52]

Part of the problem is that the male adolescent peer group does not socialize for sexual monogamy; it stresses the fact that all women are legitimate sexual objects (except mothers and sisters) and that a man is a fool if he does not take advantage of any sexual opportunity. After living in this world for several years, the man finds it difficult to think of his wife as the only legitimate sexual object. Women at the office, wives of other men, divorced women— he finds many of these women sexually attractive, and he often finds that they view him in the same light. An urban society has many opportunities for straying; the controls have to be internal because the external controls of the rural or village society are not present. A substantial number of married men find this situation somewhat more than they can manage.

In the Victorian world, a married man would solve this problem by having an affair with a younger woman or a woman of a lower social class. If he was discreet, as President Warren G. Harding was,[53] his wife would overlook the matter. And the man would be protected because marriage to this other woman was usually not possible.

Things are not so simple today. Men and women who become involved sexually in contemporary America are often from the same social class, and marriage is always a possibility. Thus, what starts out as an affair ends up in divorce and remarriage, with the father becoming separated from his children.

One can debate the morality of all this endlessly. We are only interested in the father's sex life as it affects his marriage and hence his relationship with his children. It seems clear that if his sex life with his wife is not satisfying (a) his tolerance of his marriage will be lowered and (b) his tendency to look around for another sexual partner will be enhanced. In either event, his role as father will suffer more or less.

Problems with alcohol.   There are several million fathers in the United States who have a drinking problem. A recent nationwide survey, in fact, concluded that nearly one in five families are adversely affected by alcohol.[54] They may or may not be classified as *alcoholics* (a term that is hard to pin down), but their use of alcohol interferes with the performance of their major social roles: their work, their marriage, and their relationship with their children.

If a man drinks too much, there are at least four ways in which this affects his performance as a parent: (a) the drinking becomes a real strain on the family budget, and this is true at almost all economic levels except for the very wealthy; (b) the quality of the marriage suffers; (c) when the father is home, he is not able to function normally—he is either too good to the children or is abusive; and (d) the attitude of the children toward him changes from positive to negative.[55]

For persons who have never known alcoholism at close range, the events that take place between alcoholics and their families are unbelievable. Only recently we interviewed a young mother with two children who said that during a drinking bout her husband threatened to kill her and both children. When sober, this sort of behavior was never apparent in this husband-father. The wife is now afraid of her husband and has obtained a separation.

One woman told us that her alcoholic husband had 35 different jobs in their five years of marriage; had beaten her up at least 50 times; and on 10 occasions had beaten the couple's two preschoolers bloody about the face. The husband swore to us he could not remember any of the violence; many researchers in the area of substance abuse would concur that it was possible the man "blacked out" during his drinking bouts, not remembering a thing afterwards. These women have reason to be afraid of their husbands. The first author, using news reports, tallied 27 children and 7 wives who were murdered in Wisconsin during one year by husband-fathers who were reported by the authorities to have "been drinking."

Excessive drinking by American mothers is also becoming more and more frequent in our society, but in this analysis we are focusing on only the father.

This excessive drinking by the father is by no means confined to any one social class. It may be found at all socioeconomic levels in substantial numbers.

Aggression. In the past few years increasing attention has been focused on violence in the family. Murray Straus, Richard Gelles, and Suzanne Steinmetz in their nationwide study found that half of all families experience violence by a member at least once a year; their research gained international prominence, shocking many people while others only nodded their heads wearily.[56] The father, usually the biggest person in the family, is often the one responsible for the most physical damage to others when a fight occurs. Only yesterday one of our graduate students, a very pretty young woman from a farm community, shocked her friends at a cafeteria lunch table by revealing how her father had beaten her on many occasions during her teens. She related how he had broken her wrist on one occasion; broken her ribs on another; and waved a shotgun in her face in the barn one day, threatening to kill her, her mother, and himself if she persisted in dating the boy she was dating at the time. The graduate student had decided to "come out of the closet," so to speak, and talk about what happened to her so that other young people who had been abused would be encouraged to seek help. She talked about how 12 years of therapy still had not completely erased the terror and the fear she has of men, but that she was getting better. Would she ever be completely free of her nightmare? "No, I suppose I never will," she responded with her eyes glistening. We hear these stories so often. So very, very often.

The male peer group. In his study of blue-collar workers in Boston, Herbert Gans found that these men liked to spend much of their spare time with their male buddies, away from their wives and children.[57] The first writer found the same pattern in a study of middle-aged blue-collar construction workers.[58] This separation of the sexes appears to be less extensive in the white-collar world, but it seems to exist at all social-class levels. It seems obvious that fathers cannot perform their parental duties unless they spend time with their children.

To resolve this sort of strain, the American male has to be domesticated more than he ever has been in the past. To what extent this has been accomplished, or can be accomplished, we do not know. But some men are difficult to harness, as their wives have discovered. When this is the case, it seems likely that the father's role is diminished or affected negatively in some way.

The decline in power and prestige of the American father

In the preceding chapter on the American mother, it was argued that in the last several decades the maternal role has gained in power (if not prestige) while that of the father has been eroded. A number of observers have taken this view. Erik Erikson, for example, believes that somewhere along the line the American father abdicated: "Momism is only displaced paternalism," he writes.[59] Henry Biller and Dennis Meredith declare: "The modern father has been relegated to a second-class role in the family. His importance has been ignored, not only by society, but until recently by the social scientist."[60]

Hans Dreitzel has a gloomy comment on the position of the American father. "In modern families, the father role is not an enviable one," he writes. "Confronted with the emotional frustration of his wife and the disregard of his children . . . father still has to keep fit for the next working day."[61]

In a review of the literature on fathers for UNESCO, the first author argued that the father in Western society was no longer on the throne—indeed in some cases he has become the court jester.[62]

It is interesting that most of the writers who believe in the decline of power and prestige of the father seem to feel sorry for the guy, whereas the American mother has received very little sympathy from observers. We will not attempt to explain this odd twist.

The divorced father in American society

It may well be that the major change in the father role in American society in recent years is related to the increase in divorce. If present trends continue, it may soon develop that one out of two fathers will be separated from their children. Books by Mel Krantzler and Joseph Epstein make it very clear that the role of the divorced father is very difficult.[63] Why?

For one thing the divorced father is usually separated spatially from his children—he moves out of the family home and in many cases also out of the community. Thus to be with his children he has to make special arrangements. A divorced father said to us: "When I want to see the kids, I have to call my former wife and see if it is convenient. Sometimes it is and sometimes it isn't. I had planned to be with them a lot the first year of the divorce, but it hasn't worked out that way."

The Nobel Prize author, John Steinbeck, complained bitterly that it was difficult to make plans with his divorced wife to see his children. He writes: "You can make arrangements with a dead parent. But a living and absent but available parent does untold harm and no possible good."[64]

Another very serious problem for the divorced father is that he usually has to see his former wife when he visits his children or picks them up—and often he finds this contact with the mother unpleasant. Hollywood stars may talk about their friendly divorces, but not all marriages end that way. A divorced man said to us: "I really enjoy going to see my kids and doing something with them, but I hate to see that bitch they live with."

There is also a third complication for the divorced father: He usually gets involved with another woman who may have children and he now becomes a sort of foster father for these children, which means that he has less time (and money) for his own children. If he spends too much time with his own children, his new love can accuse him of neglecting her (their) children; if he spends too much time with her (their) children, his ex-wife can accuse him of neglecting his own.

In the tavern study,[65] the first author was impressed by the number of divorced men who claimed they had good intentions about seeing their children after divorce but that the plans had not worked out well. Often, the man will end up in a donnybrook with his ex-wife when he goes for a visit with the children. And seeing the kids for a Sunday afternoon jaunt to the park or the zoo can be a bitter-sweet experience that for many men is simply better left undone.

Until recently courts were reluctant to give custody of minor children to divorced fathers—in some states you had to prove that the mother was "unfit" before the father could be given custody.[66] This is changing and some court decisions in the 1970s and 1980s have held that both parents have equal rights to custody—the only issue is which parent will be best for the child. It may well be that more divorced fathers will have their children living with them in the future. The tender-years doctrine, in which maternal superiority is presumed, has in most states been replaced by the doctrine of the best interests of the child, in which the court cannot legally favor the mother simply because she is female.

Epstein describes how complicated it is for the divorced father to have custody of minor children—he reports problems in coordinating his work schedule with his parental role; housing arrangements were not easy; help was hard to get; and he was not sure just what principles he should follow in relating to his children. He writes: "Parenthood, like sex, like love, like much else in modern life, has become hideously complicated."[67] He also reports that he found the so-called experts on child rearing not very helpful.

None of these problems will come as any surprise to divorced mothers who have to rear their children alone. But for most fathers the experience is relatively new.

The unmarried father in American society

A graphic illustration of paternal status (or lack of status) may be seen in the predicament of the unmarried father in contemporary America. Until recently, very little was known about this shadowy figure; and, in the absence of research data, this man was portrayed as a sinister monster who seduced innocent young females and abandoned them when they found themselves pregnant.

Recent studies have yielded quite a different picture of the unmarried father:[68] (1) he is usually about the same age as the unmarried mother; (2) he is normally from the same social class as his girlfriend; (3) the pregnancy is very often the result of a love affair—not a casual sexual encounter; (4) it is not always clear who seduced whom in these relationships; (5) the expectant father is concerned about the welfare of the expectant mother; (6) the boy (or man) is also concerned about the welfare of the unborn child; (7) in some cases, the male has offered to marry the girl and has been refused; and (8) unmarried fathers, as a group, are willing to participate in research projects when invited.

The legal position of the unmarried father in our society has been extremely difficult—in most states he has all of the responsibilities of a father and none of the rights. It has been argued that basically our laws today deny the existence of the unmarried father.[69] The mother is regarded as the natural guardian of a child born out of wedlock.[70] These putative fathers, as they are called, are discriminated against for two reasons: punishment for past errors and to encourage marriage which presumably would further the welfare of the child.[71] In most states putative fathers' parental rights can be terminated without their consent.[72]

Unmarried fathers in American society have clearly been the victims of outmoded laws that express Victorian myths about these men. Women are not the only persons to suffer from ancient sexist legislation in our society.

One sometimes gets the impression that being an unmarried father involves no trauma for the man. This is hardly true. One university student described his experience in high school when his girlfriend became pregnant. "I almost committed suicide," he said. "I didn't know where to turn or what to do. The girl's father threatened to kill me and my parents acted as if they wanted to disown me as their son." This situation was finally resolved with the girl having the baby in another state and placing it for adoption. The young man has never recovered from this trauma—he has had a vasectomy and does not plan to marry.

Summary and conclusion

In the past decade, there has been considerable interest in the idea that the roles of mothers and fathers are inevitably converging. Jessie Bernard talks about almost inexorable forces making this occur: the dropping birthrate coupled with the phenomenal increase of mothers of school-aged and preschool-aged children in the work force.[73]

With continued inflation has come the widespread notion that for survival both parents must work. When this happens, of course, and mom takes her lunch pail in hand, something has to give in a family. And, in short, that something is father. Mother is now joining him as breadwinner, so whether he likes it or not, he must join her as care taker of the children.

The divorce rate in the past decade has skyrocketed, and there is good reason to believe that changing women's roles has influenced this to a certain degree. But as far as researchers can tell, many men value family life highly and are making an effort to adapt to the times.[74] Even if divorce does end a marriage, the vast majority of parents will go on to remarry, and most of these people as we will see in the next chapter remain remarried.

A growing number of realistic idealists see shared parenting or co-parenting or androgynous parenting—call it what you will—as a solution to the dilemma. In many families the roles are not dictated by gender but by ability. This new freedom is seen as being highly satisfying for both parents and children alike.[75] Our society is slowly adapting to these ideas and through increased support for professional child care, flextime, and job sharing is demonstrating its commitment to alternatives to traditional parenting styles.

Bernard has proclaimed the fall from virtue of "the good-provider role" in our culture. A so-called subtle revolution has been a-borning for a long time now. We just may get to the point that William Chafe describes in his parable, as reported by Bernard:

> Jack and Jill, both planning professional careers, he as a doctor, she as a lawyer, marry at age 24. She works to put him through medical school in the expectation that he will then finance her through law school. A child is born during the husband's internship, as planned. But in order for him to support her through professional training as

planned, he will have to take time out from his career. After two years, they decide that both will continue their training on a part-time basis, sharing household responsibilities and using daycare services. Both find part-time positions and work out flexible work schedules that leave both of them time for child care and companionship with one another. They live happily ever after.[76]

Maybe they really will. And, just maybe the rest of us at some-time in the future will figure out ways, also, to live happily ever after. Until then, most of us are relegated to the difficult journey *toward* happiness, one small step at a time.

Amen.

Chapter 9

Parents without partners and other variants

In thinking about parents, it is easy to assume a model of what might be termed "the biological parent team" of mother and father. In this model two parents act as partners in carrying out the parental functions. Furthermore, both of the parents are biological as well as social parents. It is this parent-team model that is analyzed in most of the chapters in this book.

What is not realized by many observers, especially by parent critics, is the fact that a considerable proportion of contemporary American parents do not operate under these ideal conditions. These parents include parents without partners (mostly divorced or separated women, but including some men also); widows and widowers with children; unmarried mothers; adoptive parents; stepparents; and, finally, foster parents.

Some of the groups on this list are amazingly large—for example, approximately 45 percent of all children born in 1978 will experience a parental death, divorce, or separation at some point in their first 18 years of life.[1]

In this chapter we wish to examine the special problems of the one-parent family, whether it be headed by a woman or a man. It will be seen that some of these problems are severe.

Mothers without partners

One of the familiar parental types in our society is the mother rearing her children alone. As of 1980 the Census Bureau estimated that 20 percent of the children under 18 were living with only one parent, up from 12 percent in 1970.[2] Eighty-four percent of all single parents are women.[3] In an earlier America, this mother without father was seen as a heroic figure—a brave woman whose husband had died who was struggling to rear her brood by scrubbing floors, taking in family laundry, and so on. This was the brave little widow of an earlier day.

After the end of World War I, as the divorce rate began to climb, this picture—and this woman—underwent a radical change. With the rapid improvement of American medicine, marriages in the early and middle decades of life were no longer broken primarily by death; now the great destroyers of marriages came to be social and psychological, not biological.

With this shift, the public's attitude toward the mother with no father by her side changed drastically—it became ambivalent. In some cases she might be viewed with sympathy and understanding, if she happened to be your sister or a close friend, but more often she is perceived as a woman of questionable character—either the gay divorcee of the upper social-class levels or the AFDC mother living off the taxpayers at the lower social-class levels. In either case the image was a far cry from that of the heroic little widow of the Victorian era.

Statistically and otherwise, these mothers without fathers fall into five different categories: divorced, separated, deserted, widowed, and never married. All of these categories overlap, so that some mothers might at some point in their lives occupy all five positions in the list.

Our procedure in discussing these mothers in their parental role will be to identify the generic patterns and problems shared by all of these mothers, and then to look at the relatively unique patterns that cluster about any specific position.

Generic features of mothers without partners

Poverty. The median income for female-headed single parent families is less than half the median income for all families in the

United States. More than a third of all single-parent families are on welfare.[4]

In a classic study on divorced women, William Goode found financial stress to be a major complaint.[5] At any given time, approximately 40 percent of the divorced husbands in this study were delinquent in their support payments, a pattern that seems to be nationwide.[6] These percentages remain high today, as many a district court clerk, charged with administering the money, will tell you.

Poverty is extremely relative, as is deprivation. A divorced woman receiving even $1,000 a month in support payments may have to reduce her standard of living from what it was before her divorce. And if a mother is lucky enough to even receive support, the figure more often is in the $200 to $500 range.

The reasons for the financial difficulties of these mothers are not mysterious or difficult to identify. Most American men cannot afford to support two living establishments on a high level. This is one reason why some support payments are delinquent. The man usually gets involved with at least one other woman, and this costs money.[7] Often his new woman is not well off financially, and the man may find himself contributing to her support also.

Since a considerable proportion of divorced women are apparently employed at the time of their divorce,[8] they had what is commonly called a two-income family. The mother may continue to work after the father has left the home, but with two living establishments to maintain, two cars, and so on, the financial situation tends to be tight.

In a study of AFDC mothers in Boston, it was discovered that these women faced financial crises almost monthly.[9] They coped with these difficult situations by accepting aid from members of their family; by pooling their resources with neighbors and women friends in the same plight; and by occasional aid from a boyfriend.

In several counseling cases with divorced women, the writers have been impressed with the annoying feature of the relative poverty experienced by these women—one woman did not have the money to get her television set repaired and this created tension between herself and her children. Another woman, who lived in an area with inadequate bus service, could not afford an automobile. Or, try to live without a telephone as many do. Any person in our society can understand how frustrating problems of this nature can be.

Role conflicts and overload. Since these women have added the father role to their parental responsibilities, they tend to be either overloaded or in conflict over their various role commitments. The presence of a husband-father provides more role flexibility than these women now have—if the mother is ill, or has to work late, the husband may be able to be home with the children.

When these mothers are employed outside of the home, as a sizable proportion are,[10] the work hours usually conflict with those of the school system. Children leave for school too late, get home too early, and have far too many vacations for the employed mother. There are also childhood illnesses that must be coped with.

While the termination of the marriage has reduced or eliminated the mother's role as wife, she is still a woman in the early decades of life and men will be in the picture sooner or later. Thus, she may not be a wife at the moment, but she will soon be a girlfriend, and the courtship role may be even more demanding than that of wife. Many singles moan when describing the trauma of going back to the dating life. "I'm not strong enough to be 17 again," one 35-year-old mother of three noted. The pressure for sex, the ambiguity of how new men will relate to the children, questions of cohabitation versus marriage, all these and more weigh heavily on the single mother's mind.

It is the writers' belief, based on numerous interviews with divorced women, that being the head of a household is, for most women, an 18 hours a day, 7 days a week, and 365 days a year job. It would seem that only the most capable, and the most fortunate, can perform all of the roles involved effectively.

Role shifts. Since the vast majority of the mothers being discussed here—80 to 90 percent[11]—will eventually remarry, they face the difficult process of taking over the father role and then relinquishing it.[12] This is not easy for most of us; once we have appropriated a role in a family system, it is often difficult to turn it over to somebody else.

Furthermore, these mothers operate in an unusual family system in that, for an indefinite period, they do not have to worry about what the other parent thinks. They are both mother and father for the time being.

This is not entirely true, of course, in the case of the divorced woman, but it seems to be largely true, even for this group.[13] The departed father starts out with the best intentions of "not forgetting my kids," but a variety of factors tend to reduce his parental influence as time goes on.[14] Chief among these seems to be the inherent difficulties of carrying on a positive relationship with the children when the marital relationship is dead or still steaming. One study of separation and divorce found that the average mother had fully 93 percent of the responsibility for child care after the marriage was broken, while fathers had only an average of 7 percent of the care.[15] As one father lamented, "Of course, I want to see Tommy. But every time I went over to pick him up I got in a raging argument with his mother. That's no good for anybody."[15]

One divorced woman talked to the writer about the problem of "shifting gears" in her parental roles: "I found it very difficult," she said. "When my husband and I were first divorced, he continued to see the children and participated in some of the decisions about them. Then he moved to another state and we seldom saw him after that—but he did continue to send the support checks.

"At this point," she continued, "I assumed almost all of the parental responsibilities, except for the money sent by my former husband and some advice (of questionable value) that my mother chipped in from time to time.

"And then I met the man I am now married to. At first he stayed out of the children's lives, not being sure how long he and I would be going together. But as we moved toward marriage, the children became attached to him and gradually he became a foster father to them. Now he has taken over a considerable amount of parental responsibility and I am back almost to where I was before my divorce—I am just a mother again."[16]

In the study by Reuben Hill, he analyzed role shifts in a group of families in which the father had been temporarily pulled out of the home for military service. Hill discovered (a) that some of the wife-mothers could not pick up the added responsibility when the father left the home and (b) that some of the mothers could not relinquish the father role when the husband returned from the service. One has the impression that some of the mothers being discussed here have these same problems.

Once these women have remarried, there is a sort of built-in strain in that one of the parents (the mother) is a natural parent while the other (the father) is only a stepparent. This problem will be analyzed later in this chapter.

Public attitudes. These mothers are operating in deviant family situations, and for the most part the community tends to regard them and their children as deviants.[17] Except for the widow, all of these mothers are viewed with some ambivalence in our society. They receive some sympathy, some respect, and some help, but they are also viewed as women who are not "quite right"—they did not sustain their marriage "until death do us part."[18]

The never-married mother, of course, did not have a marriage to sustain, and the public has no ambivalence about her; they simply condemn her and that is that.[19]

If these mothers require support from public welfare, they will find the community's mixed feelings reflected in their monthly check—the community will not permit them and their children to starve, but it will also not allow them to live at a decent level.[20]

The well of loneliness. Any parent rearing children alone will suffer some degree of emotional deprivation. This syndrome appears repeatedly in interviews with divorced and widowed parents. The love partner has been taken away, and whether this was the result of death or divorce, the psychological impact is similar—one half of the parental team has been lost. Sooner or later all (or most) of these parents will reach out for a new life partner, but in the interim, it is a very lonely world.[21]

Historicallly, there has been a lack of institutional supports for single parents. But in the 1970s and 1980s, as their numbers skyrocketed, numerous institutions slowly began to address their special needs. Universities began to hire advisors who were sensitive to the challenges of nontraditional students, the category that single parents fit under. Churches, especially the more liberal denominations but gradually followed by more conservative sects, began to develop programs aimed at single parents, including both educational and social functions. The public schools responded slowly as the percentage of children of divorce grew in the classrooms by setting up afterschool care programs for so-called latchkey children and by gingerly talking about single-parent families in human relations discussions and classes. The human and social service sector of our society has helped by developing classes for single parents and their children and offering counseling for their individual needs; the welfare system was severely strained in the late 1970s and early 1980s by rising unemployment due to recession, and many single parents were among those caught in the squeeze between job loss and shrinking benefits. And, the economic sector has seen an influx of single parents into the work force and responded by gradually increasing support for child care in business and industrial settings, and by offering flextime and job-sharing options usually on an informal basis, but sometimes on a formalized basis. We are of the opinion that institutional response to the needs of single parents in our society has been far too slow and far too modest.

We have now examined some of the generic problems of the one-parent family system, except for the system in which the one-parent is a father, which will be looked at later. Now let us analyze the specific features of the subsystems in the one-parent family.

Specific features of the subsystems in the one-parent family

The divorced mother. The divorced mother has several advantages over the deserted mother: She at least has had the help of a domestic relations court in spelling out the financial responsibility of the father, also the legal arrangements for custody. In this sense, divorce is a lot less messy than desertion in our society.

The divorced mother is also legally free to associate with other men and to remarry if she finds the right person—advantages the deserted woman does not have.

The divorced father, it seems to us, is not in an enviable position in his role as father. He may be happy not to be married to his children's mother any more, but he often hates to be separated from his children.[22] In a sense he still has the responsibility of a father for his minor children but few of the enjoyments of parenthood. To be with his children, he has to interact to some degree with his former wife—a process so painful that he was willing to have the marriage terminated.

In the unpublished study of 80 divorced men, one of the most frequent regrets expressed by the men was their frustration and concern about their relationships to their children. As one father after a losing custody fight for his children lamented: "I lost my job, so she wanted a divorce. She got the divorce. She got the house. She got the furniture. She got the car. Now she got the kids. How much more can I lose? How much can I take?"

The divorced mother has one parental advantage that she shares with all other parents without partners: She does not have to share the daily parental decisions with a partner who might not agree with her strategy. In the Goode study of divorced women, the mothers seemed to think this was an advantage.[23] The parental partner can be of great help if he can agree with his mate on how their children should be reared, but when this is not the case one parent can probably do a better job going it alone.

All in all, then, was divorce the right path to follow? Divorced persons' replies may come as a surprise to some. Soon after the marital separation and divorce, many people will say they, in effect, "could have tried harder to make the marriage work," as the cliché goes. But later on in the process—a few years down the line—the individual's life has begun to stabilize, and the response is often quite different. For example, one study of 138 people divorced an average of 1½ years found that 40 percent felt they should have gotten out of the marriage sooner; another third felt they were happier now than before the divorce. Only 14 percent still considered the divorce a tragedy or mistake; and the final 11 percent indicated they had no choice in the matter, so they might as well accept the situation.[24]

Murray Straus estimates that a third of the divorces may involve violence—hardly conducive to successful child rearing.[25] Add to this Morton Hunt's estimate that another half of the marriages simply burned out with no emotion left at all.[26] Small wonder that divorce is often a relief to people, rather than a disaster. Most often, we'd guess, divorce is a mixture of both.

The deserted mother.   It has already been indicated that desertions in our society are more messy than divorces.[27] There are two reasons: (a) desertion is more apt to be unilateral, with the decision to pull out being made by one party alone and (b) there is no court supervision of the desertion process—it is unplanned from society's point of view.

The deserted mother is likely to have more severe financial problems than the divorced mother because support payments have not been agreed upon.

Psychologically, desertion is probably more traumatic than divorce, partly because it is more unilateral but also because it is less planned.[28] To the extent that this is true—and we recognize that the evidence on this point is not conclusive—then the deserted mother is handicapped in her parental role by her emotional upheaval or trauma.

This woman also has other problems: She is not legally free to remarry and in a sense not even free to go out with other men since she is technically still a married woman. These feelings, of course, will tend to reflect the social class and moral subculture of the particular woman.

The separated mother.   If we assume that most marital separations in contemporary America have been arrived at by mutual agreement, then this mother has certain advantages over the deserted mother: In separation there is usually some agreement about child support and child custody, issues which are not often settled in advance in cases of desertion. It would also seem that separation would usually be less traumatic in that the decision is more likely to be mutual than it is in desertion.

On the negative side the courtship status of the separated mother is ambiguous; she is not free to marry.[29] Psychologically, the separated mother is often in limbo. In our studies of separated mothers and their children, for example, we found them to be an almost invisible segment of the population.[30] While everyone seems to know a number of divorced people, finding separated people by word-of-mouth is very difficult. The separated tend to be rather quiet about the separation; they are probably correct in doing so, for Robert Weiss has estimated that half of the marital separations end in reconciliation.[31] Why upset parents, friends, co-workers with the sad news if there is a good chance of getting back together? But since they are in limbo, it is difficult to plan for the future of the children, and of the parent. The tension and indecision can be tremendous. Many times we have heard separated people talk of the desire for closure—even if closure means the end of marriage.

The widowed mother.   The one big advantage of this parent is the favorable attitude of her family, her friends, and the community toward her. This tends to be reflected in her self-image, thus giving her emotional support. Once she emerges from the period of bereavement, however, she has to face about the same problems as the women discussed previously—she probably will have financial problems; she will have to be father as well as mother; she may need to get a job; and eventually she will have to consider whether to remarry.[32] (Of course, the widowed mother, on the average, is going to be older than the divorced mother, for example; this means that her troubles may be fewer and to a lesser extent. Her financial situation may be more secure in middle- or late-middle age than a young mother recently divorced; similarly, her children will probably be older and more independent. Finally, she may not feel a great need to remarry, but simply to enjoy the companionship of her male and female friends and a modest amount of solitariness after a family-filled life.)

It is difficult to say whether widowed women suffer more or less emotional trauma than the women whose husbands are still alive but whose marriages are dead. Both have experienced "death" in one form or another—either psychological or physical.

It is undoubtedly true that some of the marriages of widowed women had also failed before the husband died, but there is no way to discover how large this group is.

The never-married mother. This is not the place to review the status and problems of the never-married mother in our society—the literature on this woman is quite voluminous.[33] It only needs to be said here that this mother has all the problems of the women discussed before plus a few of her own. She is more likely to be a member of a racial minority—one of the extra burdens she has to shoulder. She is also more likely to be on public welfare—a major burden in itself in our society. Her chances for marriage are not as gloomy as some people once thought,[34] but her chances for a successful marriage may be more dubious.

The never-married mother has one advantage over the divorced, the separated, and the deserted mothers: She does not have to juggle the ambivalent feelings of the general public toward her; she knows that they disapprove of her almost unanimously.

We are talking here, of course, of the mothers who keep their children. Those who give up their children for adoption and those who terminate their pregnancies by abortion have their own problems which will not be discussed in this book.

It is interesting to note that some women in our society have occupied *all* of the positions discussed so far. They have been never-married mothers, divorced, deserted, separated, and widowed, although not necessarily in that order. We have interviewed a number of such women and they all were remarkable persons.

One of these women was a never-married mother at 16, deserted at 18, divorced at 20, widowed at 23, and remarried at 25. Along the way she had accumulated six children and had been separated any number of times.

What was impressive about this woman was not only her lonely journey through the wars of matrimony but her intense concern for the welfare of her children. The general public would undoubtedly have viewed her as a "bad" mother, but our own judgment was that she did quite well with children—her problems were largely with husbands and boyfriends.

Another unforgettable woman participated in a research project with us on parenting. Specifically, we were looking at how life changes and stresses influence a parent's behavior. To measure changes, we were using what has been dubbed the Holmes Stress Test.[35] In this test, people gain points by having experienced a particular change in the past 12 months. For example, if you experienced the death of a spouse in the past year, you would get 100 points; a divorce is rated 73 points. Being fired from work counts 47 points; retirement is 45; pregnancy 39, and so on. Holmes and his colleagues have found that life change is stressful, and that the more points a person accumulates in a particular year, the greater the chance the person will have a physical or emotional illness. A life change score of 150 or less on the Holmes test gives the person a 37 percent chance of becoming ill during the next two years; a score of 150 to 300 raises these odds of illness to 51 percent; and a 300-plus score means the person has an 80 percent chance of becoming seriously ill. Scores of 100 to 200 are common; 300-plus is a high score. We rarely see people with scores of 500. The woman mentioned earlier in the research project on parenting came up after taking the test and noted that she scored 750 points for the past year.

We gasped. "I got a divorce in January; married in February; broke up in July, and now I'm living with another fellow. My mother died. I had major surgery and got fired from my job. I would have scored higher on the test," she added, "but they didn't have any category on it for being in a mental hospital."

She chuckled: "But I did that, too!"

It is too bad that women like this do not write books, for they could tell us all much that we need to know about life.

Father-only families

The most recent Census Bureau figures available show 13 percent of all single-parent families to be headed by the father.[36] Given the current trend toward women's and men's liberation, and the extraordinary popularity of movies such as *Kramer vs. Kramer*, it is quite plausible to predict that the percentage will increase. In fact, the Department of Health and Human Services does estimate that by 1985 about 30 percent of all single-parent families will be male headed.[37] About two thirds of these single-parent fathers are divorced; the remainder are widowers or were never married.

There are a number of studies on the emergent role of the single father, and the parallels between single fathers and single mothers are striking.[38] Our recent study compared divorced males and females with custody of the children on a large number of measures. We found that fathers held a slight edge over the mothers in income, education, and the tendency not to move from their home and community after the divorce. But we were startled when we statistically analyzed the 33 fathers' and 38 mothers' responses to 63 questions in the general areas of the history of the divorce process, feelings as a single parent, relations with the ex-spouse, and forming new social relationships. On 62 of the 63 questions, the fathers and mothers did not differ significantly.

In capsule form, we found that:

1. The process of divorce was not essentially different for fathers and mothers. Causes of the divorce were not different; the children's role in the process was not different, nor did friends or relatives behave differently toward the individuals depending upon whether they were males or females. Both groups saw the divorce as being a stressful event in their lives.

2. Both men and women were open about describing the stresses and strains of single parenthood, but agreed that if the situation were to arise again, they all would tackle it. The marriage had become an untenable position for them, and though a two-parent family to most of these people was seen as being potentially superior, a stable one-parent family in their particular circumstances was generally better for the children.

3. The fathers and mothers described their child-rearing philosophies and behaviors essentially the same. Fathers did not yell at or hit the children any more than mothers. For a few fathers with teenaged girls, sex education was a minor problem; the fathers usually had a sister or friend talk about female concerns with their daughter.

4. The fathers and mothers described their children's behaviors after the marital separation in a strikingly similar manner. The vast majority of the children were doing well at home and in school; emotionally and physically most of the children were described as being healthy.

5. Custody arrangements with the ex-spouse were similar for both men and women. Most ex-spouses had the children for holidays, weekends, and summers. The one statistically significant difference between men and women did occur in the general area of relationships with the ex-spouse. Only one mother said she encouraged her children to take sides in any continuing disagreements with the ex-spouse, while a third of the fathers encouraged this teaming up. The reason for this difference is highly speculative, but possibly fathers still harbored a bit of the old stereotype that it is an even graver error for the mother to abandon the children than the father.

6. In regard to forming new social relationships, both men and women were equally interested in remarriage. The children of both generally encouraged them in their quest. We found that neither group fit the unkind picture of the gay divorcee, hopping from bar to bar and bed to bed. To relax and socialize, most of the folks stayed home or went to friends' houses; only 10 of the 71 parents reported visiting a bar even on occasion.

Past research on fatherhood had led us to predict that fathers would compare quite favorably to mothers in a study of single parents. We were shocked, however, to see how close the two fit together. On 62 out of 63 questions, to reiterate, no significant difference.

One father called recently to ask about the research, and if he could use some of our findings in a custody battle. "I guess the question I need answered is: 'Can fathers be good mothers?' " Our reply to this man: Most likely. The data indicate, in general, that fathers are just as competent as mothers in raising children alone.

Is the one-parent family pathological?

It has been common in the past to assume that somehow both biological parents have to be in the home to assure the psychological and social health of children. In recent years this assumption has been widely challenged. In a review of the data Robert Bell makes this comment: "The existing evidence suggests that the chances of psychological damage to children resulting from the divorce of their parents is no greater than that for children in unbroken homes marked by continual marital tension."[39] Louise Despert goes further than this and argues that the damage to children is greater in "holy deadlock" marriages than in families in which divorce has occurred.[40] Despert writes: "A man and woman may have been unable to make a success of their marriage, but they can yet make a success of their divorce."[41] Mel Krantzler agrees with this statement.[42] And, apparently so do most of the parents in the United States. A survey found that two thirds of the parents responding disagreed with the notion that parents should stay together when unhappy for the sake of the children.[43]

In a conference of home economists discussing the one-parent family this conclusion was reached: "A father's absence from a family is not what causes emotional and behavioral problems in children."[44]

If one wishes to debate the number of adults required to socialize children properly, the question can be asked: Who decided that *two* parents was the proper number? Philippe Aries claims that until modern times children were reared by the community in Western society.[45] Bernard Farber agrees with Aries in saying that ". . . in almost every human society more than two adults are involved in the socialization of the child."[46]

Alfred Kadushin reviewed a mass of studies in an attempt to determine whether the one-parent family system was inherently dysfunctional or pathological. The basic purpose of this study was to determine whether adoption agencies would be justified in considering single persons for adoptions. Kadushin concluded that "the association between single-parent familyhood and psychosocial pathology is neither strong nor invariable.[47] Kadushin also makes the statement: "The material suggests a greater application of different kinds of contexts in which children can be reared without damage."[48]

Joan Aldous also was not convinced that the case against the one-parent family had been proved. In a study of Head Start children, she did not find significant differences in perception of adult male and female roles between father-present and father-absent children when race and social class variables were controlled.[49]

It is obvious to any clinician that the two-parent system has its own pathology—the two parents may be in serious conflict as to how their parental roles should be performed; one parent may be competent but have his or her efforts undermined by the incompetent partner; the children may be caught in a "double bind" or crossfire between the two parents;[50] both parents may be competent but simply unable to work together as an effective team in rearing their children; one parent may be more competent than the other but inhibited in using this competence by the team pattern inherent in the two-parent system.

We believe the so-called pathology of the one-parent family in the United States reflects the fact that society is organized for the two-parent family—the lack of adequate daycare programs, for example, stems from the notion that both parents will be in the home and that the mother will have nothing to do but stay home and take care of her children. Compare this with the Soviet Union where the assumption is made that mothers will be in the labor force and that government and industry must provide daycare facilities for all children needing them.[51]

The American school year was originally designed for farm families, with long summer vacations so that children could help with the farm work. This plan is devastating for one-parent families when the mother or father is employed outside of the home. The Russians even have a six-day school week—a boon to one-parent families. School hours do not fit the one-parent family if the parent holds an outside job. School opens after the parent has left for work and closes early in the afternoon before the parent gets home from work. We need cultural arrangements that fit the one-parent family as well as the two-parent family.

We believe that much of the research that condemns the one-parent family has reflected biased samples—children from one-parent families in the urban ghetto are compared with children from two-parent families in the suburbs. With such samples you can prove almost anything.

Mavis Hetherington takes a balanced stance in her review of the research on single-parent families:

> A conflict-ridden intact family is more deleterious to family members than is a stable home in which parents are divorced. An inaccessible, rejecting, or hostile parent in a nuclear family is more detrimental to the development of the child than is the absence of a parent. Divorce is often a positive solution to destructive family functioning; however, most children experience divorce as a difficult transition, and life in a single-parent family can be viewed as a high-risk situation for parents and children.[52]

Our research on parents and children is illustrative of Hetherington's point. We found that the toughest time for family members was directly after one parent moved out of the home; but the children on the average recovered relatively quickly. By three months after the marital separation, the mothers in our study felt the children were functioning about as well as they were just when the father left. After a year, the children appeared to be considerably happier than they were with father around. Again, "holy deadlock" may be the most difficult situation of all to endure. One in five children in our study noted that they had witnessed physical violence in their family before the father left home. "Did you fight in front of the children?" we asked. One young mother replied: "My husband tried to drown me twice in front of my preschool boys."[53]

As Hetherington argued: Neither the gloom-and-doom approach nor the political stance of refusing to recognize that many single-parent families headed by mothers have problems other than financial difficulties is likely to be productive.[54]

Gary Peterson and Helen Cleminshaw argued that one step in helping single-parent families would be the development or community divorce clinics, in which families would be able to receive counseling, educational programs on divorce, as well as information about welfare entitlements, housing, daycare, self-help groups, and lists of other supporting agencies in the community.[55]

Joint custody

"Your mom and dad aren't going to be living together anymore," the second author found himself saying to a seven-year-old girl whose parents were divorcing.

"I know. I wish they would stay together, but they just can't get along," she replied, looking down at the reeds along the edge of the lake.

"I don't like to ask you this question, but it's my job," he began, guiltily. His research on divorce and children had gotten him involved in custody disputes being heard in the district court. "So, who do you want to live with? Mom or dad?"

"Why doesn't the judge just take a big knife and cut me down the middle and give half to mom and half to dad?" the little girl replied with the wisdom of Solomon.

Divorce is often a painful business. Compound the problems with uncertainty about what to do with the children and the issues become labyrinthine in nature. One judge has told us that the toughest issue in the world to decide is whether or not to impose the death penalty. The second toughest issue? What to do with the children in a custody fight.

Women's liberation in many ways has been a boon for men. Wives have demanded more from husbands in the way of familial reponsibilities, and many men have responded positively. Others without any prompting at all have been quite active with the children.

In families such as these divorce can be particularly painful. When mother and father divorce, does one have to divorce the children, also? Many parents believe this should not be the case and work actively to preserve relationships with both parents.

The argument for joint custody goes like this: It allows the children to continue to have the support and nurturance of both parents, even though they are not living together any longer. The counterargument: If they couldn't communicate with each other well enough to hold the marriage together before, how can they expect to work out all the delicate dealings that co-parenting after divorce demands?

Aside from philosophical arguments pro and con, there is very little hard data one way or the other on the joint-custody issue. The second author and colleagues Julie Elmen and Judy Fricke are just completing a large-scale study of the issues and their early findings are relevant here.

The three researchers surveyed 738 parents in 47 states and the District of Columbia. The parents responded to newspaper articles calling for volunteers and were divided into four groups: mothers with custody; fathers with custody; joint custody; and split custody.

Joint custody was defined as both parents having relatively the same amount of responsibility for the care of the children. To measure responsibility, all the hours the parents logged in a typical week caring for the children were added up; if neither parent took more than 60 percent of the total hours, the division of labor was judged to be relatively equal between the two and the custody arrangement was labelled joint custody. (*Split custody* was defined as an arrangement in which one parent takes some of the children and the other parent takes care of the remainder of the children.)

The parents responded to a 100-item open-ended and fixed-response questionnaire. Some of the results are quite instructive:

> A positive relationship exists between parental adjustment to the custody arrangement and child adjustment to the custody arrangement.

Feelings of being overburdened by the children are significantly less prevalent among parents with joint custody as opposed to those with sole custody.

Sole-custody parents claim to be experiencing significantly greater stress in their lives than joint custody parents.

Children's adjustment to the custody arrangement did not differ between the two groups.

Joint custody parents lived closer to their ex-spouse than sole-custody parents.

Joint-custody parents reported feeling more positively toward their ex-spouse at the time custody arrangements were set up and more often reported the process of working out custody arrangements was a mutual, friendly one.

Sole-custody parents often wished their ex-spouse spent more time with the children; joint-custody parents were relatively more satisfied in this regard.

The children maintained a stronger relationship with both parents in joint-custody families as opposed to sole-custody families.

Joint-custody parents were significantly more positive about the importance for children to maintain close relationships with both parents after a divorce.

Sole-custody parents reported significantly lower gross yearly incomes.

Joint-custody parents reported more positive changes in their social lives since assuming custody than parents with sole custody (joint custody, in many instances, gave parents more free time to develop social relationships).

In sum, joint custody works quite well for many, many families. For that matter, sole custody also works quite well for many, many families. The researchers concluded that each family is unique; that no particular custody arrangement works for all families; and that the key lies in correctly judging which arrangement will fit the lifestyles and personalities of the individuals involved. A most difficult task, indeed.[56]

The Family Court of Milwaukee, Wisconsin, has come up with a Bill of Rights for children in divorce, and these are as sage a set of operating principles as any we have seen for people pondering what to do about the children:

1. The right to be treated as an interested and affected person and not as a pawn or chattel of either or both parents.
2. The right to that home environment which will best guarantee an opportunity to grow to mature and responsible citizenship.
3. The right to the day-by-day love, care, discipline, and protection of the parent having custody.
4. The right to know the noncustodial parent and to have the benefit of that parent's love and guidance through adequate visitation.
5. The right to a positive and constructive relationship with both parents, with neither to be permitted to degrade the other in the mind of the child.
6. The right to the most adequate level of economic support that can be provided by the best efforts of both parents.
7. The right to the same opportunities for education that the child would have if the family unit were not broken.
8. The right to periodic review of custodial arrangements and child-support orders as the circumstances may require.
9. The right to recognition that children involved in a marriage dissolution are disadvantaged parties and that the law must take affirmative steps to protect their welfare, including where indicated, a social investigation to determine their interrests and the appointment of a lawyer-guardian to protect their interests.[57]

Other difficult parental roles

The parents considered in this section are not necessarily parents without partners, but they do occupy relatively unique and complex positions in the parental role system. These are stepparents, adoptive parents, and foster parents. We will consider them in that order.

The role of stepparents

With about 80 percent of the divorced persons in the United States remarrying, sooner or later most children in the single-parent families will add a stepparent to their life.[58] Anne Simon noted that the 1960 decade was the first time in America in which more stepchildren were created by divorce and remarriage than by death.[59] E. M. Rallings suggested a reasonable estimate would be that 1 child in 10 is currently living with a stepparent.[60]

Some of the children in these families do not know how to refer to their stepparents—especially when the father or mother has been married more than twice. One college student, a young man of 20, said to us: "My mother has been married four times. I don't even try to remember the name of her latest husband any more—I just call them by number." Actually, after the second divorce, this boy moved in with his maternal grandparents, whom he now calls dad and mom.

A college girl said to us: "Do you have to love your stepfather? Mine wants to be real 'buddy buddy', but I can't stand him."

A divorced woman of 35, now remarried, is rearing two sets of children—two from her first marriage and two from her husband's first marriage. She finds the role of stepmother difficult and frustrating. "The other day," she told us, "one of my stepsons didn't do what I had asked him to do. When I corrected him about this he said— 'You're not my *real* mother.' I got mad and belted him one." She went on to say that she also found it difficult when one of the stepchildren accused her of being partial to her own children. This woman finds her second marriage satisfying, but she regards the role of stepmother as being perhaps the most difficult job she has ever undertaken—and especially so when there are two sets of children.

Actually, the kinds of situations in which stepparents find themselves are almost endless. In the previous case, for example, if this woman has any children by her second husband, there will be *three* sets of children. At this point she is not enthused about this prospect.

A stepmother may find herself rearing a group of children from her husband's first marriage; a stepfather may find himself in the same spot; both may have children with them from a previous marriage; one or both may have had children in more than one previous marriage; they may have children in their new marriage and thus start another set of children; and so forth.[61]

Historically, the role of stepmother has been considered the most difficult parental assignment in Western society. It was no accident that the terrible woman in Cinderella was a stepmother. Probably the stepmother role is so difficult because children in our society are relatively closer to their mother than to their father, and this means that it is very unlikely that anybody can follow the mother without experiencing some problems. The following factors can be identified as complicating the stepparent role in our society:

The stepparent is following a preceding parent. Stepfathers and stepmothers do not start with the child at birth; they follow a preceding father or mother. If the child's relationship with the first parent was positive, this creates difficulty for the stepparent—he or she has to work his or her way into the charmed circle; but if the preceding relationship was negative, this also sets up problems— hostility generated in the earlier relationship may be displaced onto the stepparent.

In many different ways, the child will be continuously measuring the new parent against the former parent.

Stepparents have a tendency to try too hard. Many college students have referred to this in term papers written for the first author in which stepparents were discussed. It seems that the stepparent is so insecure, so afraid of failure with the child, that the stepfather or stepmother pushes the relationship too fast or too hard. Time is required to heal the wounds left over from the previous parent-child relationship, and many stepparents do not give the child enough time.

Some stepparents try to replace the former parent. Simon and other writers on the stepparent role emphasize that the new parent should usually not attempt to replace the previous father or mother but should see him- or herself as a supplement, meeting needs of the child not met by the previous parent. This is especially the case in which the child continues to see the biological *father or mother*.

The complex sets of children to be reared by some stepparents. This was discussed earlier, but one can see how easy it would be for a stepfather or a stepmother to favor his or her biological offspring over the stepchildren, and even if no favoritism is involved the child may feel there is. Blood ties are very deep in human society, and not all of us can rise above this in complex stepparent situations.

For all of the stated reasons, and more, the stepparent in our society has a difficult role. Simon takes a positive attitude toward stepparents.[62] She points out that millions of children in modern America would literally have no father or mother to rear them if it were not for stepparents.

Jessie Bernard, in her classic study of remarriage, concluded similarly that given the hazards inherent in steprelationships, one might predict maladjustment of children rather than adjustment. But Bernard's data indicate that to the contrary most of the children were doing relatively well. She outlined three reasons why: (1) the children's attitude toward remarriage was favorable; (2) the new parent often proved to be a salvaging force, through understanding, wisdom, and love helping to heal the trauma of the previous marital failure; and (3) people of all ages seem to have a reservoir of resiliency, which makes it possible for them to adjust to whatever blows life brings.[63]

L. Duberman surveyed a random sample of parents in Cuyahoga County, Ohio, hoping to assess the stepparent-stepchild relationship. She termed her findings "somewhat surprising": 18 percent rated the relationship "poor," 18 percent rated the relationship "good," and 64 percent rated the relationship "excellent."[64]

Sharon Hanna and Patricia Knaub in a Nebraska study found that love and communication were the greatest strengths of stepfamilies, and discipline and handling of the children and finances as the two greatest areas of conflict. Most of the desired changes in these families involved the children. The researchers found that family strength scores were generally high, along with measures of marital satisfaction and perceptions of family adjustment. Fathers were not more satisfied with family relationships than mothers. Custodial parents were not more satisfied than noncustodial parents; and having a child together did not significantly affect the scores.[65]

A group of University of Texas at Dallas researchers also did a lot to explode the popular notion that stepfamilies are necessarily troubled. The team studied the effects of remarriage on the parent's and child's social behavior, by comparing intact, divorced, and stepfather families. A major finding: Boys in stepfather families were more competent in social behavior than boys in intact families, and stepfathers and their wives were more competent in their parenting than parents in intact families.[66]

Ruth Roosevelt and Jeannette Lofas wrote Living In Step: A Remarriage Manual for Parents and Children to address the problems of stepfamilies and founded the Stepfamily Foundation in New York City, which now has affiliates scattered around the country.[67] The book addresses issues of "natural hostility" stepparents encounter from their new children; whether the parent should side with spouse or children; how families can coexist and cooperate, even though they in a sense are competing; how to cope with being a pawn in a war between loved ones; and the traffic problems that occur with the seasonal shifts of children. The local Stepfamily Foundation affiliates offer social functions and self-help through group interaction (and commisseration) over challenges the families face in integrating the new families together. Many stepparents and their spouses find encouragement and strength at these gatherings.

All in all, remarriage generally is a beneficial experience for most divorced persons. Norval Glenn analyzed seven recent American national surveys for evidence on personal and marital happiness of persons remarried after divorce. He found a "remarkably high level of well-being among persons remarried after divorce," which indicates that divorce does not apparently happen to the maladjusted, chronically unhappy person, or that marital failure typically has pronounced long-term negative effects on the happiness of divorced persons who remarry. Glenn found consistency with the view that the high American divorce rate "is not so much a symptom of pathology in the institution of marriage as it is a reflection of rather effective mechanisms for replacing poor marriages with better ones."[68]

Adoptive parents

Roughly 2 percent of all children in our society are adopted. Of these children, about half are adopted by relatives and half by nonrelatives.[69]

Unlike foster parents (to be discussed shortly), adoptive parents have all of the rights that biological parents have once the final adoption papers are signed by the court having jurisdiction. Adoptive parents not only have the same rights as natural parents but also the same responsibilities.

Some features of adoptive parenthood are relatively unique: Adoptive parents are screened by the adoption agency and must pass relatively strict requirements before a court will permit them to adopt a child. Furthermore, adoptive parents are literally on probation for a period of from six months to a year, and during this period their child can be taken away by the court if the adoptive parents do not seem to be performing their parental role properly. Biological parents do not have to pass tests (except being fertile) before becoming parents, and once they have a child, it is difficult to take the child away from them.

There are other problems facing adoptive parents: Many children will eventually want to know who their real parents were. Will a search for the biological parents put a strain on the adoptive parent-child relationship? Will the adoptive parents lose the child to the birth parents? Arthur Sorosky, Annette Baran, and Reuben Pannor argued that all adoptees have a desire to know about their origins, and that they are more preoccupied with existential issues and feelings of isolation in the adolescent years than nonadoptees. This research team studied reunion cases of adoptees and birth parents and concluded:

> What stand out most in our study of reunion cases are the positive benefits the majority of the adoptees gained. Most were enriched by a new, meaningful relationship with their birth relatives. More important was the effect upon the adoptee who was able to resolve the conflicts of his/her dual identity.
>
> Regardless of what kind of relationship, positive or negative, existed between the adoptee and adoptive parents prior to the reunion, the effect of the experience was in some way enhancing to that relationship. The feelings of the adoptees toward their adoptive parents became more concretely positive and assumed a new meaning, even when the reunion resulted in an ongoing relationship between the adoptee and the birth parents. The realization emerged for the adoptees that their adoptive parents were their only true psychological parents and that the lifelong relationship with them was of far greater importance than a new connection with the birth parents. [70]

Katrina Wehking Johnson of the University of Notre Dame wrote that she was tempted to applaud the research by Sorosky, Baran, and Pannor for its timeliness, relevance, and significance; but she cautioned that enthusiasm for their book, *The Adoption Triangle*, should be tempered with the recognition that the methodology for the study was vague, they used a biased sample, and idealized adoption reunions. She points out that the researchers drew their sample from hundreds of letters from birth parents and adult adoptees, relating their personal experiences about their reunions, and that those uninterested in, or hostile to, the search for birth parents would have had little motivation to be included in the study. A further criticism is that the authors emphasized the biological tie between birth parents and children; Johnson, both an adoptive parent and a biological parent, found this insistence disturbing for it seemed to place more emphasis on inheritance rather than nurturance in the development of children into healthy adults. Johnson concluded that sampling difficulties and the biological emphasis of the authors should not be overlooked when one is trying to draw inferences on what effects unsealing adoption records will have on the majority of adoptees, birth parents, and adoptive parents. The returns, in short, are not all in.[71]

How do you tell an adopted child that "We are not your real parents" without disturbing the child emotionally? How do you convince the adopted child that it is just as much loved as if it had been born to the adoptive parents?[72]

Another difficulty of adoptive parents is that they suffer from a sort of guilt complex which makes them feel that they have to be "perfect" parents—in a sense they have to prove to the adopted child that they are as good as (or better than) biological parents. This is also a problem of stepparents. Feelings of this nature do not make parenthood very easy.

Adoptive parenthood has many positive features: These parents are voluntary parents—they did not have a child because of an unplanned pregnancy but because they wanted a child; to some extent adoptive parents have some choice over the child they will accept for adoption, whereas biological parents have to accept what the obstetrician delivers; adoptive parents are on probation for several months before the adoption becomes final, and if the adoption does not seem to be successful, the child can be returned to the custody of the court. Finally, since adoptive parents are screened before being accepted for adoption it seems likely that they are reasonably competent persons, a statement that one can hardly make about some biological parents.

Research seems to indicate that the great majority of legal adoptions in the United States are considered to be successful—a term that is hard to define in regard to parenthood. Kadushin and Seidl, for example, found that 97 percent of the adoptions they surveyed were successful in that the final adoption papers were approved by the court and the child remained permanently with the adoptive parents.[73]

Transracial adoption, usually a white family adopting a nonwhite child, came into being as an alternative to continued institutionalization of large numbers of minority children. Rita Simon and Howard Alstein wrote that by 1976 the practice of transracial adoption as an alternative to homelessness was dying out—largely because of minority opposition. A common charge was implicit racism and cultural genocide. The debate raged hotly, as one letter to the editor of *Ebony* illustrates:

> This is a white racist society caused by whites and whites alone, and their act of adopting blacks is insulting and psychologically damaging and dangerous. For 400 years, we have been constantly bombarded with overt and institutionalized racism, which white people to this present day have done little to correct. I wonder how Jews would feel if ex-Nazis rushed to adopt little Jewish orphans.[74]

Curiously, as minority protest intensified and took its toll on transracial adoption, researchers came to surprisingly hopeful conclusions in several evaluation studies of the families.

David Fanshel surveyed a group of adoptions involving American Indian children adopted by non-Indians and reported that approximately 90 percent of these transracial adoptions were considered to be successful.[75]

Rita Simon and Howard Altstein focused on racial identity, awareness, and attitudes of the adoptive nonwhite children and their white siblings. They found that "transracial adoption appears to be a mechanism whereby children can develop racial 'color blindness.'" Children, in short, could be aware of race, respect race differences, and be comfortable with their own race in these unique families.[76]

Constance Abraham and the second author surveyed transracial adoption families and compared them to same-race adoption families and found that there were no differences in how well the children were adjusting to the adoption, nor did sibling relationships differ. The experiences of the children in both types of families were generally successful.[77]

The final evaluation of transracial adoption cannot be made, though, for several years until many of these children grow up.

> If the fears expressed by black and Indian children opponents of transracial adoption are realized, that these children will be white on the inside and black on the outside, and that they will be perceived by both white and black as pariahs, transracial adoption will be remembered as a dismal and emotionally costly experiment. If the hopes and expectations of the parents involved in transracial adoption are realized, and their children are emotionally whole, well-adjusted, and able to move easily within and between black and

white communities, society's failure to maintain and support the program will be remembered with deep regret. Time, thus, will determine transracial adoption's final evaluation. [78]

Kadushin even found that adoptions of older children, usually
considered to be risky, tended to turn out favorably. [79] It would seem
that adoptive parents perform as well as, if not better than, biological parents.

Adoptive parents in the United States have suffered from a number of preconceived beliefs held by child-welfare agencies: that
older children would not benefit from adoption; that women who
work outside of the home would not make good adoptive mothers;
that children from one religious background could not be reared
properly by adoptive parents from another religious faith; that older
persons would not do well as adoptive parents; that persons should
not be permitted to adopt children from another race; that single
adults could not rear adopted children properly; that divorced persons should not be permitted to adopt children, and, finally, that
homosexual persons could not serve as adequate adoptive parents.
In recent years all of these assumptions have been challenged.

One wonders what would happen if biological parents were
screened as carefully as adoptive parents before conceiving a child.
How many could pass the tests? It is a good question.

Foster parents

A relatively new type of parent in American society is the foster
parent utilized by social work agencies to take care of children
whose biological parents are unable or unwilling to assume parental responsibility. For example, a parent may be abusive or neglectful, making a court-ordered foster placement necessary. Or the
child's parents may have died suddenly in a car wreck with no
surviving relatives. For various reasons these children cannot be
placed for adoption and yet cannot live in their own homes. The
latest figures show more than a quarter million children are living in
foster homes in the United States. [80]

Kadushin points out that foster parents have largely replaced the
children's home in our society: As of 1923 about 65 percent of the
homeless children in the United States were living in institutions
built for such children, whereas today the vast majority are living in
foster homes. [81]

This is not the place to review the whole foster-home movement, but in view of the increase in foster parenthood in our society in recent decades, a few observations are in order.

Foster parents have no parental rights. Although about 75 percent of all foster-home placements turn out to be permanent—the child never returns to his own parents—the foster parents usually have no right to permanent custody of the child.[82] As a rule, they cannot adopt the child, nor can they prevent the agency from taking the child away at any time for any reason. The agency is not required to "show cause" when it decides to remove a child from a foster home; there is no appeal to the courts.

About the only clear-cut right the foster parent has is the right to be paid—about 95 percent of them receive compensation for taking care of the child.[83]

The foster-parent role is ambiguous. Foster parents are supposed to express instant love or affection for the foster child, but at the same time they are not supposed to become so attached to a child that they cannot give the child up at any time.

The role is ambiguous in that it combines a comercial arrangement with an expectation of affection or a willingness to perform beyond the call of duty. When a child is sick, the workday is 24 hours, with no overtime from the agency.

The foster-parent role is ambiguous in that while the job pays, it does not pay very well—and yet the care of the child is supposed to be first class. The pay varies from state to state, but generally it is about $200 per month, even for hard-to-place children such as teenagers or the emotionally disturbed. The time, anyway, is considered voluntary—the state pays out the money to cover room and board.

Every natural parent and every adoptive parent knows that nobody could pay enough to properly rear a child—even $1 million would not cover the heartaches and the anguish experienced by most parents at one time or another.

The foster-parent role is also ambiguous in that what is planned as a temporary placement may turn out to be permanent, while a placement that was intended to be permanent may be terminated in a few days if things do not go well.

It is the authors' belief that the foster-parent role is one of the most complex roles attempted by any parent in our society, and the research seems to support this belief.[84]

Summary and conclusion

It would seem that a sizable proportion of American parents operate under conditions that are far from ideal. The picture does not coincide with the dream that most of us have when we start a family.

If nearly one half of American marriages are not really successful—whether or not they end in divorce—this fact alone would mean that millions of fathers and mothers will have to try to care for their children under difficult circumstances. It is not only divorce but other forms of marital failure which complicate this picture.

In this chapter we took a look at parents operating under unusual circumstances. Not all of these fathers and mothers are without parental partners as the chapter title suggests, but all of them face family situations that are somewhat different or unique.

The assumed pathology of the one-parent family was questioned. Although we believe a stable two-parent family is superior to a stable one-parent family, we realize that divorce may be the only reasonable alternative for many troubled parents.

Chapter 10

Parents, mass media, and the youth peer group

In this chapter an attempt will be made to analyze the impact of the mass media and the youth peer group on children. It is the thesis of this chapter that these forces compete seriously with parents in their attempt to influence the values and behavior of their sons and daughters. It is also our belief that the power of the mass media and the youth peer group over young Americans is much greater today than it was in the 19th century or the early decades of the 20th century. The rest of the chapter will be devoted to an examination of these propositions.

Parents and television

Today's young adults in America are the first generation reared under the influence of television. The average young person in the United States will have watched television for approximately 22,000 hours by the time he or she has completed high school compared with spending about 11,000 hours in the classroom.[1] During that period the child will have been exposed to about 350,000 commercials.[2]

Victor Cline, professor of psychology at the University of Utah, has discovered that the average American child will have seen over

13,000 human beings murdered or maimed on television by the time
the child is 15 years old.[3] A survey of research by the *Chicago
Tribune* revealed that of 762 leading characters on prime time television, half committed acts of violence on one or more programs.[4]

Some observers believe that television has become a major force
in socializing children. Alistair Cooke, who has produced numerous
television programs for both commercial and educational networks,
has been quoted as saying: "Television ranks next to the mother and
father—far ahead of school and church. Children watching television learn so much about the world that appeals immediately to
their emotions, but I'm not sure it involves their intelligence, their
judgment."[5]

S. I. Hayakawa, an authority on language and semantics and a
well-known hawk during the Vietnam War, has made the observation: "The trouble with today's youth may be that they are the first
humans to grow up having watched television all their lives."[6]

The net effect of television on children is not yet known. Children
certainly learn from watching and some of what they learn is undoubtedly helpful to them in growing up. On the other hand, some
of what they see on the tube may be quite damaging. Alberta
Siegel, a psychologist at Stanford University, is concerned about the
violence children are exposed to on television. "Like other primates,
man learns by watching," she has said.[7]

Professor Cline of the University of Utah has done laboratory
experiments with children which lead him to believe that violence
on television desensitizes children to violence—an effect he considers to be dangerous.[8] Other researchers are not convinced that
the negative effects of television on children outweigh the positive
effects.[9]

An English advertising executive, who has also worked in mass
media in the United States, believes that commercial television,
because of its concentration on contemporary experiences, has
helped contribute to the generation gap in contemporary society.
He writes: ". . . the young today cannot share their parents' response to events which deeply moved the parents in the past."[10]

In his study of the television industry, Robert Metz, who writes
about mass media for the *New York Times*, was appalled at the
crass commercial nature of the industry. In discussing children's
programs with network executives, Metz learned that the network
asked only one question about a program beamed at children: How
many kids watched the show last week?[11] The reason, Metz argues,

is that rates for commercials are based not on the quality of a program but on the number of viewers.

A recent survey of physicians found that 94 percent believed there is too much violence on television. Besides heightened aggression, the doctors cited nightmares, epileptic seizures, and injuries resulting from imitating TV incidents as problems stemming from video violence.[12] Not long after this American Medical Association survey, a Miami teenager charged with killing an elderly neighbor of his during a robbery was said to be insane from seeing too much television violence, according to his attorney. The boy "became intoxicated with the TV dramas and lived them as if they were his own life," the lawyer said. "Kojak," "Police Woman," and a film about mass murderer Charles Manson were responsible for "diseasing his mind and impairing his behavioral controls." The boy took the money from the robbery and treated four friends to a weekend in Disney World.[13]

Manson echoed these sentiments: "We are what you made us," he said, speaking of society in general. "We were brought up on your TV. We were brought up watching 'Gunsmoke,' 'Have Gun Will Travel,' 'FBI,' and 'Combat.' 'Combat' was my favorite show. I never missed 'Combat.'"[14]

Muriel Cantor observed that the television networks tell advertisers that their programs influence behavior, but they tell Congress and parents that their programs don't influence children. She noted that obviously one can't have it both ways.[15]

John Murray, a child psychologist at the Boys Town Center in Omaha, reviewed 3,000 studies in the past 25 years on the effects of television on the young. With Barbara Lonnborg, he wrote *Children and Television: A Primer for Parents*, which summarized the massive research findings in a very readable way and offered strategies for parents in their battle to counter TV's negative effects. First, the negative effects:[16]

1. The average preschooler watches about four hours of television a day. This has a negative effect on the child's school performance, reading ability, and play activities.

2. The accumulated evidence from hundreds of research projects on television violence leading to aggressiveness in children indicates that the tube is "a powerful tutor," in the words of Albert Bandura.

3. Television gives a child an unrealistic portrait of the world, a TV

world where "crime occurs 10 times more often than it does on the streets, where men outnumber women three to one, where young people are only one third and the elderly one fifth of their actual proportion of the population, where women rarely work outside the home, and most are younger than the men they deal with, and where children often fail at the things they attempt to do." Also, drug abuse, alcoholism, and sex are brought to the child's attention sooner than many parents might wish. Sexual innuendoes, for example, increased from 1 per hour of prime-time TV in 1975 to 11 per hour in 1978.

4. The average child is exposed to 20,000 television commercials each year. Under the age of six or even eight years old, most children don't understand that advertising's goal is to sell products. The kids tend to believe the ads and beg their parents to buy sugary cereals and action toys so often falsely portrayed.

Values portrayed by the mass media

In some societies, such as the Soviet Union, the mass media are expected to present material that supports the basic values of the society.[17] When this is the case, parents do not have to concern themselves with the exposure of their child to movies, television, radio, and the other mass media. This is not the case in the United States. It is the writers' contention that in our society much of the material presented to children and young adults by the mass media is in conflict with the basic values held by parents. The pages to follow will present this point of view.

Sex

Teenagers are in the process of discovering the world of sex—their bodies and their glands are propelling them toward sexual maturity, even though psychologically and socially most of them are far from being mature.

Now there is nothing wrong with sex—as most Americans will testify—and, given the lack of an adequate sex-education program in the United States, somebody has to help these youngsters get some idea of what sex is all about. American novelists have been mining this field for a long time, but in recent decades television and the drive-in movie have muscled their way into this market with great enthusiasm.

Unfortunately, as the writers see it, sex in the movies and on television is usually on a physical level visually and verbally, yet is presented to the audience as love—in other words, the signals or cues are confusing. In one sense we are watching physical and genital attraction between a man and a woman, but in another sense we are expected to believe that these two people are in love. Sex and love, however, are two different things.

In a newspaper series, a professional observer of the Hollywood motion picture industry made the following statement: "Pictures that depict—indeed glorify—infidelity, nudity, sexual license, and vulgarity are being turned out in profusion. They have achieved box office success for several film companies that had previously been near bankruptcy. . . . Actors and actresses who break the established moral codes in their personal behavior find the screen moguls automatically disposed to boost the price of their services."[18]

Almost at random we select a motion picture advertisement of the following nature:

SLAVES TO THEIR OWN STRANGE DEVICES!
PLAYTHINGS OF EACH OTHER'S UNHOLY PASSIONS!

Photographs in the advertisement show a teenage boy and girl.[19]

Violence

Survey after survey has shown the massive dose of violence presented to young and old alike on television and in motion pictures.[20] America is, of course, a violent society, and the mass-media owners are always eager (a bit too eager) to point out that "We only give the customers what they want." On the same kind of logic, prostitutes and drug pushers could plead the same defense. Human beings have many self-destructive tendencies, and all human societies do what they can to hold these to a minimum level. It is difficult to see how modern films and television programs are helping to achieve this end.

The impact of movies, many of them violent, on American youth is considered to be enormous. The film, *Rebel Without a Cause*, by James Dean is thought to have influenced the dress and lifestyle of an entire generation.[21] Even 10 years after his premature death, teenage James Dean Clubs existed in almost every state in America.

The idealization of immaturity

In a study of teenage subculture,[22] one of the major points developed is that today's teenager no longer worships adult heroes—his idols are just as juvenile and immature as he is. In commenting on this in the *Saturday Review*, the education editor, Paul Woodring, put this point in the following words:

> The adolescent of an earlier age was eager to grow up, and the heroes he chose to emulate, while not always admirable, were usually adult. Today's teenager often chooses a model no older and no more mature than himself—a juvenile who has achieved wealth and fame at an early age with the help of just a little talent or beauty plus a hard-driving publicity agent. It is not difficult to understand why such models are chosen—they provide the basis for elaborate daydreams of what is seemingly possible for any adolescent who "gets a break," without much long waiting or hard work, without going to college or even completing high school. By comparison the prospect of a career emulating that of Abraham Lincoln or Florence Nightingale seems decidedly dull.[23]

In the face of such daydreams, parents often find it difficult to sell their children on the facts of life—that for most Americans hard work and years of training are required to compete in the society.

In the 1960s, many of the young grew their hair long and dressed shabbily. One important purpose of this behavior was to thumb a collective nose at maturity and parental values that the young felt had sold them out on Vietnam. If anyone is lulled into a false sense of security thinking such rebellion is dead, we suggest they study carefully the current younger generation's "new wave" of music, punk haircuts, and sneering disaffection with social values. The dynamics are strikingly similar. And though the young cannot charge the old with genocide in Vietnam, they can argue quite convincingly that the tremendous problem of youth unemployment in an inflationary spiral is yet another example of the American dream gone haywire.

Materialism

The well-known semanticist, S. I. Hayakawa, is quoted as saying that the antimaterialism of today's youth may be a reaction to television's message that "material possessions are everything, that this headache remedy, this luxurious carpeting, this new model car [will bring happiness]."[24]

American parents are themselves inclined to be materialistic—as is the whole society—but we often have the feeling that parental materialism cannot compare with that portrayed in the mass media.

The first author still has vivid memories of two mass magazine advertisements of a few years ago that seemed to have hit a new low. In one, a mother, surrounded by her husband and children, is looking at a new car and says: "Our new Plymouth is the greatest thing that ever happened to this family."

In the other advertisement, aimed at the Christmas trade, a father is shown heading for home (at least we hope so) pulling a child's sled on which reposes a case of a famous brand of whisky. The first author likes a drink as well as most Americans, but somehow this picture was revolting.

One of the interesting features of mass-media materialism is the effort made to make it seem free. You just get out the credit cards and off you go to Hawaii, with no cash needed. This is similar to what Woodring was writing about in the quotation earlier—no real effort is required to enjoy the fruits of the affluent society.

Hedonism

One dictionary defines *hedonism* as "the doctrine that pleasure is the principal good and should be the aim of action."[25]

Without debating the merits of this philosophical system, it does seem that the mass-media message in our society is essentially hedonistic. This reflects the fact that the ultimate aim of most mass media is that of entertainment and escape. Advertisers assume that Americans see enough reality in their everyday life; when they watch television they want to escape reality and be amused.

To the extent that this is true, teenagers (as well as most other Americans) are exposed to an unreal world when they turn to the mass media.

It may well be, of course, as David Riesman suggests, that the drift of our entire society is in the direction of hedonism.[26] With mechanization and automation, the major problem in the affluent society may well be what people do with their leisure rather than what they do at their place of work.

Parental values versus mass media values

The writers believe that most American parents do not agree with the basic values portrayed in the mass media aimed at young persons. The pages to follow attempt to support this argument.

Parents on violence

Most American parents, regardless of what they may have done in their own lives, hope (and pray) that their children will not attack or kill other human beings. As Margaret Mead observed, Americans are "counter punchers"—children are taught not to start a fight but also not to run away from one. They are to fight back if they are attacked by someone else.[27]

This is not the world of television and the movies. It is true, of course, that the bad guys always lose on "Gunsmoke" and "Bonanza," and Hollywood has a code that crime does not pay—but nevertheless the violent, ruthless person, like the devil in old-fashioned sermons, often emerges as a sort of "inverted hero." He may lose the girl, and even his life, but meanwhile he has captured the audience. The old gangster films made by Jimmy Cagney and Humphrey Bogart illustrate what we are talking about. Evil, for some reason, is just a lot more interesting than good.

We grant that researchers are divided as to the long-range effects of such films on children, but our point is that most American parents would prefer that their children not be subjected to such a heavy dose of aggression and violence. A Gallup poll, for example, found that most parents believe there is a link between television violence and criminal or other antisocial behavior (by a 67 percent to 29 percent margin). And that most parents favor restricting violent television programs to the hours after 10 P.M. (by a 70 percent to 24 percent margin).[28]

Suppose somebody did a series of television films showing children how to shoplift from supermarkets and other stores more effectively. Even if *most* children who saw the series never actively engaged in shoplifting as a result of the series, would it be in the public interest to show such films? Actually the series might even *lower* the crime rate for juvenile shoplifters by helping them avoid detection, but one can be sure that merchants would create such an uproar that the series would be banned. Parents often feel the same way about various aspects of the mass media, but they seldom are able to obtain any redress. They simply don't have the clout the Chamber of Commerce has.

Mass-media owners have a pat answer to parents who protest: "Don't permit your child or teenager to watch our programs—or read our comics—if you don't approve of the content." Any parent who has tried to shield children from violence on television or crime in movies knows how difficult this solution is. In the DeFrain family, the TV is in the basement. The children go there to watch it, often when mom and dad need a breather from them. The parents need help from the media, for it is most difficult to try to monitor every program.

Actually, television and radio frequencies belong to the society, not the station owners, and the licenses granted the operators specify that the wavelength must be used "in the public interest."[29] Stations that do not adhere to this policy may have their licenses revoked.

Using the same argument as the mass-media owners, why should the sale of marijuana or heroin be prohibited? Why should the sale of alcoholic beverages to minors be illegal?

In their report on life in the Soviet Union, Leona and Jerrold Schecter claim that they did not have to worry about what programs their children watched on Russian television—the programs often bored the children but never presented antisocial behavior.[30] The same cannot be said of the mass media in our society. The Schecters still preferred life in the United States to that in Russia, but this does not mean that they approve of some of the programs on the mass media in America.

Sexual restraint

In the mid-1970s, Betty Ford, the president's wife, was severely criticized by some Americans, and highly praised by others, when she said that she would not be surprised if any of her children were having premarital affairs. In a study of blue-collar tavern patrons, the first author found scarcely any parents who did not realize the possibility, if not the probability, that their children would have sexual relations before marriage.[31] But most parents, regardless of their own sexual histories, do hope that their children will use sex constructively in their lives, and that they will subscribe to some sort of decent sex code. One element of such a code is that sex should be combined with affection and/or love.

It seems to us that television, the movies, and many mass magazines do not portray sex in this way. It is often presented as an
overwhelming physical attraction between a man and a woman,
with the individuals having little or no choice about what they do
about the attraction. And the relationships are entered into after
such a brief courtship that it seems hardly appropriate to describe
the interaction as love.

It may well be that young Americans can still recognize love
when they find it, but we have to question how much help they
received from the mass media in this matter.

Lifetime monogamy

Although the divorce rate in the United States increased in the
1970s, the majority of Americans have been married only once and
it seems to the writers that American parents still consider lifetime
marriage the ideal—even if it didn't work out for them they hope it
will for their children.

In the mass-media world, however, it is a rare star performer who
has not been married more than once—from Frank Sinatra to Elvis
Presley to the Beatles, divorces are the norm. This is perfectly legal
and moral in contemporary America, but it hardly presents a very
positive image of lifetime marriage for young persons.[32]

Planning for the future

Most parents in our society have come to accept the old banker's
cliché that "the future belongs to those who prepare for it." Even
though the parents may be in debt, they realize that some thought
has to be given to the day of reckoning—not only in regard to
financial matters, but also in regard to sex, alcohol, education, and
so forth.

The mass media present a vague picture of the future consequence of present action. We see beautiful men and women drinking beer every few minutes on television but nobody ever gets fat.
We see all the handsome males and females smoking their cigarettes on television but nobody ever gets lung cancer. We see entire
families taking off for Hawaii with nothing in their pockets but a
credit card, yet nobody ever goes bankrupt. That is a never-never
land.

Commercial nature of the mass media

It needs to be remembered that the mass media in American society are operated for profit. This means that the ultimate test of their effectiveness is not what they do to people but how much money they make. In commenting on this, a television executive writes: "Because television can make so much money doing its worst, it often cannot afford to do its best."[33]

Earlier in this chapter it was stated that by the time an American young person emerges from high school he or she will have been exposed to about 350,000 commercials on television alone. The ultimate impact of commercials on children (or adults) is not known, but one survey of the research concluded: "70 percent of commercials are based on fear. If you don't do this, he won't kiss you again. The easiest way to get people to do something is to scare them to death."[34]

It seems incredible today that in 1929, according to Milton Mayer, the National Association of Broadcasters adopted a code which said that "commercial announcements shall not be broadcast between 7 and 11 P.M."[35]

Positive aspects of the mass media

It is undoubtedly true that children and young adults learn many different things from television, movies, radio, and magazines and that some of this learning is essentially useful and positive in the lives of these persons. Both television and the movies, for example, have been outstanding in recent years in their portrayal of racial problems.

We have to wonder, however, to what extent the basic values of parents are supported by the mass media. At present the writers' votes would have to be negative. Greed, hype, jiggles, and violence still predominate.

Parents and the youth peer group

In his study of American society, The Lonely Crowd, David Riesman takes the position that there has been a significant increase in the power of the youth peer group in recent decades. He writes: "There has been an enormous ideological shift favoring submission to the group . . . the peer group becomes the measure of all things; the individual has few defenses the group cannot batter down."[36]

James Coleman, after studying social life in 10 high schools, was impressed by the extent and power of teenage society. He writes: "Our adolescents today are cut off, probably more than ever before, from the adult society . . . our society has within its midst a set of small teenage societies, which focus teenage interests and attitudes on things far removed from adult responsibilities, and which may develop standards that lead away from those goals established by the larger society."[37] Coleman did not find that these high school students ignore or even reject the values of their parents—his main point was that parents are in constant competition with teenage society and are never sure when their wishes will prevail with their adolescent children.

Ralph Keyes, author of *Is There Life After High School?*, argues that,

> High school is uniquely American and Canadian. In other cultures the family continues to matter more during adolescense. The big problem is that we assume that high school is an academic experience, yet what you learn in class is the very least part of the experience. What you learn in the hallways is important.[38]

One can shrug off this competition with the old bromide: Good parents have no trouble with teenagers—only poor parents do. Within limits this may be correct, but the stiff competition from the teenage society still poses severe problems for parents who have only tenuous relations with their adolescent children.

In another context Coleman makes this statement: "The adolescent lives more and more in a society of his own; he finds the family a less and less satisfying psychological home. As a consequence, the home has less and less ability to mold him."[39]

Salvador Minuchin and associates, in an intensive study of low-income families, concluded that older siblings may influence their younger brothers and sisters more than the parents do. This can be dangerous.[40]

In his book, *Future Shock*, Alvin Toffler comments on the increased influence of the youth peer group: "Robbed of adult heroes . . . children of streamlined, nuclear families are increasingly flung into the arms of the only other people available to them—other children. They spend more time with one another, and they become more responsive to the influence of peers than ever before."[41]

In a very scholarly study of the campus revolts of the 1960s and the 1970s, Kenneth Keniston concludes that parents and their middle-class children were separated by three basic issues during this period: (1) the drug revolution—the belief of young people that marijuana and other drugs might be better than alcohol; (2) the sex revolution—the idea that young adults were as entitled to sex as married persons are; and (3) the revolt against the establishment—the refusal to support the war in Southeast Asia, the rejection of military service, and the disenchantment of young persons with leaders such as Richard Nixon.[42] Keniston argues that very few middle-class parents were able to agree with their children on the above issues.

Differences of opinion continue into the 1980s. A recent Gallup poll indicates that 58 percent of the boys and 62 percent of the girls aspire to lifestyles quite different from their parents. The majority view was succinctly phrased by a Winthrop Harbor, Illinois 14-year-old girl: "I don't want to have five kids, and I don't want to live in Winthrop Harbor." How would the lifestyle differ? The young would like to go out more often and do more things (34 percent); have more money (28 percent); follow a different line of work (26 percent); live in a different area (21 percent); have more free time (20 percent); stay single longer (16 percent); understand their children better (16 percent); have fewer children (15 percent); have a bigger, nicer home (15 percent); have a happier marriage (14 percent); and be less strict with their children (10 percent).[43]

It is often assumed that the power of the youth peer group is typical of all Western societies and is not unique to the United States. Jesse Pitts disagrees with this and argues, for example, that the French middle-class family exercises more control over its children and young adults than the family does in America. Life does not have to be this way.[44]

The youth counterculture

In the chapter to follow, detailed attention will be given to the so-called generation gap in American society, but at this point it is necessary to make a few observations about what amounts to a counterculture evolved by young people in the United States during the 1960s and the early 1970s.[45] To the extent that this counterculture still exists, it poses substantial problems for parents.

In its purest form, the counterculture is a revolt against the middle-class way of life—more specifically, against the upper-middle-class way of life.[46]

Measuring the extent of an amorphous mass such as the counter-culture is, of course, basically impossible. No Gallup or Roper poll down through the years ever quixotically tried to trace its rise or alleged decline, so it is difficult to know exactly how pervasive the phenomenon was in the 1960s and 1970s, or the extent to which it remains today. Most observers tend to argue that the counterculture still exists into the 1980s, but either is smaller or simply more accepted by society in general and of lesser interest.

For example, an estimated 1 million people live in communal arrangements today, but much less is written about communes, because, as sociologist Ben Zablocki of Rutgers University puts it: "Communes are being perceived as less radical."[47]

This could also be said of long hair, rock music, drugs, premarital sex, antiestablishment views, and a number of other phenomena which caused such heated debate in the 1960s. Judith and Jack Balswick note that, "The emphasis in our institutions of higher education on humanism and self-direction during this decade may account for some of this apparent lack of alienation of the present-day youth."[48] As the styles and beliefs of the young gain wider acceptance, albeit grudging acceptance, these styles and beliefs do not have to be so vigorously defended by the young and extremes tend to diminish of their own weight.

We could find no literature indicating an increase in the number of alienated youth since the 1960s. But it would be foolish to conclude that young people have reverted automatically to adopting the values of the older generation. The world rarely moves backward in time.

Rejection of materialism

The youth counterculture takes the position that parents have become slaves to money, material possessions, and the rat race that is usually associated with these. In matter of fact, as Bernard has pointed out,[49] young Americans today are the most affluent and the greatest spenders of their age ever seen in American society, but on the surface they reject the symbols of middle-class life. They may be attending a college that costs their parents $8,000–$12,000 a year, but they dress as if they were in the poverty group.

Drugs and alcohol

Many of the parental generation were addicted to alcohol, and the youth counterculture is determined to explore other drugs besides alcohol. This began as a debate over marijuana but eventually involved drugs that parents had never heard of. Young people have argued, correctly, that alcohol is itself a very dangerous drug, but most parents feel that at least they know the dangers of alcohol, while they do not know the hazards of drugs their children are experimenting with. Marijuana use has reached what some call epidemic proportions. The U.S. Department of Health and Human Services has calculated that 31 percent of all children age 12 to 17 have used marijuana at least once (double the figure for a decade ago); and 68 percent of all 18- to 25-year-olds.[50] Another study found alcohol to be used by 95 percent of college students in New England. The majority of men (69 percent) drink weekly or more often, as do half of the women. More than a third of the men said they became drunk at least once a month, and one sixth of the women. One fifth of the men had been in physical fights or trouble with the authorities because of their drinking; and 1 in 10 had lost a friend, had an automobile accident or other alcohol-caused accident in which someone was hurt.[51]

Politics

Most American parents are committed to one of the two major political parties, whereas many of their children have been disillusioned with both the Democrats and the Republicans. Robert Kennedy, Eugene McCarthy, and George McGovern attracted large numbers of young persons, but all of these charismatic figures were either assassinated or overwhelmingly defeated in the political arena. No political parties of the Left or the Right have been able to attract any large numbers of young Americans, which means that many of those of the counterculture are politically alienated. Many of these have psychologically withdrawn from the world of politics—they have become a type of anarchist: You do your thing and I'll do my thing.[52]

The writers have no quarrel about the rights of the younger generation to revolt against social conditions that it regards as inefficient, unjust, or immoral. Our point is that individual parents should not feel that they are personally responsible for these feelings and this behavior in their children: They should not feel guilty, as most of them do. Perhaps the parents who should feel guilty are those whose children did *not* struggle against the war in Vietnam, and who have not spoken out against racism, poverty, environmental degradation, nuclear buildups, and the other ills in American society.

The problem is that parents have been brainwashed into thinking that they are responsible for anything their children do. We read articles in the newspapers and magazines that "College students who use marijuana come from unhappy homes."[53] This is like saying that girls who make out were not loved by their parents.

Parents need to recognize that American society is in the midst of a social revolution—and probably a social revolution that is long overdue. How the revolt will turn out nobody knows—nobody ever knows how a social revolution will turn out. But it is ridiculous for parents to think that they can stop the revolution or to feel inadequate because some of their sons and daughters are on the barricades.

Furthermore, the extent of the social revolution is still vigorously debated today, and the extent to which young people have joined the revolution may not be all that great. Joseph Adelson, a University of Michigan psychology professor who apparently delights in drawing the ire and fire of liberals, argued that the picture of the angry and embattled youth of the 1960s was a "caricature" based upon a "tyranny of the visible." Observers tended to look at the squeakiest wheels, in effect, at those clamoring for attention and change, at those who were the most exotic. Adelson concludes that as a whole, adolescents "are *not* in turmoil, *not* deeply disturbed, *not* at the mercy of their impulses, *not* resistant to parental values, *not* politically active or rebellious."[54]

Again, charting the size and shape and demeanor of the counterculture probably will prove impossible. How many? How angry? How alienated? Who knows? Maybe, who cares?

But, for a lot of parents these issues are major problems in their own individual family lives. For many more parents, these issues could be major problems if they were aware of what their children were up to. (For example, do the parents of the second author's marriage and family relationships class students know that fully a third of the students have had intercourse without the benefit of contraceptive protection?) For all parents, the responsibility for the actions of their children does not necessarily have to rest on their shoulders. Tracing the threads of life back to a culpable person is extremely difficult, and an often highly unuseful exercise.

Dress

The counterculture involves almost a complete revolution in dress, compared with the clothes worn by their parents, with blue jeans and various outfits becoming the symbol of revolt and rejection.

This revolution in dress was accompanied by the hair revolution: long hair and beards for the males and very long hair for the females. Some parents have adjusted to the change in hairstyles, but it has been a serious issue in many families in regard to sons, and stories of males being kicked out of home or disowned because of hair are still not all that uncommon.

Sex

While the so-called authorities are still debating about whether there has been a second (or third) sexual revolution in American society,[55] the openness of sex beginning in the 1960s and continuing into the 1980s, as well as the new pattern of college men and women living together outside of marriage, has shocked hundreds of thousands of parents. The older generation has charged "moral disintegration," which young persons have resented. The counterculture argues, with some logic, that open sex is just as moral as concealed sex. Federal census and health statistics indicated that out-of-wedlock births increased 50 percent in the past 10 years to at least one in every six babies in the United States (47.5 percent of all black and other minority babies were born to unwed mothers, and 8.7 percent of white babies).[56] Clearly, the times are a-changing, and a gulf between parents and children—if it actually exists—would certainly be most apparent in the area of sex. A good part of the problem lies in the fact that most young people cannot really imagine their parents as sexual beings. Comments from the young such as these are common: "I can't even imagine what type of sex life my parents have!" "Let's face it, very few people can actually imagine their parents copulating at all, let alone figure out the small details."[57] And if students can't imagine their parents having sex, they probably can't talk with them about sex very easily. Talk, incidently, could be quite useful today, for sex on campus is evidently commonplace. The second author surveyed 120 college juniors and seniors in his marriage and family relationships class and found that 82 percent of the men and 78 percent of the women had experienced intercourse. Furthermore, the class proved its worldliness to the professor by alleging that 61 percent of the men and 55 percent of the women had engaged in oral sex. It might be added that the state of Nebraska, where this survey took place, is not noted as a land of flaming radicals. What's happening in Berkeley?

Parental strategies for coping with the mass media and the youth peer group

It is the writers' belief that most American parents have not evolved any successful strategies for dealing with the mass media or the youth peer group. Some parents, of course, seem to overcome almost any odds—their children attend colleges rife with drugs and never use anything stronger than aspirin. We do not know whether these fathers and mothers are just lucky or very skillful in handling young people, but suspect a combination of the two. In interviewing such parents we often get the impression that even they do not know the secret of their success.

Mass-media strategies

When children are young, parents often censor the movies they may attend or the television programs they may watch. Some parents even refuse to own a television set. One mother said to the first author: "We didn't buy a TV set for two or three years because we didn't like the programs offered for children. Then we found that the kids were watching television at their friends' house—which meant that we had nothing at all to say about what programs they were seeing. So we finally bought a set and tried to establish some standards as to what shows they could tune in."

Basically, in this strategy parents are trying to isolate a child from what the parents consider an evil or dangerous world. The weakness in this approach is that it does not prepare the child to deal with such matters when he or she finally encounters them—and sooner or later the youngster will be exposed to almost every facet of the society, good or bad.

Murray and Lonnborg offer some suggestions for what parents can do:

1. Limit the time a child spends in front of the tube. Getting rid of the television altogether may not be an option for many families. But restricting a preschooler's hours in front of it to a half an hour or hour a day and no more than two hours for an elementary school child would be helpful.

2. Monitor programs to see which are violent, and either turn off the set when they're on or sit down with the child, all the time explaining that it is just an act, what motivated a person to violence, how else they might have behaved, and what the painful consequences of violence are.

3. Discuss with the child how life on the screen differs so drastically from real life—the life they see in their neighborhood, in their school, in their family. Help them develop critical thinking skills by showing how to distinguish good acting from bad, good and bad dialogue and plot.

4. Talk with the child about advertising. On shopping trips show the child how the toy that looked so fantastic on the television looks in reality. Talk about nutrition and how television peddles expensive sugary foods rather than inexpensive natural fruits and vegetables.

5. Join others, such as the PTA, in collectively trying to influence the television industry. Praise the networks and local stations for good work, and let them know when you are displeased.[58]

Peer-group strategies

There apparently was a time in American history when parents could supervise the peers their children associated with. This no longer seems to be possible. In a marriage course of 450 students, the first author asked how many of the students felt that their dating in high school had been "supervised" by their parents—that the persons they dated had to be approved by their parents. Only one student came up after class and reported that her parents had always exercised a veto power over boys she could go with.

A popular strategy today is to move into a better neighborhood, on the assumption that as the houses (and the mortgages) get bigger, the children (and their parents) get nicer. Almost any parent can recite the limitations of this strategy: The deepest revolt against parents is often in the upper-income suburbs.

Some parents rely on traditional methods—they immerse their children in the church and attempt to internalize the old virtues: honesty, hard work, patriotism, sacrifice, virginity, and so on. This may or may not work. One devout Roman Catholic mother said to the first author: "I took my four kids to mass every Sunday, sent them to parochial schools, had them say their prayers every night—and what good did it do? My daughter is on the pill, my sons never go to church, and I'm the only good Catholic in the family."

Parents try the Boy Scouts, Girl Scouts, YMCA, YWCA, private schools, expensive colleges—all with the hope that their children "will stay out of trouble." One physician known to the first author invested $5,000 sending his son to a private college because the father had read such "terrible things" about students at the state university. Within two semesters, the son was so hooked on drugs at the private college that he had to be withdrawn. The father now wonders where you send a son so that "he won't get involved with drugs." It's a good question.

Summary and conclusion

In this chapter, an attempt was made to look at mass media from the point of view of parents. It seems to the writers that the major conflict between the values of parents and those of the mass media stems from the fact that parents have learned to live cautiously, with one eye (if not both) on the future, whereas the mass media present a world in which the more interesting people live dangerously and largely in the present.

There are both positive and negative effects of mass media on children, and the research on such influences is far from conclusive as yet.

The chapter also discussed the youth peer group, the counterculture, and the impact of these on parents. The basic thesis was that there has been a vast increase in the power of the youth peer group and that relatively few parents have evolved successful strategies for coping with this force.

Chapter 11

Parents and social change

Kingsley Davis, in his classic paper on parent-youth conflict, discusses social change first.[1] He writes:

> The first important variable is the rate of social change. Extremely rapid change in modern civilization, in contrast to most civilizations, tends to increase parent-youth conflict, for within a fast-changing order the time interval between generations, ordinarily but a mere moment in the life of the social system, becomes historically significant, thereby creating a gap between one generation and the next.[2]

We are assuming that Davis was correct in this observation, but we wish to push the analysis further than he does in an attempt to see *how* rapid social change affects parents in our society. Before proceeding, however, it may be helpful to make a few observations about the concept of social change.[3]

The concept of social change

Social change is not synonymous with social progress. In social science analysis, social change is not equated with social progress or social deterioration. It can easily be proven, for example, that the divorce rate in America has increased since 1900, but the evaluation of this change is quite a different proposition. Almost all of the changes discussed in this chapter are of this same nature: They have had both positive and negative impact on American parents.

One spin-off of rapid social change is confusion over values. Toffler argues that:

> Seldom has a single nation evinced greater confusion over its sexual values. Yet the same might be said for other kinds of values as well. America is tortured by uncertainty with respect to money, property, law and order, race, religion, God, family, and self.[4]

But to eliminate such confusion would be to deny the principles of freedom of thought and speech on which this country was founded. And with the quieting of the clash of ideas comes the death of a creative, vital society. There lies the trade off.

The rate of social change is not constant.   Societies and their way of life (their cultures) do not change at a fixed or steady pace. The United States, for example, has probably changed more from 1900 to the present than it did in the previous two or three centuries. In many ways, the rate of change seems to be cumulative—it follows a curve of acceleration. According to Toffler, "It has been observed that the last 50,000 years of man's existence were divided into lifetimes of approximately 62 years each, there have been about 800 such lifetimes. Of these 800, fully 650 were spent in caves." Almost all the material objects we use were developed in the last, the 800th lifetime. Even the printed word has only been common for the last six lifetimes.[5] When the rate of social change accelerates, parents find it more and more difficult to "understand" their children once the young people reach junior high school and the years of early adult status. In reverse fashion, as social change becomes more rapid (and perhaps deeper) children and young adults tend to find their parents "impossible." One college woman said to the first author: "I have to hide my birth-control pills when I go home for Christmas—my mother would have a stroke if she knew I took them."

Social change is not even or symmetrical.   It would be nice and convenient if all the aspects of a culture changed at the same rate of speed, but this is usually not the case. One aspect of the culture often changes rapidly while other parts change slowly. It is quite likely, for example, that American women have been changing more rapidly in the last few decades than American men have. To the extent that this is true, agreement on how to rear children becomes difficult between mothers and fathers.[6]

Social change is not usually planned. In most societies, major social changes are not actually planned; they simply evolve in response to some need or they occur as the result of some crisis in the system. An example would be the American public welfare system, which is currently being subjected to severe criticism. Until the economic disaster of the 1930s, the United States had no modern public welfare system. Voluntary or private social work agencies met family emergencies and did most of the family counseling, with local public welfare agencies meeting the minimal economic needs of the chronically indigent. When this system broke down because of mass unemployment in the 1930s, a new system of local-state-federal public welfare services was hastily improvised. Today it is becoming increasingly clear that this system, designed to help the temporarily unemployed of the 1930s, is not adequate for the 1980s. The clients of today are different and their needs are different.[7] The failure of the welfare system to be properly planned and organized has posed great problems for low-income and minority-group parents, as we have seen in earlier chapters.

The Reagan administration's response to the situation has been to cut the budgets of social programs while giving whopping boosts to the military. The theory being, of course, that a safety net would remain for the truly needy, while alleged cheaters would be culled. Unfortunately, cutting budgets on a computer printout is a lot easier than looking at each individual case by case and making an honest effort to see who really needs help. State and local governments are now faced with this problem, and calls have already gone up for a moratorium on more cuts until the country can adjust to the present ones. The welfare drama continues.

The total results of social change are not often anticipated. In social systems, also families, a change in one part of the system forces change in other parts, for the simple reason that the various aspects of the system are interrelated. Prohibition is often cited by American social scientists as a prime example of the unanticipated results of social change. It was not realized in advance that prohibiting the legal sale of alcoholic beverages would channel hundreds of millions of dollars of revenue into the underworld, thus creating a vast empire of syndicate gangs that still poses problems in urban America.[8]

A good example of unanticipated change in the American family would be the impact of the automobile on parents and children. Not only was the budget of the family drastically altered, but supervision of dating couples became literally impossible. Chaperones at dances, for example, became mere symbols once couples could come and go in automobiles.

Social change is often not desired—it is forced on people. It is very doubtful that millions of American men really want to give women equality. In a very real sense, this change is being forced on men. This means that social changes of this nature always create conflict, and even after the battle is over, pockets of resistance will be found.

Only recently the first author heard a so-called educated person make this remark at a public meeting. "Don't you agree with me," he said to a mixed group of men and women, "that the American family began to decline when the women began to wear the pants?" The women present greeted this remark with cold silence, but a few male heads nodded in agreement.

Parents are often caught by this ambivalence about social change. Some parents may go along with the change, while others try to resist it. One parent may accept the change while the other is still fighting it. Another possibility is that the children will welcome the change while the parents deplore it. The going steady dating system that swept through American high schools after World War II has been popular with young people but not with parents.[9]

Social change is usually not reversible. It is rare indeed when a social system, or a family, reverts to a previous state of organization. The American divorce rate, for example, never returned to the prewar level after World Wars I and II. Some sort of permanent change had taken place in the American marriage system during these national crises.[10]

This same principle does not seem to hold for parent models, however. There is, at least in the United States, a certain cyclical pattern to child rearing. Max Lerner, for example, comments that the extreme permissiveness of American parents that developed during the 1920s and the 1930s seems to have tapered off in the 1950s and 1960s.[11]

These fads or fashions in parent models pose certain problems for fathers and mothers—should they go along with the current fashion or stick to older patterns? What if one parent is contemporary while the other is traditional? American parents have been plagued with dilemmas of this sort in recent decades.

With this background let us now turn to an analysis of a massive social change that American parents are still struggling to cope with—urbanization.

The impact of urbanization on American parents

We do not intend to commit the error so common in sociology textbooks—to present the modern city as the den of iniquity. It is true that all of our crime syndicates are to be found in our large cities, but it is also true that all of our great art museums are found in these same cities. Later in this chapter we will present some of the positive aspects of the city as it affects parents, but at this point we wish to analyze some of the problems American parents found themselves facing once they had left the farm and had settled in the city.

Pluralistic nature of the city.   The city has been the great melting pot in our society. This means that urban fathers and mothers have had to function in close proximity with parents of diverse ethnic, religious, and racial backgrounds. While this is a source of richness and variety in urban life, it is also a potential source of conflict. Sons and daughters form friendships across cultural and racial lines, and parents are not always sure how to react to this. Young people also fall in love across these lines to the consternation of parents.

In such a pluralistic community, children are exposed to all sorts of "competing models"—such as Catholics, Jews, Italians, blacks, middle class, or lower class. Children exposed to such a variety of people may question why their own parents think and behave as they do, and this may threaten the parents.[12]

Of course, urban communities tend to be segregated by social class and by race, but to some extent the pluralistic nature of the metropolitan community has to be faced by all who live there, parents as well as their children.

The increased leisure of urban youth.   One great advantage of the farm parent has always been that the children could be kept busy. The opposite situation faces urban parents: School adjourns at 3:30 and children roam the streets; during vacations or the long summer period, urban children find themselves with time to spare. In the more affluent neighborhoods or suburbs, this problem is easier to cope with, but in the low-income areas solutions are difficult to find. The present school year was never designed for urban parents and it conflicts with the work schedules of both fathers and employed mothers. The urban school should offer at least a half-day program during the summer months, plus some evening and weekend programs.[13]

A more powerful youth peer group.   One of the results of more leisure time and close physical proximity in the city has been the rise to power of the youth peer group.[14] Urban children may spend 30–50 hours a week talking and playing with members of their peer group, and out of this youth society emerge norms of behavior and loyalties that challenge the power and influence of parents. This is a relatively new development of urban America that rural parents did not have to cope with. The second author, for example, had a stunning interview with a young adult who was about to testify in court against one of his peers, an alleged drug dealer. The young man was very, very afraid; his hands shook as he talked. He explained that it was something he had to do because he had gotten off drugs and to prove to himself that he could completely shake the drug habit he was not even going to lie about anything again in his life. His life up to that point had been "one big lie." So when asked to testify he was put in a terrible dilemma. He knew he must not lie if he really wanted to preserve his newfound sense of integrity, but that if he did tell the truth on the witness stand, the close-knit federation of drug dealers in the community would soon know that he was untrustworthy. The young man feared for his life.

The impersonality and anonymity of the city.   Parents in the urban community often do not really know with whom their children are associating. Not only do they not know their children's friends, they also do not know the parents of these other children. Very often all they know about the peer group of their children consists of what the children choose to tell them. This means that in planning their strategy or making decisions concerning the peer group, parents are forced to operate with inadequate or biased data. Any business executive today will tell you that the most modern computer is no better than the information fed into it. The same principle applies to parents.

In an interesting passage in his textbook on the family, Bernard Farber points out that parents are forced to take a risk in almost every decision they make—they never have complete knowledge or understanding of any particular child, nor do they ever have all of the facts affecting the particular problem facing them.[15] While this observation applies to all parents, it seems especially to be a condition faced by fathers and mothers in the modern urban community. One mother said to the first author: "All I know about the boys my daughter dates is what she tells me. How am I supposed to help her choose her boyfriends when I don't know anything about them?" It is a good question.

The pervasive nature of urban mass media. It is true that no American today, except a few hermits and some religious minority groups, can escape the massive attack of the mass media—radio, television, newspapers, magazines, and billboards. To some extent, rural parents have to contend with such forces also, but not to the same extent as urban parents. There is something about the physical crowding of people that heightens the communication process.

In a very real sense, urban parents today operate in an atmosphere of the circus or the carnival. Their children are surrounded by hundreds of pitchmen selling some product or some idea. It is only the very skilled father or mother who can prevail against the highly paid men and women from Hollywood and Madison Avenue.

The urban ghetto. The problems of minority-group parents were analyzed in a separate chapter, but a few words about urban slums and the problems they pose for parents are appropriate here.

As the affluent white families migrate to the suburbs, the central city of the metropolitan community comes to be composed primarily of low-income whites, blacks, Puerto Ricans, Mexican-Americans, and American Indians. This central city is badly financed because the well-to-do taxpayers live out in the suburbs. This means that schools and other public services are not maintained at desirable levels. Housing is almost universally substandard—the *U.S. Riot Commission Report* said that at least 70 percent of the housing occupied by black families does not meet minimum standards.[16]

It is clear that only superior parents could rear children successfully in such an an environment. It is not odd that school dropout

and juvenile delinquency rates are high in such areas—the amazing thing is that such behavior is not universal. The question really
is not: "Why do the children fail?" But, rather, "How do some manage to succeed?"

The positive aspects of urbanization

The city is often portrayed as the center of evil in our society, but
in a very real sense it has been the center of hope—for the millions
of immigrants from Europe who got here too late for the free land;
and more recently for the American black family.

With all of its problems for parents, the urban community actually
offers many advantages: better school systems, with special classes
for the handicapped child; better social welfare services, both private and public; better medical and public health facilities; more
tolerance for racial and religious minorities; and a greater chance
for vertical social mobility.[17]

It can be argued, with considerable logic, that the improverished
rural parent in contemporary America is in an even more difficult
position than the urban ghetto parent. There is no place in the rural
agricultural economy for most of the low-income farm children; their
parents lack the knowledge and experience to help these children
make a successful move to the city; and, finally, the rural community lacks the network of health, welfare, and educational services
available to low-income urban parents.[18]

It is an interesting fact that the minority group that has achieved
the highest socioeconomic position in the United States—the Jews—
is almost entirely metropolitan in residence. And contrary to what
millions of Americans think, the majority of these Jewish families
entered the socioeconomic system at the bottom. It was their utiliza-
tion of urban services, such as the urban university, that enabled
them to attain a comfortable position in our society.[19]

We have been analyzing the impact of urbanization on parents.
Because of the massive move to the city since World War I, farm
parents now constitute less than 10 percent of all parents in the
United States. In a sense they have become a minority group—not
only in a statistical sense but also sociologically.

The special problems of rural parents in
modern America

It could well be true that rural parents in our society are in a more
difficult position than urban parents. In some ways the rural revolu-

tion in the United States in recent decades has been deeper and more widespread than changes taking place in the city. The mechanization of the farm has greatly reduced the demand for farm laborers, and the increased productivity per farm worker has meant that in each of the recent decades the percentage of the American population engaged in agriculture has declined. In 1930, almost 25 percent of the total population lived on the farm. By 1940 this figure had dropped to 23 percent. In 1950, 15 percent; 1960, 9 percent; 1970, 5 percent. Latest figures indicate that by 1979 the farm population has fallen to 2.8 percent.[20] An astounding decline. In human terms, for example, this means that in the area where the second author's father grew up around Alexandria, Nebraska, there were 17 farms in 1930. Fifty years later only 6 farms remain.[21]

All of this means that a majority of our farm youth today will be forced to resettle in the urban world.

Historically, the farm family in the United States has been romanticized. The image most of us have is that of the prosperous middle-class farm owner—the one usually portrayed on the cover of mass magazines at Thanksgiving. Americans do not like to think about the lower-class farm families—the farm tenants, the sharecroppers, the farm laborers, or the migratory farm workers. These families, on the average, are probably worse off than most low-income urban families.[22]

In the next few pages we wish to focus on some of the special problems faced by farm parents.

The urbanization impact. Because of mass media, the automobile, the consolidated school, and general population mobility, farm children are increasingly being subjected to urban values and the urban way of life. This means that a considerable amount of social distance is being created between farm parents and their children. To the extent that the parents are attempting to internalize rural values and a rural way of life in their children, the parents are struggling against the stream—the whole drift of the society is in the other direction.

Farm parents are preparing their children for an urban-industrial world. Farm parents today face many of the problems American immigrant parents used to face; they have to prepare their children for a world they do not understand themselves. On the farm, historically, a man who was willing to do hard physical labor could get by. Formal education was not very essential. The ability to handle animals was more crucial than the ability to handle people.

These conditions do not prevail in urban America, and to a considerable extent they no longer prevail in rural America either. Trade unions, sex equality, racial integration—ideas that have never been too popular in rural America are dominant today in urban America. Farm children will have to understand and adjust to this world of the city, but their parents may not be too much help in the process.

The rural economy. There is simply no place for most of the farm children in the farm economy of tomorrow. Only the well-educated, well-financed farm youth can hope to survive in the agricultural world of tomorrow. Farms of today are larger, more expensive, more mechanized, and more scientifically managed than ever before. The poor farmer has no place in such a world unless he plans to earn his living in a nearby city and run a small farm as a sort of hobby or moonlight operation.

The rural social class barrier. Because of the farm revolution, the farm boy or farm girl from a low-income family has little chance for vertical social mobility. Migration to the city offers the best hope for most of these children. The better informed farm parents know this. The children of the others will have to find it out the hard way—by experience.

A farm father said to the first author: "I have operated this dairy farm for over 30 years with only two weeks vacation in all that time. I have made a good living and want to turn the farm over to my son. He says he wants no part of it—too much work. I can't understand what's happening to kids today." This man sold his farm and retired.

Parental defense mechanisms against social change

How do successful parents—those who seem to have relatively few problems in rearing their children—cope with rapid social change? In the opinion of the writers, there are at least four basic strategies utilized by these parents.

Early parenthood. Women today are having most of their children by the time they are 30 years old. Many of them can be heard to say: "I want to have them while I am still young enough to enjoy them." Though it is correct that many women defer parenthood until later in life, as the media has pointed out recently, the majority still opt for early parenthood.

There are, of course, many potential disadvantages in assuming the parental role at an early age, but one of the advantages is that it does reduce the social distance between parent and child.

The buddy system of parenthood. In a sense these parents adopt the attitude that "if you can't lick 'em, join 'em." They virtually become teenagers themselves and seek to bridge the generation gap in this way.

To some extent such parents resemble the social workers assigned to work with street gangs in our larger cities—they mingle with the young people and try to influence the group from within. One college girl described a mother of this type in this way: "My mother is a real pal. You can do almost anything with her—she fits right into the group."

Some parents seem to achieve a certain amount of success with this buddy approach, but others simply make themselves look and feel ridiculous.

Do not try to understand the younger generation—it is hopeless. One mother told the first author: "I don't even try to understand my children's generation anymore. My only concern is that they understand me."

These parents take the position that basic values do not change in our society and they hammer away at these in rearing their children. "Honesty and decency and cleanliness don't change," one father said to the first author. "As long as you stick to things like that you can't go wrong. And you'll never be out of date."

Essentially, these parents hold themselves aloof from the current fashions in child rearing and stick to the "eternal verities." They remind one of a woman who refuses to raise or drop her hemline just because Paris says to wear the skirts short or long. One woman said to us: "What do I care about what Paris says? My knees are big and bumpy and I don't intend to show them if I can help it." Some parents adopt this approach in their roles as fathers and mothers.

The radar system of child rearing. David Riesman argues that most American parents hedge against social change by using the "radar system" of child rearing.[23] Not being sure of what is right or wrong, these parents train their children to "fit in," to "be adjusted." They equip their children with a built-in radar antenna that provides them with a constant flow of signals as to what is happening in their significant reference groups, and all these children need to do to be adjusted is to alter their values and their behavior to fit the current fashion. Almost all of us do this in choosing our clothes, but Riesman says that "fashions" now include values and norms as well as hemlines or shoe styles.

William Whyte develops a similar argument in analyzing the "social ethic" of the middle-class suburbanites reported on in his best seller, *The Organization Man.*[24]

Riesman believes that parents in an earlier America really did not care what other parents were teaching their children.[25] These pioneer fathers and mothers, says Riesman, knew what was right and they internalized these values and norms in their sons and daughters. In any new or difficult situation, then, all these children had to do was to look *inward* to find the solution to their dilemma.

This system of child rearing may work well in a deeply religious society in which parents can operate with "revealed truths" that are assumed to be "eternal." But in a society in which the revealed truths come from the secular priests, who seem to change their truths almost every decade, how can parents find any absolutely certain values or norms to internalize? The answer seems to be that they cannot.

Faced with this neat little problem the smart parent falls back on an even more eternal principle—the law of the jungle, which is to *survive.* "Don't be a sucker, or a martyr," the child is told. "Go along with the group and you can't get too far out of line." In a sense this represents the wisdom of the old sergeant (or the old chief petty officer) when he tells the raw recruit: "Keep your nose clean and you won't get into any trouble."

Riesman has an interesting comment on the inner-directed method of child rearing. "Homing pigeons," he writes, "can be taught to fly home, but the inner-directed child must be taught to fly a straight course *away* from home, with destination unknown; naturally many meet the fate of Icarus."[26]

It was said earlier that some parents try to solve the problem of social change by teaching their children what the parents consider to be permanent values such as honesty, decency, and integrity. But do these words mean today what they meant yesterday? Is a girl today a "nice" girl if she has an abortion? If she begins taking oral contraceptives while she is still single? If she lives with her boyfriend?

Is a young man today a "nice" boy if he experiments with marijuana, alcohol and other drugs? If he has numerous sexual affairs while single? If he lives with his girlfriend?

It is difficult to see whether fathers and mothers in contemporary America would find any eternal truths to teach their children. In a Protestant church known to the first author, a careful survey of the membership conducted on an anonymous basis by an outside research organization found that about 60 percent of the members were "not sure they believed in God."[27] This seems strange since to join this church new members have to stand up in front of the congregation and take an oath that they *do* believe in God.

What should contemporary parents teach their children about lifetime monogamy versus serial monogamy and divorce? By the mid–1970s, the president of the United States was married to a divorced woman; the vice president of the United States was a divorced man married to a divorced woman; the most famous Roman Catholic family in our society, the Kennedy family, had a divorced daughter; the Henry Ford family, long a symbol of virtue in America, had several divorces on its record; many of the culture heroes (such as Johnny Carson) were divorced people. By 1983 it looked like the Kennedys would add another divorce to its list, and the president himself was a divorced man.

Are parents to teach their children that divorce is "bad"? What should a Roman Catholic mother teach her daughter about modern means of birth control? The church disapproves of these methods of preventing conception, but surveys show that the new generation of Catholics does not support the church on this issue.[28]

Parents who cannot cope with social change

Although the point is difficult to document, it seems likely that parents who cannot cope with social change must face insuperable barriers in rearing children in contemporary America.

Riesman makes the point that some parents may be preparing their children for a world that no longer exists. He writes: "Parents who try in inner-directed fashion, to compel the internalization of disciplined pursuit of clear goals, run the risk of having their children styled clear out of the personality market. Inhibited from presenting their children with sharply silhouetted images of self and society, parents in our era can only equip the child to do his best, whatever that may turn out to be."[29]

A college woman student said to the first author: "My parents asked me not to drink when I came to college. I have tried to follow their advice but it is very difficult—a typical date on this campus is to go to some tavern and drink beer. Some of the guys are offended if you refuse to drink." This girl wants to be popular, but she finds it difficult to achieve this goal and follow the teaching of her parents.

Another woman student wrote in a term paper: "My parents are against premarital sex—but it seems to be popular on this campus. You have to learn how to turn down a guy when he makes a pass without being nasty. It is a very delicate art."

It is true, of course, that parents may teach their children almost any set of values they wish to, but if they deviate too much from the current model, they run two types of risk: They may damage their relationship with their child; or their child may be isolated from his or her peer group and be considered odd or peculiar. This is not always undesirable, but it does pose special problems for adolescents with their great fear of nonconformity.

Some parents seem to have difficulty coping with social change because one parent is more contemporary than the other. Not all married couples change at the same rate, so that a traditional father may find himself paired with a more contemporary mother—and this can pose problems in a role such as parenthood that demands teamwork. Actually one of the complexities of the parent role is that we usually have to work at it *in pairs*. This is not easy when we have differential social change between parents.

Some studies indicate that mothers in our society may be more contemporary than fathers.[30] If this is true, then a built-in strain between American parents would be expected. The writers do not believe that the current research is adequate to conclude that this is the case.[31]

Of course, if the American father is as "shadowy" in our family system as some observers seem to think, then whether he is modern or traditional would not make much difference. As we stated in an earlier chapter, however, we doubt very much that fathers in our society have ceased to affect the rearing of their children. Especially since the latest wave of feminism, fathers seem very much alive and well.

Parents and resocialization

In a society dedicated to rapid social change and progress, as the United States is, the dilemma of parents is clear: They themselves grew up in the world of yesterday, a world that is now largely dead, even if not buried, and this is the world they internalized; they rear their children in the world of today, a world they only partially understand and only partly accept; but they are rearing their children for the world of tomorrow, a world that nobody understands as yet. These conditions are some of the reasons why even intelligent and capable parents often feel confused and bewildered in contemporary America.

In his paper on parent-youth conflict, Davis refers to the phenomenon of *decelerating socialization*.[32] By this he means that parents have already passed the peak of their learning curve by the time they become parents. Thus their efforts to keep up with the world of their children are handicapped by their relatively slow rate of learning in their 20s and 30s. At the same time their children are at the peak of their learning curve.

The situation is even more complex than Davis described it, because the learning of adults (parents) actually involves *resocialization*—that is, they have to unlearn what they absorbed earlier in order to take in the new knowledge.[33]

In a famous paper the anthropologist Ruth Benedict analyzed this process of resocialization.[34] She used the term *discontinuity* to describe what happens. A girl learns that sex is bad and something to avoid, yet later as a wife she is supposed to think that sex is good and something to be enjoyed. How does she ever make the transition from stage 1 to stage 2?

Parents face this type of situation almost daily.[35] Something they were taught as children that would "never change" is suddenly out of style—for example, that college students do not get married until they have completed their undergraduate degree. Another good illustration would be the old saying that "Violence never solves anything." Some black parents are finding this old truism harder and harder to sell to their children.

Parents and future shock

In a book that was on the best-seller lists for over a year, Toffler argued that millions of Americans suffer from what he called "future shock."[36] By this, Toffler means that many of us are so appalled by the signs of the future that we find ourselves depressed and unable to make sense of our world. A striking example would be the prediction that 180 million persons would be killed if a nuclear war broke out between the Soviet Union and the United States.

The writers believe that a great many American parents suffer from future shock in trying to comprehend the behavior of some of their children. The following case studies, based on actual incidents related to the first author by parents or children, will illustrate the point.

Cohabitation at the college level

An upper-middle-class couple received a telephone call from the private college their daughter was attending that the girl had not used her dormitory room or the college dining hall for two weeks. The dean of women's office inquired as to whether the daughter might have returned home. The parents replied that to the best of their knowledge the girl was still on campus. Further investigation revealed that the daughter had been attending classes but had moved off campus into an apartment with three male students, one of whom was her "boyfriend."

What are parents supposed to think when they find their daughter living with three men? Her story was that she was having an affair with one of the male students but had had no sexual contact with the other two male residents of the apartment. The parents were prepared for the fact that their daughter might be having an affair in college—this was not unheard of in their generation—but for her to move into an apartment with three men was beyond their comprehension.

When the shock had subsided, the parents withdrew their daughter from college and persuaded her to come home until the next fall. She then returned to the same college and eventually graduated. She is now married but not to the student she was having an affair with. Her relationship with her parents has returned to what could be called "normal."

In addition to the shock of this event, the parents in this situation suffered a substantial financial loss in that the college refused to refund any room or board payment.

Honor students and hard drugs

A son who had graduated at the top of his suburban high school class and had won national recognition in college-placement tests was discovered to be experimenting with various drugs—marijuana, "speed," LSD, and cocaine. The parents had become conditioned to the fact that marijuana is relatively common on university campuses, but it had never occurred to them that their son would experiment with LSD and cocaine, which they understood to be quite dangerous. Their son told them that other honor students from the same high school had been taking these drugs with him. All of the students in the group were from so-called nice families of the upper-middle class.

When their shock had subsided, these parents persuaded their son to see a university drug counselor, who convinced the son that LSD and cocaine were nothing to fool around with. The parents now feel that the crisis has passed and that the son and his friends are over the hard-drug phase of their lives. No permanent break has occurred between the son and his parents.

A nice Catholic girl

Parents with an Italian background, both devout Roman Catholics, learned that their daughter at the state university had been living with her boyfriend when they had understood that she was sharing an apartment with a girlfriend. They also found out that their daughter had had an abortion.

This situation produced what seems to be a permanent break between the daughter and her parents. The father and mother terminated the daughter's allowance and refused to help her complete her degree, even though she was an honor student. The girl is now working and attending the university on a part-time basis.

In this case the social distance between the parents and the daughter was too great for compromise: The parents could not accept the daughter's social world and she could not accept theirs.

An interracial love affair

An undergraduate white woman student told the first author that she has been dating a black student for over a year. Her parents live in the South and she has not had the courage to tell them of this campus experience. The girl now thinks she is in love with this black student and she is frightened about the future. "I think my father will have a stroke or heart attack if I tell him or if he finds out. I don't know what to do." This relationship apparently began as a mild campus experience and then became serious. The woman student is positive that her parents would never forgive her if she continues the affair or considers marriage with this person. The feelings of the black student and his family were not clear.

A gay and a lesbian

A male student told the first author that he had written to his parents announcing that he had concluded that he was homosexual and was living with his lover off campus. He immediately received a phone call in which his mother offered to pay the bill if he would go to a psychiatrist and get himself cured. The student said he didn't want to be cured. He liked his homosexual lifestyle.

Another student told the first author that she went home and told her parents she had become a lesbian. The mother began to cry, and the father became furious. He told the daughter never to come home again, that she was not considered a member of the family anymore. Living in the liberal atmosphere of the university community, this girl had thought that homosexual men and women were beginning to be accepted. She could not have been more wrong in terms of how her parents felt.[37]

An abortion

One female student told the first author that she had gone home to tell her parents that she was having an abortion. "My father called me a 'slut' and a 'whore' and told me to get out and not come back again." This girl was traumatized by the experience. She felt that abortions had been declared legal by the U.S. Supreme Court in 1973, and that her parents would accept the high court's decision. It turned out that her father's attitude on abortion had not changed at all, court or no court. Abortion to him was murder. Pure and simple. A decade after the court's decision, our society remains terribly divided over the issue.

Discussion of the generation gap

In an interesting book Lewis Feuer argued that every society experiences a generation gap to some extent but that in every society there are historical periods in which the gap is accentuated.[38] Feuer cited the Russian period from about 1880 to 1920 as an example of a time when parents and children in that society tended to be alienated from each other. In many ways the 1960s was such a period in the United States. Edwin Newman said that adults in general were distrusted by young people in the 1960s because it was the older generation which got us into the Vietnam war.

> Because people of age and experience and position led us into Vietnam, they made age and experience and position look ridiculous. This conferred a kind of blessing on youth and inexperience and not being in the establishment.[39]

When crises arise with older children, parents have to decide whether they are prepared to face a permanent break with their son or daughter. In some situations known to the writers, parents have taken a position from which they eventually have had to back down. This is illustrated in the following situation. A Jewish undergraduate woman came to the state university without any sexual experience. In her freshman year she lived in a dormitory and began having an affair with a "nice Jewish boy." Every weekend they would spend together either in his room or her room. They thought they were in love but did not know how deep or how permanent the relationship might be.

In her sophomore year, this girl decided that she wanted to share an apartment with her boyfriend and he felt the same way. "I didn't like the sneaky relationship we had had in the dorms," she said. They found an apartment they could afford and moved in.

Being an extremely honest person, this girl wrote to her parents and told them where and how she was living. She assured them that this boy was the only man she had ever slept with and that they might eventually be married—as yet she was not sure.

Her parents were shocked. They could not understand how a nice Jewish girl could do such a thing. They also refused to help her continue at the university.

This girl, an honor student in high school and college, was prepared for her parents' reaction. She obtained a job and continued her education with a reduced load. She had no intention of moving out of the apartment.

When the winter recess came, the parents wrote and asked the daughter if she would bring her boyfriend home so that the parents could meet him. One stipulation was the couple were not to sleep together during the visit.

The girl and the young man agreed to the arrangement. The parents were so impressed with the boyfriend and the apparent happiness of their daughter that they offered to help her complete her education. She accepted the offer.

This story ends with the girl's mother insisting on a big wedding when the couple decided to get married in their junior year. Both of the young people went on to graduate school and so far the marriage appears to be successful. The relationship with the parents (on both sides) is excellent.

This girl said: "I am not a sex radical. I do not believe in bed hopping but I also don't believe in hypocrisy. Furthermore, I have seen a lot of poor marriages and I wanted to avoid that if possible."

Actually, this girl was a mixture of traditional and modern: She believed in monogamy and sexual fidelity but she also believed in the right of young persons to test their compatibility for marriage. Persons who regard this girl as a radical should be aware that a survey of junior and senior women at Cornell University concluded that 34 percent of the girls had tried living with a male student while in college and that 80 percent of these reported the relationship to have been a "positive experience."[40]

In an interesting discussion of black and white college students who have been deeply involved in the civil rights struggle in the South, Robert Coles argues that some of the old terms, such as *normal* or *mature* or *radical*, are no longer helpful in understanding today's generation.[41] Coles cites a young black man who was fully aware that he might lose his life in the racial struggle but had come to the conclusion that he was willing to pay this price if necessary to change the racial situation in America. Coles' point is that this young man is not *immature*—he is *determined*.

In the case of the Jewish girl discussed earlier, two further points need to be made: (1) In a book called *The Vanishing Adolescent*, Edgar Friedenberg points out that young people are doing things in high school and college that their parents did not do until they were much older.[42] If the girl in this situation had begun living with a man in graduate school, the parents might not have been so shocked.

But undergraduates are now doing what graduate students did in earlier decades. (2) The current generation is much more open about its sexual behavior. Parents have taught their children to be honest and are often not prepared for the consequences.

It's always nice to know you're not alone. That's the principle almost every group therapy experience or parent education program operates on, and many middle-class parents reading this book may be interested to also take a look at The Rockefellers: An American Dynasty. In that book, Peter Collier and David Horowitz revealed that a tremendous generation gap exists in this family of the super-rich. The newer generation of Rockefellers harbors a number of radicals, while their parents remain staunchly arch-conservative.[43]

It is a serious error to believe that better communication will resolve the problems created by the generation gap. It is certainly true that improved communication at the verbal level will clarify intergenerational conflicts, but this does not necessarily resolve them. In fact, in some situations more complete communication will reveal that parents and their children are even farther apart than they had thought.

But there is some evidence that the gap closes as time passes and children's hair greys like their parents. Kent Jennings and Richard Niemi, political science professors, interviewed 1,669 high-school seniors and their parents during the student movement days of the mid-60s. Eight years later the professors went back and reinterviewed most of their cross section of American youth and parents, asking the same questions. The professors learned that in most respects there had been a coming together of opinions, reading and viewing habits, and political opinions. "The flow of the two generations over time has . . . worked to bring them closer together now than they were eight years previously," they said. "To the extent that differences increased, they took form in the rising generation's having emerged with slightly to moderately more liberal political views, greater independence of partisanship and higher Democratic voting behavior." The researchers thought this was genuinely amazing, considering that the parents and the children grew up in such totally different worlds: The older generation was formed in the Depression and World War II years; the younger in the age of affluence and an all-pervasive media beaming visual truths about world events in every home in a way that had never happened before in history.[44] In short, there is some hope for parents that their children will not reject their values totally for long; hope that many of the verities of one generation will be passed on, eventually, to another. But, not complete hope, by any means. The world rarely goes backward, for better or worse.

In his discussion of the American family of the future, Toffler makes this statement: "We have it in our power to shape change. We may choose one future over another. We cannot, however, maintain the past. In our family forms, as in our economic, science, technology and social relationships, we shall be forced to deal with the new."[45] The writers agree.

Summary and conclusion

In this chapter the nature of social change was analyzed and the point was made that rapid social change increases the social distance between parents and their children. It was also argued that fathers and mothers are not always equally contemporary in their view of the social scene.

The concept of *future shock* was borrowed from Toffler to help understand some of the more disturbing aspects of social change in America.

It should be made clear that the writers concede the right of the new generation to remake the world—we are only looking at the stress between parents and their children as the new behavior and the new values have their impact on families.

Chapter 12

Counseling with parents

In his book, *Games People Play*, Eric Berne makes the following statement: "Raising children is primarily a matter of teaching them what games to play."[1]

In this chapter on counseling with parents, we are adopting a stance somewhat similar to that of Berne. Counseling with parents is primarily a matter of helping them see explicitly what parental model they have been using; examining that model with the parents to see how well it fits them and their children; suggesting alternate models that might work better for them; and, finally, teaching parents how to implement the model decided on. The rest of this chapter will attempt to explain how this counseling system works.

The attitude of the counselor

Before proceeding to parental models and their implementation, a few words need to be said about attitudes that social workers, marriage and family therapists, teachers, ministers, judges, psychologists, and psychiatrists tend to have toward parents.

Parents are often assumed to be inadequate parents before they get a fair hearing—the child has been doing something wrong, therefore the parents must be doing something wrong. This may turn out to be true, but the counselor should not assume that parents are the only factors involved in the behavior of children.

Counselors who have never been parents tend to underestimate the complexity of parenthood in our society.

Middle-class counselors may have a bias against or lack of understanding of parents from the blue-collar world. Herbert Gans found this to be true in a study of working-class families in Boston and the first author came to the same conclusion in a study of parents in a blue-collar tavern.[2]

Counselors need to be careful that they do not become "child worshippers"—people who will do almost anything to parents behind the defense of helping the child. Parents are people too and they have as much right to consideration as children have.

Parent models

Whether they realize it or not, all parents adopt one parent model or another. In the rest of this chapter, we wish to examine some of these models to see what their essential characteristics are and to discuss how parent counselors can use the models in working with parents.

The martyr model

Many parents, without realizing it, adopt the martyr model. "Nothing is too good for my children," they will say, or "I would do *anything* for my child." The following characteristics are usually found in this model.

Parental guilt. For some reason these parents usually exhibit guilt, and the counselor needs to explore this with them.

Overprotection. Guilt is often accompanied by overprotection. The parent is afraid that something will happen to the child and attempts to set up a "super safe" world for the child. This, of course, almost invariably produces problems for all parties concerned—parents as well as children.

It is our impression that divorced parents, or those whose marriage has failed even though it is still intact, are especially subject to the guilt-overprotection syndrome. Parents with handicapped children will often exhibit this pattern also.

It hardly needs to be said that these martyr parents spoil their children. They cannot set realistic goals for their children, or if they do, the goals are not adhered to.

Revolt or meek submission by the child. A healthy reaction by children living under this parental model is that of revolt—they almost instinctively reach out for a normal life, and this inevitably brings them into conflict with the parent or parents. At this point the martyred parent assumes the posture: "Look what you are doing to me—and after all I have done for you." Berne analyzes this game as it is enacted between marital partners.[3]

A child that does *not* revolt against the martyr model is a troubled child—he will be crippled for life if he does not revolt. This might not be true in some societies, but it is certainly true in the open-class, competitive, impersonal society American children will graduate into.

The famous Irish writer, Sean O'Faolain, has this to say about the martyr model: "Like all women who become slaves to their children, my mother not only exhausted her own emotions but ultimately killed the emotions of everybody around her."[4]

Hostility and resentment by the child toward the parent. In the event of revolt this will be open and obvious. In cases of submission it will be covert and repressed. Martyr parents can never understand this reaction by their children: "Look at that attitude after all I have done for them."

It is the writers' belief that the martyr model is perhaps the most destructive one found in American parents. In some ways it is even more destructive than the model of parent neglect—the neglected child is at least free and has a chance of finding a substitute parent.

On an ethical level, it is simply not right that a parent should serve as a martyr for a child. It denies the parents the right to a life of their own as adults; furthermore, it places the child in the inevitable role of the ungrateful offspring.

Some of the most difficult counseling situations in working with martyr parents are found when one parent adheres to the martyr model while the other one rejects it. This can be described as a split model situation. When this is found the counselor has to be careful not to be seduced by the martyred parent, and to see the split as an asset—it means that conflict is present and out of this conflict change can be generated.

The best strategy in dealing with martyr parents is to be honest and direct. Unless they can be made to see what they are doing to themselves as well as to their children the prognosis is not good. These parents have thick defenses, and the counselor will often need to be provocative and/or assertive to get any movement.

The buddy or pal model

A certain number of parents in contemporary America seem to have adopted the buddy or pal model—they apparently feel that this is a solution to the gap between the generations.

Some students of the family have been rather caustic in their comments on this model. Robert Bell, for example, has this to say:

> The middle-class belief that a parent should be a "pal" to his children reflects a social value which gives importance to a common world for parents and children. The belief in a common world has developed around notions of democracy between parents and children and implies they are equals socially, psychologically, and intellectually. If this is true, it is a devastating picture of the parents because it implies that they are still teenagers.[5]

Bell goes on to point out that the pal approach to parenthood is not the only area in which the lines between generations have been blurred in our society.

In a sense the parents who adopt the buddy or pal models are following the old saying, "If you can't beat 'em, join 'em." They are trying to infiltrate the youth peer group and work from within. In some ways they resemble the social workers assigned to work with juvenile gangs on the streets of our large cities.[6] These social workers have no authority; they simply attempt to influence the gang leadership. This is not only a difficult role but also a dangerous one—and the writers have a hunch it is no easier for parents.

It is possible that the pal or buddy model received its impetus from the rush of early marriages that followed the end of World War II. The first author interviewed a mother of 20 a few years ago who was taking care of her two preschool children. She just laughed when we asked her if she felt mature enough to be rearing a family.

"Nobody is grown up in this house," she said. "My husband is 20 also, and he certainly isn't very grown up." After a pause she looked at her children and said: "*I guess we're all growing up together.*"

It struck us that her generation—at least some of them—do not accept the traditional idea that you have to be grown up to get married. On the contrary, all you need is somebody who wants to grow up with you. The writers do not know how many young parents in America subscribe to this point of view, but for those that do the pal model may be functional. They would only be kidding themselves if they pretended to be mature adults rearing a family.

Another impetus for the pal or buddy model may have come from the rejection of middle age or old age in our society. Americans do not revere older people or assume that they have any great store of wisdom to offer young people. If anything, we tend to pity older people—and by older the society means anybody over 40. Thus, by the time American parents are dealing with adolescents, they are near or over the dividing line between youth and old age. Many of them are tempted to conclude that they might as well pretend to be a pal or buddy because there is nothing to gain by acting your age. Millions of women in our society use this strategy with some success, and some parents apparently use it also.

The writers happen to believe that the pal or buddy model of parenthood is difficult and risky. Its major problems follow.

It is extremely unrealistic. Our society holds that parents are responsible for the rearing and guidance of their minor children. Parents can be imprisoned for neglect or mistreatment of their children. They can also have their parental rights terminated under certain circumstances.

In view of the generation gap in our society, it seems unlikely that any children are going to be fooled by the pal model of parenthood.[7] They know who the enemy is—and their motto seems to be: "Never trust anybody over 30."

As we pointed out earlier, the pal or buddy model may be realistic for some teenage parents who are still children themselves, but the model hardly fits the vast majority of American parents.

The roles called for in the model are quite complex. Few of us can cross generation lines effectively and convincingly enough to make this model work. One has to penetrate or infiltrate the youth peer group, understand its subculture, and be accepted by the group. Pal parents cannot fall back on parental authority when the going gets tough—they have to sustain the pal role consistently if the model is to work. Very few parents can achieve this level of role performance.

The pal model requires superior parents to make it work. In World War II, the first author had an opportunity to study at close range two types of officers in the U.S. Naval Air Corps.[8] The traditional officer maintained considerable social distance between himself and his enlisted men—a model that the Navy had found to be effective over the years. This traditional model was well defined and made no great demands on the imagination or creativity of the officer. All he had to do was to follow the rules and not much could happen to him. In the bomber air groups, however, with their long missions and close physical proximity, some officers abandoned the traditional model and adopted a pal or buddy model—their enlisted men did not have to salute officers, first names were used, regulation clothing was not insisted on, and so forth.

It was the first author's impression, based on three years of participant-observation, that only the *superior* officers could adopt the buddy model and get away with it. If the officer was average or below average in ability, the flight crew soon deteriorated and order had to be restored by some subordinate, such as a chief petty officer, if the crew was to function properly.

It is our belief that the same conditions hold for parents. Only the superior parent can play the buddy game with his or her children without losing their respect and their obedience.

The pal or buddy model involves considerable risk. This was quite clear in the Naval Air Corps in the opinion of the first author. Several tragic plane and crew losses might have been avoided in the first author's air group if crews had been held under more strict discipline.

We have the impression that the pal model is equally risky for parents. If things do not go well, they have to retreat to a more formal, authoritarian parent model—and this retreat or shift in role is extremely difficult to manage without damaging the parent's image in the eyes of his or her children.

A professor known to us had been using the buddy model with a graduate seminar. Among other things, he told members of the class that they did not have to come to class if they did not want to. One day this professor went to class and found only one student out of 15 present. He was furious and immediately posted a notice that attendance would be compulsory in the future. The class reacted with resentment, and the semester was completed in the atmosphere of an armed truce.

One of the advantages of the traditional authoritarian parent model is that it allows the father or mother to relax the rules occasionally without damaging the relationship with the children—in fact, the relationship should be enhanced. This is not the case when the pal model has been adopted.

In their study of marriage, George Bach and Peter Wyden make the following statement about parents and children: "It goes almost without saying that true intimacy can exist only between peers who wield more or less equal power, never between parent and child."[9] The writers think there is much to be said for this position.

The police officer or drill-sergeant model of parenthood

Some parents seem to conceptualize their role as that of the police officer or drill sergeant. They are alert to punish the child for the most minor offense, making sure that s/he obeys the rules at all times. These parents seem to believe that this system of parenthood will keep their children from getting into trouble. In some ways, this police-officer model is a foolproof defense system for the parents: If the child does get into difficulty the parents can always say, "We told him or her not to do it."

In our opinion, this model will not work for most parents in the United States for the following reasons:

Americans tend to be "cop haters." Almost any book on police in the United States, or even casual reading of the daily newspaper, will reveal how unenviable the position of the police officer is in our society.[10] Except on television shows, the police are the bad guys. In a recent incident in the Midwest, a group of citizens stood by while a patrolman was beaten up by several men who had been creating a disturbance. Not one citizen offered to help the officer.[11]

From the earliest colonial days, Americans have been allergic to authority, and the allergy seems to be increasing, not decreasing.

The adolescent peer group is too powerful. Parents may get away with the police officer model while their children are quite young, but eventually the parents will be confronted by the adolescent peer group—and as we have seen in earlier chapters, this is a formidable opponent in contemporary America.

In some ways the police officer and drill sergeant have an advantage over parents: The legal structure is usually on their side. Parents are not always sure of a friendly reception in court—many judges, social workers, and psychologists will identify with the helpless child. As Max Lerner says, there are no "bad children in our society—only bad parents."[12] In this sort of atmosphere it is difficult, if not impossible, for the extremely strict or harsh parent to win in our society.

A great deal of love is needed to make the police-officer model work. If the parent can achieve the image of the "benevolent despot," strict or even harsh discipline will be tolerated by many children. But warmth and love have to be so obvious and plentiful that the child can never doubt that the parent has the child's best interests at heart.

It is our impression that many parents who adopt the police-officer or drill-sergeant model simply do not have enough love for the child to make the severe discipline tolerable. Or if they do have the love, it does not get communicated to the child.

Parenthetically, it can be said that much of the open hostility of the poor and minority groups in our society toward the police stems from the fact that these people are convinced that the police do not have their best interests at heart—they view the police as their enemy, not their friend.[13] It appears that many American parents who adopt the police-officer model are viewed in a similar way by their children.

The pluralistic nature of our society, discussed in earlier chapters, also poses problems for parents using the police-officer model—the norms are not that clear or that specific; there are often divergent or competing norms of behavior, and the child may challenge the right of the parent to select a particular norm to be enforced. Here, again, the police officer and drill sergeant have an advantage over parents—the laws governing communities and the regulations in the armed forces are more specific than those with which parents operate.

This model is not functional in our society. If the United States is actually an open-class, competitive society, then a premium would be placed on parental models that emphasize such qualities as initiative, aggression, and competitiveness—qualities that appear to be minimized in the police-officer or drill-sergeant model. It needs to be remembered that the police and the armed forces are primarily concerned with maintaining order and discipline, hence the model is functional for those systems. But, to the extent that America is still an open-class, competitive society, the model is dysfunctional for parents; it would not meet the basic needs of either the society or the child.

It is possible, however, to view the situation in an entirely different light—that America has become primarily a socioeconomic system of large bureaucratic organizations, both public and private, and that these systems maximize obedience, discipline, reliability,

and conformity, qualities that appear to be attainable with the police-officer or drill-sergeant model.

Daniel Miller and Guy Swanson found that the middle- and
lower-class parents in their sample appear to be preparing their
children to "fit into" large bureaucratic organizations.[14] When one
remembers that the most expansive sector of the U.S. economy in
recent decades has been that of public employment, these parents
may be preparing their children very realistically for the America of
today and tomorrow.

In reading David Riesman and Lillian Whyte, one gets the same
message—American parents are preparing their children to live
and work harmoniously in a tightly organized mass society.[15] Whyte
does not like what she sees—nor does Riesman—but the picture
they report is quite clear: American society today has more room for
the conformist than it has for the innovator.

Melvin Kohn argued that one's social class influences one's behavior to a great degree. A higher-class position brings with it the
expectation that one's decisions and actions have consequence; a
lower-class position brings with it the assumption that one is at the
mercy of people and forces beyond one's control or understanding.
Self-direction, then, is a possibility for higher-class people, but not
lower-class people, whose only approach to life should be conformity. Kohn, of course, does not argue that these beliefs are correct or
moral; rather, he describes them on the basis of the data he collected from more than 4,000 people.[16]

It may well be that the police-officer or drill-sergeant parental
model is functional for the lower class and most of the middle class
in our society, but that it is dysfunctional for other groups. This
appears to be the finding of Miller and Swanson.[17]

The writers believe that the police-officer or drill-sergeant model
has limitations that are not necessary. This will be seen later in the
chapter when the fifth and last parental model is analyzed. But
before that let us look at the fourth model, the teacher-counselor.

The teacher-counselor parent model

This is the developmental model.[18] The child is conceptualized as
an extremely plastic organism with almost unlimited potential for
growth and development. The limits to this growth and development are seen as the limits of the parent and other teachers to tap
the rich potential of the child. Parents themselves are regarded as
expendable—only "the child" counts. Discipline may be firm but

never harsh—and punishment should be psychological, not physical or corporal.

The good teacher-counselor (parent) always puts the need of the child first—within the tolerance limits of the classroom or the school system itself.

This model has deep historical roots in our society—Jesus is usually presented as a teacher or counselor; Benjamin Franklin and Abraham Lincoln, both folk heroes in America, reflect some of the teacher-counselor image. The dedicated and underpaid schoolteacher is a warm symbol in the United States, and in these days of social work and psychiatry the image of the counselor casts its shadow across the land.

This model reflects the progressive-school era inspired by John Dewey, the psychiatric viewpoint pioneered by Sigmund Freud, and the educational philosophy of Jean Piaget. The child is seen as fragile and plastic but capable of infinite growth and development if enough parental love and guidance are applied. The uniqueness of each child is stressed—not his similarity with other children.

At the middle-class level, this model has probably been dominant in the United States in recent decades. While it has many fine features, the writers believe it also poses the following problems:

Parents are not viewed as ends in themselves.   In this system the needs of the child are always paramount. Parents are expected to sacrifice themselves gladly for the welfare of our children. Such a value system, in the opinion of the writers, can have devastating effects on fathers, mothers, marriages, society, and even the child. It is a great burden in later life for a son or daughter to be told, "I sacrificed everything for you." This takes us back to the martyr model discussed earlier in this chapter.

This model is often too permissive.   American parents are accused of spoiling their children.[19] This is easy to do in the teacher-counselor model because of the great stress placed on the uniqueness of each child and his or her needs—relatively little is said about the needs of the parent or the needs of society. Thus, the child may get the impression of being the center of the universe.

The model tends to produce anxiety and guilt in parents.   Middle-class parents in contemporary America appear to be afflicted with anxiety and guilt. Lerner doubts that *any* human society has ever produced parents as anxious and threatened as those in our society.[20] Some of the reasons for this have been explored in earlier chapters in this book. Orville Brim argues that one of the chief products of the massive parent-education program in the United States has been parental guilt.[21]

The writers believe that most American parents are reasonably conscientious and competent in their parental role and hold the teacher-counselor model partly responsible for these fathers and mothers being made to feel guilty and inadequate.

The model tends to view parents as experts. When parents try to become experts, they are courting trouble—they can never really learn all of the mystique known to the psychiatrist, the psychologist, the home economist, or the social worker, and if anything goes wrong they will be told: "But that's not what we said. You misunderstood us." In a very real sense, a little knowledge is a dangerous thing.

What also happens is that the professionals (the designated experts) begin to judge parents by professional standards—parents should know this or that or something else.

This model does not adequately present the needs of the society. Since the model focuses primarily on the needs and development of the individual, the requirements of the community and the larger society are necessarily downgraded. This has been one of the factors that has produced a generation that displays relatively little respect for parents or other representatives of the social order.

It would seem that, in any society, a balance must be struck between the imperatives of the society and the needs of the individual—and it is our judgment that this parent model fails to pass this test.

The athletic coach model

It seems to the writers that some of the most successful parents in our society use a model derived from the role of the athletic coach. As we have analyzed this model, it appears to have the following characteristics:[22]

Physical fitness. The players must be physically fit for the contest. This involves not only vigorous physical activity but also abstention or moderation in smoking, drinking, late hours, and so on.

Mental fitness.   The athlete must be psychologically fit—that is, he or she must have confidence in his or her ability and a feeling that he or she can compete successfully.

Knowledge of the game.   The player must know the rules of the game and the penalty for violating them. At times he may knowingly and deliberately violate the rules—but only after calculating the chances of getting caught and the potential gain if he or she is not caught.

Basic skills and techniques must be painfully learned.   There are no "born" star athletes—they may be born with potential, but only hard work will permit them to realize that potential. A player who refuses to practice, no matter how gifted, will not be tolerated on the squad.

The player must have stamina.   The player must not give up or reduce his or her effort—even when tired. As Woody Hayes, coach of the Ohio State football team, once said: "Victory in football means getting up one more time than your opponent does."[23]

Aggressiveness and competitive spirit.   The athlete must desire to compete and to win. There are no "happy losers" among first-rate athletes or their coaches.

The player must accept strict discipline.   Regardless of the status on the team—star or substitute—each player must submit to strict discipline. Violation of basic regulations usually results in suspension or dismissal from the squad.

Subordination of self to the success of the team.   Each player is expected to put the success of the team ahead of personal glory. Failure to do this not only brings repercussions from the coach but also from the other players.

The coach is expected to have the welfare of the players in mind at all times.   In order for the tight discipline system in this model to work, the coach must never order a player to do anything that might threaten his or her welfare—an injured player, for example, no matter how essential to the team, must never be ordered to play if the player's future may be jeopardized. Most coaches would not even permit a person to play—even though he or she requested permission—if further injury at this time could result in permanent damage.

The coach cannot play the game—this must be done by the player. The coach's position here is quite analogous to that of parents: Once the game has begun, it is up to the players to win or lose it. The coach has some advantages over parents—he or she can send in players and can substitute one player for another. But the coach faces the same prospect as parents of sitting on the sidelines and watching players make mistakes that may prove disastrous.

Discussion of the athletic coach model

The writers submit that this model has much to recommend it to American parents. The overwhelming popularity of competitive sports in our society seems to indicate general acceptance of the model among large numbers of youth as well as by the general population.

The model seems to contain a nice balance of assertiveness, competitiveness, and cooperation. The developmental theme is included in the expectation that each player will realize his or her full potential. The model emphasizes success but the players, as well as the coach, must also learn how to live with defeat.

The model has some limitations, however, due to the fact that the role of parent is not exactly the same as that of an athletic coach. Some of these limitations are as follows: (1) The coach has had professional preparation for his or her role—most parents have not. (2) The coach can select the players from a pool of talent—parents have to work with the children they have, talented or not. (3) The coach can substitute one player for another—parents cannot. (4) The athletic contest for which the coach is preparing the team is more specific than "the game of life" for which parents are preparing their children. The athletic contest is less subject to deep social change than is the society for which parents are training their children. The time span is shorter for the coach also. He or she does not have to wait 20 years to see whether the efforts paid off. (5) The coach can quit if the situation seems hopeless—parents are not supposed to resign their roles as father or mother. Coaches can also be discharged or fired—something that is legally possible for parents but not common. (6) Coaches are expected to like or at least to respect their players—but parents are supposed to love their children.

In an interesting passage, Brim says that "If a social role *requires* characteristics such as friendliness or love, it is almost self-defeating."[24] He goes on to say that "Certain acts might be required in a role . . . but that love and similar expressions of feeling cannot be deliberate or contrived."[25] In this respect the athletic coach has an advantage over parents.

Even with these limitations the writers believe that the athletic coach model has many features that parents might use with positive results.

The use of these models in counseling parents

It would seem that these models can be used by counselors to help parents see what they are doing. The technique is similar to that used in the client-centered counseling system developed by Carl Rogers—the counselor reflects back to the parents the model they are using.[26] At an appropriate time, the counselor should point out that several parent models are available in our society and that perhaps this father and/or mother might do better using another model.

This approach assumes that the parents desire to improve their role performance and are willing to consider modification of their behavior. If this proves not to be the case, then the counselor would have to explore other problems that would seem to be blocking the treatment.

Some trends in parent counseling

In recent years, communication theory has emerged as a basic approach in working with parents.[27] In this system many of the problems facing parents are considered to be the result of inadequate or distorted communication between parents and their children, or between the parents themselves. The counselor analyzes the communication network in the family and helps various members of the group to improve their communication skills—not only the messages or signals they send but also the interpretation of messages emanating from the other members of the family unit. The improvement of communication does not necessarily solve parent problems, but it at least clarifies them.

Another influential group in parent counseling in the last decade has been the behavior-modification practitioners.[28] In this approach the parent problems are reduced to specific acts that are dysfunctional for the family system. Parents are taught how to encourage and sustain behavior in their children that will produce a better functioning family unit. According to Sheldon Rose, the parent-counselor role in the behavior-modification system is conceptualized as that of teacher rather than therapist.[29] The parent then assumes the role of pupil or learner.

Norman Epstein has described a system of parent counseling that seems to be eminently practical.[30] Using a limited number of group sessions, and delimiting the goals of the counseling program, parents are viewed as persons whose managerial tactics have not been successful with their children. In this approach, marital problems are not treated, since it is assumed that all parents have marital problems. Personality problems are viewed in the same light: All parents have personality problems. This leaves the Epstein group free to focus on parental problems—what the parents are doing in trying to cope with their children, what the results of these efforts have been, and what can be done to change the coping efforts to get better results.

In all of these approaches, group counseling seems to be preferred to the traditional individual-psychotherapy model. Another emphasis is on the delimitation of counseling goals. The writers believe both of these trends to be in the right direction.

The earlier chapter on the American father pointed out that counseling agencies often make relatively little effort to involve fathers in counseling sessions. There appears to be a trend away from this now toward more concern about the father's influence in the family. The writers hope this tend will continue,[31] but if we believe James Dobson, who has been quite influential to parents in the past few years, there is a long way to go. He writes: "Who reads the books on family living? Eighty percent are women. Who attends seminars on meaningful family life? The majority are women."[32] We would add that from our experiences in marriage and family counseling and the experiences of many colleagues, it is the women who usually drag the men kicking and screaming in for professional dialog.

Some of the most exciting developments we have seen in the past few years use professionals in only support roles while nonprofessionals and parents themselves form the nucleus for positive growth in a troubled family.

Self-help groups, such as Parents Anonymous which is modeled after Alcoholics Anonymous, can be powerful in effecting change. When parents get together and see they are all about in the same boat, a great weight can be lifted. As we have encountered so many times in our own work:

> You mean, *your* kid (pick any of the following) spits, bites, whines, fights with his sister, chews tobacco, wrecked her car, threw up on your best blouse, and so on?
>
> You better believe it. I could have killed (pick any of the following) him, her, them, it.
>
> Gee whiz! I thought I was the *only* parent in the whole wide world whose kid (pick any of the following) . . .

The professional's role in such a group is still important, but different from tradition: as an organizer, teacher, orchestrator, putter-together, sometime go-fer, oft-time searcher for the "Gee-Whiz! Phenomenon." By setting up the proper environment for the parents, the professional makes it possible for growth to occur.

With the vast amount of interest in family violence in the past few years have come some very creative developments for treating families in which child abuse occurs. So-called lay-therapy models are springing up all over the country. With an estimated 2 to 4 million cases of child abuse occurring nationwide each year there are simply not enough professionals nor money to go around. So, many communities have hired professionals to supervise a vast cadre of volunteers who go out into the homes of troubled parents and, in effect, befriend folks. This friendship model of therapy can work wonders. To a troubled person, the fact that someone cares about them can be a boost to battered self-esteem; the proof of the caring is in the simple fact that the volunteers do not make one nickel out of the deal. Lay therapists cannot carry the whole weight, of course; a complete battery of social supports is necessary in preventing the reoccurrence of abuse, including income supplements, educational and job opportunities for parents, professional counseling for parents and children where necessary, transportation help, housing support, respite care of the children to relieve weary parents, and a host of other creative aids to down-and-out parents. But, it is clear that communities who have a lay-therapy program added to the other multitude of social supports are more effective in preventing further child abuse.[33]

And, Sharon Stitt may become a role model for many other parents interested in grassroots operations to make life easier for their compatriots. In 1977 she started "Parent Place" in Seattle. The divorced mother of four who dropped out of high-school says the operation, in the very modest setting of a remodeled "temporary" military hospital vintage World War II, is number one to support parents, to help them realize "They are not alone."

"Parent Place" is a place of relaxation. It operates on a shoestring budget, like so many good things in the world, and it welcomes "runaway" moms and dads, if only for an hour or two. "It's a kind of a place of relaxation," Stitt explains. "There are no teenagers lying around smoking." Parents who drop in for casual talk or more formal group meetings range in age from 17 to 84.

The agency has received a few modest grants and would like to become a United Way affiliate. But Stitt has reservations, for red tape often is wrapped around money: "I can't understand when a person wants to speak with a counselor, they have to go through everything from grandma's maiden name to the witness stand. We are very proud of our system which is professional, but far from bureaucratic."[34]

Parent-training programs

Another encouraging development for parents in recent years has been the proliferation of parent-training programs. In the opinion of the writers, parent-training programs have several distinct advantages over parent counseling or parent-therapy programs: (1) in parent training the emphasis is on the prevention of problems rather than treating them after they develop; (2) there is no stigma attached to attending parent-training programs, but some stigma is usually associated with counseling or therapy services; (3) parent-training programs tend to focus on problems that all parents must face sooner or later—not on problems that are unique to a given family.

One of the most popular parent-training programs, Parent Effectiveness Training, reports that a quarter of a million parents have taken their course in all 50 states under the direction of over 7,000 certified instructors.[35] These statistics are indeed impressive compared to the national situation only a few years ago. Don Dinkmeyer developed Systematic Training for Effective Parenting along similar lines and estimates that a million people have been influenced through his workshops and book sales.[36]

We must not be too smug in thinking that parent training or education is a new phenomenon. Rather, it seems because of the mass media to be better developed and more visible. In fact, James Croake and Kenneth Glover point out that the first recorded meeting of a group of parents in the United States was in 1815 in Portland, Maine. "Maternal associations" were forming and study groups met regularly to discuss child-rearing problems before 1820.[37]

It scarcely needs to be said that some parents will need counseling and/or therapy even though they have attended parent-training programs. Such parents should not feel guilty or incompetent—their problems are simply more complex than those that most of us have to deal with. For the mass of parents, however, it is hoped that the group training programs will be sufficient.

Summary and conclusion

The conclusion of a book often turns out to be its bottom line. What does it all boil down to? The reader just waded through hundreds of pages, but can it all be distilled into one memorable passage?

We'll let Kelley Brigman do that work for us. Brigman, a creative professor at Mankato State University in Minnesota, got tired of reading all the doom-and-gloom literature in the media. He doesn't consider himself a Pollyanna by any means. In fact, Kelley is a divorced single parent with custody of the children and has his hands full teaching and finishing up a doctorate. But he wanted to see if he could get a bit more objective picture of what is happening in families, so he surveyed a cross-section of family life professionals all over the country. The professionals came from the fields of sociology, psychology, social work, home economics, family studies, child development, and marriage and family therapy. Some were teachers, some worked in agencies, some were therapists. All had a good deal of experience with families and in studying family issues.

Brigman did a lot with his data, but the most interesting thing he came up with was to create a composite statement that reflects the majority of the responses from the professionals:

> The family in America is in a state of rapid change as it adapts to a changing and hostile social environment. It is experiencing some confusion because it is undergoing an identity crisis, but it is actively redefining itself and new and more viable family forms and roles are

emerging. Some families are dysfunctional, some are troubled, but the majority are basically happy and well adjusted. Some of our disappointments occur because we simply expect too much from family life. Family life is the preferred lifestyle of the overwhelming majority of American people and even though there are some problems, we value family life enough to work to overcome them. Family life in America is alive, remarkably healthy and strong. It is as good as or better than it has ever been. It is here to stay. "The family is still the most important institution on this earth and likely to remain so." "The family will survive and it will continue to be the place where people's intimate and emotional needs are met, where sex is shared and where children are raised, socialized and placed in society."[38]

Or maybe, as we are fond of embellishing Mark Twain's alleged notion: Life *is* hard. But nobody ever came out of it alive, anyway.

Notes

Chapter 1

1. Norbert Wiener, *I Am a Mathematician* (New York: Doubleday, 1956), p. 224 (italics not in original). Wiener, a child prodigy, is often given credit for being the brain behind the development of the modern computer.

2. All of the case illustrations used in this book refer to actual parents, but certain details may have been altered to protect their anonymity.

3. Max Lerner, *America as a Civilization* (New York: Simon & Schuster, 1957), p. 562. We cite this book often in this study because we regard it as one of the better attempts to delineate American civilization. For another analysis, see Robin M. Williams, Jr., *American Society*, 3d ed. (New York: Alfred A. Knopf, 1970).

4. For a discussion of the failure of parent specialists to consider the social conditions under which parents function, see Orville G. Brim, Jr., "Causes of Parent Behavior," *Education for Child Rearing* (New York: Russell Sage Foundation, 1959), chap. 3. This is the definitive analysis of parent education in the United States and is cited often in this book. David Harman and Brim followed up Brim's earlier work two decades later with *Learning to Be Parents: Principles, Programs, and Methods* (Beverly Hills: Sage Publications, 1980). The two books complement each other. One sociologist who made a consistent effort to understand the social forces affecting parents was the late James H. S. Bossard of the University of Pennsylvania; see his *The Sociology of Childhood* (New York: Harper & Bros., 1948), also other volumes he wrote over a period of years.

5. Kingsley Davis, "The Sociology of Parent-Youth Conflict," *American Sociological Review* 5 (August 1940), pp. 523–35. Although published in 1940, this paper was being reprinted as late as 1965; see Hyman Rodman, *Marriage, Family, and Society* (New York: Random House, 1965). It is also available in *Social Perspectives on Behavior*, ed. Herman D. Stein and Richard A. Cloward (Glencoe, Ill.: Free Press, 1958). In many ways, this paper was the original impetus behind the present book.

6. Davis, "Sociology of Parent-Youth Conflict."

7. David Riesman et al., *The Lonely Crowd* (New Haven: Yale University Press, 1961), p. 49.

8. Davis, "Sociology of Parent-Youth Conflict."

9. See Chapter 11 of this book for an extensive analysis of parents and social change.

10. We are in the same position as Davis, Lerner, and Williams in that, while we believe American parents to be more uneasy than parents in most other modern

societies we are unable to prove the assertion. For the Williams discussion, see "Kinship and the Family in the United States," *American Society*, chap. 4.

11. Bell points out that in most human societies parents are not expected to rear children who are "different" from the parents; they are only expected to produce images of themselves. See Robert R. Bell, *Marriage and Family Interaction*, 4th ed. (Homewood, Ill.: Dorsey Press, 1975), p. 469.

12. For a discussion of the "cult of the child," see Lerner, *America as a Civilization*, pp. 560–70.

13. An interesting description of the process of families "splitting up" as the sons left for the West may be found in Lura Beam, *Maine Hamlet* (New York: Wilfred Funk, 1957).

14. Ivan F. Nye, "Runaway Youth: Problem or Symptom?" *Family Strengths 3: Roots of Well-Being*, ed. Nick Stinnett, John DeFrain, Kay King, Patricia Knaub, and George Rowe (Lincoln: University of Nebraska Press, 1981), pp. 225–41. See also F. Ivan Nye and Craig Edelbrock (eds.), "Runaways," a special issue of the *Journal of Family Issues*, 1980.

15. Alvin Toffler, *Future Shock* (New York: Random House, 1970), pp. 207–8.

16. U.S. National Center for Health Statistics. *Vital Statistics of the United States* (Washington, D.C.: U.S. Government Printing Office, 1974, 1980). In 1979, 5.6 percent of all households were headed by a single male, and 11.7 percent by a single female, for a total of 17.3 percent. See U.S. Bureau of the Census, *Current Population Reports*, Series P-20, No. 349, Table No. 55, 1979.

17. For discussion of parents in unusual circumstances, see Chapter 9, "Parents without Partners and Other Variants."

18. Of U.S. working women, 43 percent have children under age 18 at home. Broken down further, 20 percent of working women have preschool children, and 23 percent have school-aged children. See Helen Znaniecki Lopata (ed.), *Family Factbook* (Chicago: Marquis Academic Media, 1978), p. 96. For a valuable analysis of the family system in which the wife-mother is employed outside of the home, see Lynda Lytle Holmstrom, *The Two-Career Family* (Cambridge, Mass.: Schenkman Publishing, 1973); an earlier study is that of F. Ivan Nye and Lois Wladis Hoffman, *The Employed Mother in America* (Chicago: Rand McNally, 1963). For a good discussion of the challenges and possible solutions for these families, see Barbara Chesser's article, "Building Family Strengths in Dual-Career Marriages," *Building Family Strengths: Blueprints for Action*, ed. Nick Stinnett, Barbara Chesser, and John DeFrain (Lincoln: University of Nebraska Press, 1979), pp. 361–71.

19. In 1970 the U.S. Census Bureau found 72 percent of all Americans living in urban communities. The bulk of the nonurban residents were not farming but merely living outside of the city. According to reports by the federal government, only 8 percent of American families were engaged in farming in the early 1970s. Officials at the Census Bureau told us that by 1980, 73.7 percent were living in urban areas, and 26.3 percent nonurban. The farm population had further dwindled to 6.1 million, only 2.7 percent of the total U.S. population of more than 226 million.

20. There is considerable controversy about the net effect on children of such mass media as television. This material will be reviewed in Chapter 10, "Parents, mass media, and the youth peer group."

21. The studies of the youth peer group will also be discussed in Chapter 10.

22. A faculty committee at the University of Wisconsin in 1967 decided that the university should no longer accept the role of *in loco parentis* (substitute parent)

in dealing with its students. This may be possible for a university, but fathers and mothers cannot yield responsibility just because the going gets rough.

23. The development of child-rearing experts is treated in Lerner, *America as a Civilization*; Brim, *Education for Child Rearing*; Daniel R. Miller and Guy E. Swanson, *The Changing American Parent* (New York: John Wiley & Sons, 1958), and James W. Croake and Kenneth E. Glover, "A History and Evaluation of Parent Education," *The Family Coordinator*, April 1977, pp. 151–58.

24. See, for example, the research of William H. Sewell, "Infant Training and the Personality of the Child," *American Journal of Sociology* 58 (1952), pp. 150–59; and also Martha Wolfenstein, "Trends in Infant Care," *American Journal of Orthopsychiatry* 23 (1953), pp. 120–30.

25. E. E. LeMasters, "Parenthood as Crisis," *Marriage and Family Living* 19 (1957), pp. 325–55. The writer was first made aware of the widespread interest in parental problems by the reception given this paper. Feature stories appeared in such newspapers at the *New York Times* and the *Chicago Tribune*; the paper was summarized for a group of newspapers in Australia; several hundred reprints were requested from all over the world; as late as 1968 (11 years after publication), feature stores were still appearing in mass magazines and metropolitan newspapers based on the findings of this paper. The study also proved a catalyst for a long line of research which continues up to the present. A short listing of related studies follows:

Everett D. Dyer, "Parenthood as Crisis: A Re-Study," *Marriage and Family Living* 25 (1963), pp. 196–201; Daniel F. Hobbs, "Parenthood as Crisis: A Third Study," *Journal of Marriage and the Family*, August 1965, pp. 367–72; Daniel F. Hobbs, Jr., "Transition to Parenthood: A Replication and an Extension," *Journal of Marriage and the Family*, August 1968, pp. 413–17; Candace S. Russell, "Transition to Parenthood: Problems and Gratifications," *Journal of Marriage and the Family* 36 (1974), pp. 294–301; and Donna L. Sollie and Brent C. Miller, "The Transition to Parenthood as a Critical Time for Building Family Strengths," in *Family Strengths: Positive Models for Family Life*, ed. Nick Stinnett, Barbara Chesser, John DeFrain, and Patricia Knaub (Lincoln: University of Nebraska Press, 1980), pp. 149–69.

26. For a discussion of the parental role played by siblings in the large family, see Salvador Minuchin et al., *Families of the Slums* (New York: Basic Books, 1967), p. 219.

27. See Helena Z. Lopata, *Occupation: Housewife* (New York: Oxford University Press, 1971), pp. 200, 205–6.

28. Virginia Satir, "Marriage as a Human-actualizing Contract," in *The Family in Search of a Future*, ed. Herbert A. Otto (New York: Meredith Books, 1970), p. 58.

29. See Margaret Mead, *And Keep Your Powder Dry* (New York: William Morrow, 1943), p. 109.

30. Riesman et al., *Lonely Crowd*, p. 47.

31. See Lawrance Thompson and R. H. Winnick, *Robert Frost: The Later Years* (New York: Holt, Rinehart & Winston, 1967), pp. 68 and 3.

32. See Katharine Tait, *My Father, Bertrand Russell* (New York: Harcourt, Brace, Jovanovich, 1975), p. 118. Also, *The Autobiography of Bertrand Russell: 1944–1969* (New York: Simon & Schuster, 1969), p. 88.

33. From Bill Cosby, *My Father Confused Me. What Must I Do?* (Capitol Records, 1977).

34. Kenneth Keniston, *All Our Children: The American Family Under Pressure* (New York: Harcourt Brace Jovanovich, 1977).

35. Even though family income has increased in recent years, the cost of rearing a child has skyrocketed. In 1975 the National Organization for Non-Parents estimated that rearing one child might cost up to $300,000 if the mother had been earning $10,000 a year and quit her job to be a full-time mother (*Milwaukee Journal*, September 16, 1975). There are, of course, numerous ways to figure out the financial cost of rearing children. Besides deciding whether or not to count a homemaker's loss of income if she chooses to stay home with the kids, one must also decide whether or not to figure in the cost of a college education for them. So estimates may vary widely; but no estimate we have come across is modest. The range is from $70,000 to $400,000 (in 1981 dollars).

36. Norman B. Ryder, "Contraceptive Failure in the United States." *Family Planning Perspectives*, 5 (1973), p. 133.

37. See Oscar Handlin, *The Uprooted* (Boston: Little, Brown, 1952).

38. The first author's father, for example, grew up on a small farm and attended school for only three years; his mother lived in a small rural village until her marriage; later the parents moved to a small city of 12,000 population, where they reared their four children. In contrast, the first author grew up in an urban world and reared his children in an urban world. The second author's father grew up on the farm and fled to the city after high school, with attendant challenges of country clothes, country language, and empty spaces in his mouth where front teeth should have been (the result of rural Depression-days poverty). His son, the second author, had no such challenges to meet as a city youth in the mid-60s.

39. For a systematic analysis of the problems of minority group parents in our society, see Chapter 6.

40. For a penetrating analysis of the changing functions of the American family, see Robert F. Winch, "The Family in America and Its Functional Matrix," *The Modern Family*, 3d ed. (New York: Holt, Rinehart & Winston, 1971), part II.

41. For a description of the Swedish sex education program, see Birgitta Linner, *Sex and Society in Sweden* (New York: Pantheon Books, 1967); Anne McCreary Juhasz, ed., *Sexual Development and Behavior* (Homewood, Ill.: Dorsey Press, 1973); and Maureen J. McConaghy, "Sex-Role Contravention and Sex Education Directed Toward Young Children in Sweden," *Journal of Marriage and the Family*, November 1979, pp. 893–904.

42. See Jesse R. Pitts, "The Structural-Functional Approach" in *Handbook of Marriage and the Family*, ed. Harold T. Christensen (Chicago: Rand McNally, 1964), pp. 51–124.

43. The most extensive articles were by Sally Wendkos Olds, "Do You Have What It Takes to Make a Good Marriage?" *Ladies' Home Journal*, October 1980, pp. 76, 78, 202, 204; and David Milofsky, "What Makes a Good Family?" *Redbook*, August 1981, pp. 58–62. A more academic description of the research appears in Nick Stinnett, Greg Sanders, and John DeFrain, "Strong Families: A National Study," in Stinnett et al., *Family Strengths 3*, pp. 33–41.

44. Davis, "Sociology of Parent-Youth Conflict."

45. Lewis S. Feuer, *The Conflict of Generations* (New York: Basic Books, 1969), p. 68.

Chapter 2

1. Thurman Arnold, *The Folklore of Capitalism* (New Haven: Yale University Press, 1937).

2. John Kenneth Galbraith, *The Affluent Society* (Boston: Houghton Mifflin, 1958). For another treatment of folklore, see William J. Lederer and Don D. Jackson, *The Mirages of Marriage* (New York: W. W. Norton, 1968).

3. Albert Ellis, *The Folklore of Sex* (New York: Charles Boni, 1951).

4. E. E. LeMasters, *Modern Courtship and Marriage* (New York: Macmillan, 1957).

5. Dorothy Rodgers, *A Personal Book* (New York: Harper & Row, 1977), p. 175.

6. Frank's remarks come from a dialogue the second author and his graduate students had via teleconference call with Farrelly in the spring of 1979. Farrelly lives and works in Madison, Wisconsin, and is the co-author of *Provocative Therapy*, a refreshing approach to counseling.

7. Persons who think it is fun to be a great writer should read *O'Neill* by Arthur and Barbara Gelb (New York: Harper & Bros., 1962). This is the story of the tormented life of the great playwright. Or take a look at any one of numerous biographies of John Steinbeck, another Nobel Prize winning author of *The Grapes of Wrath*, *Tortilla Flat*, and many other stunning novels.

8. Brooke Hayward, *Haywire* (New York: Alfred A. Knopf, 1977), p. 200.

9. Kenneth Keniston, *All Our Children* (New York: Harcourt Brace Jovanovich, 1977), p. 18.

10. E. E. LeMasters, "Parenthood as Crisis," *Marriage and Family Living* 19 (1957), pp. 325–55.

11. A more recent study of new parents came to different conclusions; see Daniel F. Hobbs, Jr., "Transition to Parenthood: A Replication and an Extension," *Marriage and the Family* 30 (August 1968), pp. 413–17. Although Hobbs refers to his study as a replication of the earlier study by LeMasters, an important difference is that the LeMasters sample was limited to middle-class parents. This does not appear to be true of the Hobbs sample.

12. Someone else commented to the first author that marriage may also be the only game of chance in which both players *can win*.

13. In their study of married couples in Detroit, Blood and Wolfe report that only 3 percent of the sample said they would not want any children if they had their life to live over again; see Robert O. Blood, Jr., and Donald M. Wolfe, *Husbands and Wives* (New York: Free Press, 1960), p. 137. It is interesting to note that of the 909 spouses interviewed for this study not one was a male.

14. See Nick Stinnett, "In Search of Strong Families," in *Building Family Strengths: Blueprints for Action*, ed. Nick Stinnett, Barbara Chesser and John DeFrain (Lincoln: University of Nebraska Press, 1979), pp. 23–30; and Nick Stinnett, Greg Sanders, and John DeFrain, "Strong Families: A National Study," in *Family Strengths 3: Roots of Well-Being*, ed. Nick Stinnett, John DeFrain, Kay King, Patricia Knaub, and George Rowe (Lincoln: University of Nebraska Press, 1981), pp. 33–41.

15. On the difficulties of child rearing in the Churchill family, see Jack Fishman, *My Darling Clementine* (New York: David McKay, 1963). This is the story of Mrs. Winston Churchill and her married life. See also Randolph Churchill, *Twenty-one Years* (Boston: Houghton Mifflin, 1965), the story of his childhood; and his *Winston S. Churchill* (New York: Houghton Mifflin, 1966). The latter volume details how seldom Winston Churchill saw his upper-upper-class parents when he was a child.

16. At various times, almost all of the Roosevelt children seem to have had fairly serious problems when they were growing up; see Joseph P. Lash, *Franklin and Eleanor* (New York: W. W. Norton, 1971).

17. William J. Goode, *After Divorce* (New York: Free Press, 1956).

18. Boyd C. Rollins and Harold Feldman, "Marital Satisfaction over the Life Cycle," *Journal of Marriage and the Family* 32 (1970), pp. 20–28.

19. Charles R. Figley, "Children and Marriage," *Journal of Marriage and the Family* 35 (1973), pp. 272–82.

20. Norval D. Glenn and Sara McLanahan, "Children and Marital Happiness: A Further Specification of the Relationship," *Journal of Marriage and the Family*, February 1982, pp. 63–72.

21. Leonard Benson, *Fatherhood: A Sociological Perspective* (New York: Random House, 1968), p. 114.

22. Jessie Bernard interview quoted in the *Milwaukee Journal*, June 18, 1972. See also her study, *The Future of Marriage* (New York: World Publishing, 1972).

23. S. M. Miller, "On Men: The Making of a Confused Middle-Class Husband," in *Family in Transition*, ed. Arlene and Jerome Skolnick, 2d ed. (Boston: Little, Brown, 1977), p. 244.

24. Interview reported in the *Milwaukee Journal*, September 23, 1974. This study was a doctoral thesis.

25. See Stella Chess, Alexander Thomas, and Herbert Birch, *Your Child Is a Person* (New York: Viking Press, 1965).

26. See Julius Segal and Herbert Yahraes, "Bringing Up Mother." *Psychology Today*, November 1979, pp. 90–96. Alexander Thomas and Stella Chess expand on these ideas in *Temperament and Development* (New York: Brunner/Mazel, 1977).

27. Lynn Wikler, "Chronic Stresses of Families of Mentally Retarded Children," *Family Relations* 30 (1981), pp. 281–88.

28. See Chapter 4, "Role Analysis of Parenthood."

29. A well-known family sociologist, William J. Goode, takes the position that we have no reliable history of the American family; see his paper, "The Sociology of the Family," in *Sociology Today*, ed. Robert K. Merton et al. (New York: Basic Books, 1959), p. 195. Even today we believe we are yet to see one.

30. In the pioneer study of marital adjustment and its prediction, the conclusion was reached that couples with no children or one child rate their marriages significantly higher than couples with two or more children; see Ernest W. Burgess and Leonard S. Cottrell, Jr., *Predicting Success or Failure in Marriage* (New York: Prentice-Hall, 1939), pp. 258–59; see also a later study, Ernest W. Burgess and Paul Wallin, *Engagement and Marriage* (Philadelphia: J. B. Lippincott, 1953), pp. 712–13.

31. For an extensive discussion of the nonparent movement in the United States, see Ellen Peck and Judith Senderowitz, eds., *Pronatalism: The Myth of Mom & Apple Pie* (New York: Thomas Y. Crowell, 1974); also Jessie Bernard, *The Future of Motherhood* (New York: Dial Press, 1974). A good recent study is by Sharon K. Houseknecht, "Childlessness and Marital Adjustment," *Journal of Marriage and the Family*, May 1979, pp. 259–68.

32. Ellen Peck, *The Joy of the Only Child* (New York: Delacorte, 1977).

33. Judith Blake, "Family Size and the Quality of Children," *Demography* 18, no. 4 (1981), pp. 421–42.

34. Sharryl Hawke and David Knox, *One Child By Choice* (Englewood Cliffs, N.J.: Prentice–Hall, 1977).

35. Lerner, *America as a Civilization*, pp. 560–70.

36. See Orville G. Brim, Jr., "The Influence of a Parent on Child," *Education for Child Rearing* (New York: Russell Sage Foundation, 1959), chap. 2.

37. This discussion is in the section cited previously.

38. Arthur A. Campbell, "Trends in Teenage Childbearing in the United States," in *Adolescent Pregnancy and Childbearing: Findings from Research*, ed. Catherine S. Chilman (Washington, D.C.: U.S. Department of Health and Human Services, NIH Publication No. 81-2077, December 1980), p. 5.

39. See David Riesman et al., "From Morality to Morale: Changes in the Agents of Character Formation," *The Lonely Crowd*, rev. ed., (New Haven: Yale University Press, 1961), chap. 2. See also Lerner, "Children and Parents," *America as a Civilization*, pp. 560–70.

40. This statement is based on an unpublished study of college seniors done by the first author at Beloit College, Beloit, Wisconsin, in 1958.

41. One of the most penetrating analyses of the new American generation that we have seen is Kenneth Keniston, *Youth and Dissent* (New York: Harcourt Brace Jovanovich, 1971).

42. See Sigmund Freud, *Sexuality and the Psychology of Love* (New York: Collier Books, 1963); almost any page will do.

43. Each year the United States records roughly half a million births to unwed mothers. See John Stewart Dacey, *Adolescents Today* (Santa Monica, Calif.: Goodyear, 1979), p. 226–29. Kinsey reported a significant amount of adultery by both wives and husbands in his sample—but considerably higher rates for husbands than for wives; see Alfred C. Kinsey et al., *Sexual Behavior and the Human Female* (Philadelphia: W. B. Saunders, 1953), pp. 409–45. In this second volume, Kinsey summarizes the data on men from the first volume and compares them with data on women. Morton Hunt followed up on Kinsey's research in the 1970s and found that at least half of the younger American men interviewed would probably engage in extramarital intercourse at some time during their marriage. Possibly more than a third of the women would eventually have sex with a man other than their husband. See Morton Hunt, *Sexual Behavior in the 1970s* (Chicago: Playboy, 1974), pp. 258, 261.

44. For the Italian view of sex as too overpowering for individuals to control, see Luigi Barzini, *The Italians* (New York: Atheneum Press, 1964); also Irving R. Levine, *Main Street, Italy* (New York: Doubleday, 1963).

45. In the 1940s a study in Indiana concluded that 20 percent of all first births in that state were conceived before marriage; see Harold T. Christensen, *Marriage Analysis* (New York: Ronald Press, 1950), p. 153. A 1970 survey by the Department of Health, Education and Welfare estimated the premature conceptions at closer to one third of all first births.

46. See Bruno Bettelheim, *Love Is Not Enough* (New York: Free Press, 1950).

47. See the *Proceedings* of a conference on *The Single-Parent Family* held February 11–14, 1976, at the University of Iowa.

48. See Alfred Kadushin, "Single-Parent Adoptions: An Overview and Some Relevant Research," *The Social Service Review* 44 (1970), pp. 263–74.

49. Joan Aldous, "Children's Perceptions of Adult Role Assignment," *Journal of Marriage and the Family* 34 (1972), pp. 55–65.

50. See Alvin L. Schorr, *Poor Kids* (New York: Basic Books, 1966).

51. For a discussion of these issues, and some alternatives from parents who are trying a new lifestyle in which fathers are more involved in parenting and mothers have added a job or career to their lives, see John DeFrain, "Androgy-

nous Parents Outline Their Needs," *The Family Coordinator*, April 1979, pp. 237–43.

52. William R. Wineke, "Margaret Mead: All Adults Responsible for Young." *Wisconsin State Journal*, June 2, 1979, section 4, p. 2.

53. The first author was a participant in this study and received the results in a personal communication. The study was conducted in June 1972.

54. Strictly speaking, we are referring to two separate functions here: that of reproduction or replacement, and that of socialization or training for adult roles; see Kingsley Davis, *Human Society* (New York: Macmillan, 1949).

55. George Peter Murdock, *Social Structure* (New York: Macmillan, 1949).

Chapter 3

1. Benjamin Spock, "What About Our Children?" in *Family Strengths: Positive Models for Family Life*, ed. Nick Stinnett, Barbara Chesser, John DeFrain, and Patricia Knaub (Lincoln: University of Nebraska Press, 1980), pp. 137–48.

2. According to Foote and Cottrell there were 1,031 papers published on the American family during the period 1945–54; see Nelson N. Foote and Leonard S. Cottrell, *Identity and Interpersonal Competence* (Chicago: University of Chicago Press, 1955), pp. 231–90. For a content analysis of the articles on child rearing and parenthood appearing in mass magazines, see Jerry J. Bigner, "Parent Education in Popular Literature: 1950–1970," *The Family Coordinator* 21 (1972), pp. 313–19.

3. Michael J. Geboy, "Who Is Listening to the 'Experts'? The Use of Child-Care Materials by Parents," *Family Relations* 30 (1981), pp. 205–10.

4. John DeFrain and Linda Ernst, "The Psychological Effects of Sudden Infant Death Syndrome on Surviving Family Members," *Journal of Family Practice* 6 (1978), pp. 985–89; and John DeFrain, Jacque Taylor, and Linda Ernst, *Coping with Sudden Infant Death* (Lexington, Mass.: Lexington Books, 1982).

5. This early version of environmentalism is found in J. B. Watson, *Behaviorism* (New York: W. W. Norton, 1925). For a review and critique of this personality theory, see Calvin S. Hall and Gardner Lindzey, *Theories of Personality* (New York: John Wiley & Sons, 1957), chap. 11.

6. In a well-known text, the anthropologist Gillin devotes the first 171 pages to man's organic nature and his biological relationships to other mammals and other primates; see John Gillin, *The Ways of Men* (New York: Appleton-Century-Crofts, 1948). In a cursory survey of sociology textbooks, the writer found little coverage of man's organic nature and his relationship to other animals. For example, out of 556 pages of text, Sutherland and Woodward devote 15 pages to man's organic nature; on page 101 they refer to "the elimination of heredity folklore"; see *Introductory Sociology*, ed. Robert L. Sutherland, Julian L. Woodward, and Milton A. Maxwell, 5th ed. (Philadelphia: J. B. Lippincott, 1956). Another well-known text gives 2 pages out of 642 to man's organic nature; see Leonard Broom and Philip Selznick, *Sociology*, 2d ed. (Evanston, Ill.: Row, Peterson & Co., 1958). A widely used text by Arnold Green, *Sociology*, 2d ed. (New York: McGraw-Hill, 1956), devotes 14 out of 557 pages to man's organic nature. A follow-up review by the second author revealed the situation had not changed much. Joseph H. Fichter devoted one page to the "nature versus nurture" question in *Sociology* (Chicago: University of Chicago Press, 1971). Robert Bierstedt devoted a whole chapter to "The Biological Factor" in his book *The*

Social Order, 4th ed. (New York: McGraw-Hill, 1974), but really only about a page and a half of this discussion is germane to the question of the biological roots of behavior. And D. Stanley Eitzen in his book *In Conflict and Order: Understanding Society* (Boston: Allyn & Bacon, 1978) notes that three disciplines focus on behavior: biology, psychology, and sociology, but that the organic bases for behavior are the domain of the biologist. Edward Wilson is surely onto something here, indeed.

7. Edward O. Wilson, *On Human Nature* (Cambridge, Mass.: Harvard University Press, 1978), pp. 67, 19. Sociobiology was born in 1975 with the publication of Wilson's *Sociobiology: The New Synthesis* (Cambridge, Mass.: Harvard University Press). The reader is also referred to Daniel G. Freedman, *Human Sociobiology: A Holistic Approach* (New York: Free Press, 1979), Pierre L. van den Berghe, *Human Family Systems: An Evolutionary View* (New York: Elsevier Press, 1979), and Ashley Montagu, *Sociobiology Examined* (New York: Oxford University Press, 1980). Sociobiology is not without its critics, of course. See, for example, Jill S. Quadagno, "Paradigms in Evolutionary Theory: The Sociobiological Model of Natural Selection," *American Sociological Review* 44 (February 1979), pp. 100–9. Quadagno argued that evolutionary theory, the basis for sociobiology, assumes that life evolves in a positive, adaptive direction—onward and upward, so to speak. She noted that it sometimes goes backwards, too. In response to Wilson, she said: "Explaining parent-offspring conflict over such matters as going to bed early, studying hard in school, not fighting with siblings, and refraining from gambling, drinking and premarital sex in terms of the ultimate evolutionary significance is intellectual gamesmanship." In effect, she accused Wilson of taking a good theory and extending it to its logical absurdity. ". . . In terms of method and logic, sociobiology is not applicable to the study of human social behavior," Quadagno concluded.

8. For some of the other thoughtful reviews or critiques of sociobiology, see the following: Rene Dubos' article critiquing sociobiology in *The Sciences* (New York Academy of the Sciences, January 1982), pp. 26–28; Richard C. Lewontin's article on sociobiology in *The Sciences* (New York Academy of the Sciences, July/August 1981), pp. 23–26; Howard E. Gruber, "How Are We Possible?", *New York Times Book Review*, October 18, 1981; Mary Midgeley, *Beast and Man* (Ithaca, N.Y.: Cornell University Press, 1978); Alan Fix, a review of *The Selfish Gene*, *Contemporary Sociology*, Winter 1978; and Stephen Jay Gould, "This View of Life: The Problem of Perfection," *Natural History*, December 1977, pp. 32–35.

9. It is interesting to note that in the survey of personality theories by Hall and Lindzey, *Theories of Personality*, the index lists only two pages devoted to man's organic nature (p. 569). The terms *organism* and *organismic* are used frequently in the various chapters but refer to gestalt theory—that numerous factors are involved in human behavior—but these references do not spell out man's biological inheritance as the above analysis by Gillin does. For an excellent review of man's organic nature, see Weston LaBarre, *The Human Animal* (Chicago: University of Chicago Press, 1954). A mass of material on the similarity of human behavior to that of other animals has appeared in recent years; see Konrad Lorenz, *On Aggression* (New York: Harcourt, Brace & World, 1963), Robert Ardrey, *The Territorial Imperative* (New York: Atheneum Publishers, 1966), Eugene Linden, *Apes, Men, and Language* (New York: E. P. Dutton, 1974), John Napier, *Monkeys Without Tails* (New York: Taplinger, 1976), and others. The point of view that human behavior can successfully be resolved into its biological components, components that may then in turn be described as chemical and electrical events, had been labeled *reductionism*. There has been such an

upsurge of interest in reductionism lately that at least one author, Stanton Peele, hopes the pendulum will swing back the other way a bit. Peele argues that a growing consensus is emerging that the best hope for understanding and treating psychological problems lies in the recent work of biologists, geneticists, and neuroscientists. "Yet not only has biochemical and neurological research not explained basic aspects of human behavior and mental disorder—it has fundamental problems in attempting such explanations. A psychology that accepts and accounts for subjective human experience is presented as a counterpoise to the reductionist thrust." See Stanton Peele, "Reductionism in the Psychology of the Eighties: Can Biochemistry Eliminate Addiction, Mental Illness and Pain?" *American Psychologist* 36 (1981), pp. 807–18.

10. For a good (and rare) discussion of this, see Alex Inkeles, "Personality and Social Structure," in *Sociology Today*, ed. Robert K. Merton et al. (New York: Basic Books, 1959), pp. 249–76; see also Dennis H. Wrong, "The Over Socialized Conception of Man in Sociology," *American Sociological Review* 26 (1961), pp. 183–93.

11. For a critique of the "cultural explanation" of human behavior, see Elliott Liebow, *Tally's Corner* (Boston: Little, Brown, 1967), pp. 208–9. In commenting on the shift from genetic or biological explanations of behavior to a cultural theory, Brim writes: "One characteristic after another of the person was transferred, so to speak, from the domain of inheritance to the territory of environment"; see Orville G. Brim, Jr., *Education for Child Rearing* (New York: Russell Sage Foundation, 1959), p. 33.

12. Richard J. Gelles, "Applying Research on Family Violence to Clinical Practice," *Journal of Marriage and the Family* 1 (1982), p. 16.

13. Vincent notes that Kinsey's data are often questioned on sampling grounds but other studies with even more bias in their sample are quoted without criticism; see Clark Vincent, *Unmarried Mothers* (Glencoe, Ill.: Free Press, 1961), pp. 27–28.

14. See Brim, *Education for Child Rearing*, various chapters. This is the most complete critique of scientific research on child rearing that the writers have found. An earlier work by Orlansky also contains a voluminous review and evaluation of the research material given out to parents in our society in recent decades; see Harold Orlansky, "Infant Care and Personality," *Psychological Bulletin* 46 (January 1949), pp. 1–48. The sociologist Sewell has done well-designed field research on children which failed to support many Freudian theories about breast feeding and other child-rearing practices; see William H. Sewell, "Infant Training and the Personality of the Child," *American Journal of Sociology* 58 (September 1952), pp. 150–59. Wolfenstein, through an analysis of federal government bulletins on child rearing, has been able to demonstrate that the advice given parents has fluctuated from one decade to the next; see Martha Wolfenstein, "Trends in Infant Care," *American Journal of Orthopsychiatry* 23 (1953), pp. 120–30. Alvin Toffler's *Future Shock* (New York: Random House, 1970), refers to the great fluctuations in advice given to parents over the last several decades (see pp. 137–39).

15. James Walters and Nick Stinnett, "Parent-Child Relationships: A Decade Review of Research, *Journal of Marriage and the Family* 1 (1970), pp. 129–30.

16. James Walters and Lynda Henly Walters, "Parent-Child Relationships: A Review, 1970–1979," *Journal of Marriage and the Family* 4 (1980), 807–22.

17. Robert B. McCall, "Challenges to a Science of Developmental Psychology," *Child Development* 48 (1977), p. 333.

18. For Brim's discussion of the father's role, see Brim, *Education for Child Rearing*, pp. 36–38 and 69–70. For Pollak's analysis of the neglect of fathers in child-guidance clinics, see Otto Pollak, *Social Science and Psychotherapy for Children* (New York: Russell Sage Foundation, 1952).

19. See William J. Goode, *After Divorce* (New York: Free Press, 1956), p. 21.

20. For a review of several studies of parents that did not include interviews with any fathers, see Chapter 8 of this volume, "The American father."

21. Looking at how well fathers are represented in recent research published in two major family journals and looking at how the paternal role is conceived by authors of books on how to rear children, we concluded that changes have occurred.

22. See Marshall B. Clinard, *Sociology of Deviant Behavior*, rev. ed. (New York: Rinehart, 1968), p. 133.

23. See Geoffrey Gorer, *The America People* (New York: W. W. Norton, 1964), p. 70.

24. Jessie Bernard, *The Future of Marriage* (New York: World Publishing, 1972), pp. XV–XVI.

25. William H. Whyte, Jr., *The Organization Man* (New York: Doubleday Anchor Book Edition, 1957), p. 26.

26. Betty Friedan, *The Feminine Mystique* (New York: Dell Publishing, 1963), p. 117.

27. See Stanislav Andreski, *Social Sciences as Sorcery* (London: Andre Deutsch, 1972). The *Time* magazine quote is from the September 25, 1972 issue, p. 71. See also an attack by Seymour Freidin and George Bailey, *The Experts* (New York: Macmillan, 1968).

28. Cecilia Stendler, "Sixty Years of Child Training Practices," *Journal of Pediatrics* 36 (1950), pp. 122–34.

29. Martha Wolfenstein, "Trends in Infant Care," *American Journal of Orthopsychiatry* 23 (1953), pp. 120–30.

30. Daniel B. Fishman and William D. Neigher, "American Psychology in the Eighties: Who Will Buy?" *American Psychologist* 5 (May 1982), pp. 533.

31. Charles E. Lindblom and David K. Cohen, *Usable Knowledge: Social Science and Social Problem Solving* (New Haven: Yale University Press, 1979).

32. Spock, "What About Our Children?" p. 147.

33. Urie Bronfenbrenner, *Two Worlds of Childhood* (New York: Russell Sage Foundation, 1970).

34. The writers recognize that not all psychiatrists are followers of Freud. We cite Freudian theory here because we feel it has had the most impact on American parents. Miller and Swanson, for example, report that of 146 articles on psychoanalysis indexed in *The Reader's Guide to Periodical Literature* for the years 1910–35, only 27 were basically negative. They concluded that millions of American parents must have been subjected to psychoanalytic influence during this period; see Daniel R. Miller and Guy E. Swanson, *The Changing American Parent* (New York: John Wiley & Sons, 1958), pp. 185–86. On the history of American social work, see Roy Lubove, *The Professional Altruist* (Cambridge, Mass.: Harvard University Press, 1965).

35. Edward A. Strecker, M.D., *Their Mothers' Sons* (Philadelphia: J. B. Lippincott, 1946); Strecker blames the psychiatric casualties of our military forces in World War II on the American mother.

36. Robert Locke, "Psychiatry's Worth Is Questioned," *Wisconsin State Journal*, June 8, 1978, p. 1. See Gross' book, *The Psychological Society* (New York: Random House, 1978).

37. For a devastating attack on Freudian theory, see Richard LaPiere, *The Freudian Ethic* (New York: Duell, Sloan & Pearce, 1959). A more detached critique will be found in R. R. Sears, *Survey of Objective Studies of Psychoanalytic Concepts*, Bulletin no. 51 (New York: Social Science Research Council, 1943).

38. Clarence Darrow, the great criminal lawyer, is credited with developing the theory of environmentalism as a defense for certain types of crime—such as the famous Loeb-Leopold murder trial of the 1920s. But Darrow did not equate the influence of parents with environment—he indicted the entire society in which the child was reared; see Arthur Weinberg, ed., *Attorney for the Damned* (New York: Simon & Schuster, 1957); also Irving Stone, *Clarence Darrow for the Defense* (New York: Doubleday, 1941).

39. Brim develops this thesis in *Education for Child Rearing*, chap. 2; and David Harman and Brim update these thoughts in *Learning To Be Parents: Principles, Programs, and Methods* (Beverly Hills: Sage Publications, 1980), chap 2.

40. See Lerone Bennett, Jr., *Black Power USA: The Human Side of Reconstruction 1867–1877* (Chicago: Johnson Publishing, 1967).

41. Hall and Lindzey review Freud's use of the concept of instinct (see *Theories of Personality*, pp. 36–41).

42. Stella Chess, Alexander Thomas, Herbert G. Birch, *Your Child Is a Person* (New York: Viking Press 1965), p. 49.

43. Jerome Kagan, "The Parental Love Trap," *Psychology Today*, August 1978, p. 61.

44. Richard Q. Bell and Lawrence V. Harper, *Child Effects on Adults* (Hillsdale, N.J.: Lawrence Erlbaum and Associates, 1977).

45. Arlene Skolnick, "The Myth of the Vulnerable Child," *Psychology Today*, February 1978, pp. 56–65.

46. The first author first heard this expression used by the late Howard Becker, sociologist at the University of Wisconsin. We do not know the origin of the phrase.

47. These influences are summarized in Brim, *Education for Child Rearing*, chap. 2. For an analysis of learning after the years of childhood, see Orville G. Brim, Jr., and Stanton Wheeler, *Socialization after Childhood* (New York: John Wiley & Sons, 1966).

48. See Ernest Jones, *The Life and Work of Sigmund Freud* (New York: Basic Books, 1961), p. 12. This is the one-volume version edited by Lionel Trilling and Steven Marcus.

49. See, for example, Sheldon Rose, *Treating Children in Groups* (San Francisco: Jossey-Bass, 1972).

50. Jerome Kagan and Robert E. Klein, "Cross-Cultural Perspectives on Early Development," *American Psychologist*, November 1973, pp. 947–61.

51. Stephen J. Suomi, Harry F. Harlow, and William T. McKinney, Jr., "Monkey Psychiatrists," *American Journal of Psychiatry* 128 (1972), pp. 927–32.

52. See Brim, *Education for Child Rearing*, p. 34.

53. See Leo Rosten, *The Many Worlds of Leo Rosten* (New York: Harper & Row, 1964), p. 207. Although Rosten's reputation is based largely on his writing for Hollywood films and popular magazines, he also holds a Ph.D. in social science from the University of Chicago.

54. Leontine R. Young, *Out of Wedlock* (New York: McGraw-Hill, 1954). Her data are based on interviews with unmarried mothers, but she does not compare this

group with a control group from the general population. Thus, her findings may well be true of the unmarried mothers she interviewed, but the same characteristics might be found in a matched sample from the general population.

55. See Clark E. Vincent, "Psychological and Familial Factors," *Unmarried Mothers* (New York: Free Press, 1961), part III.

56. The classic example of poor sampling that produced totally misleading findings was the famous poll taken by the now defunct *Literary Digest* which predicted that a man named Alf Landon would defeat Franklin D. Roosevelt in the 1936 presidential election. Landon carried two states.

57. In a complex and pluralistic society such as ours, each person is exposed to a variety of subcultural norms, which may deviate from those of the larger society.

58. Roger J. Williams, "The Biology of Behavior," *Saturday Review*, January 30, 1971, p. 19; Williams is professor of chemistry and biochemistry at the University of Texas at Austin.

59. Robert Ardrey, *The Social Contract* (New York: Atheneum Publishers, 1970), p. 47.

60. See, for example, Don D. Jackson, ed., *Communication, Family, and Marriage* (Palo Alto, Calif.: Science & Behavior Books, 1968).

61. David Mechanic, *Mental Health and Social Policy* (Englewood Cliffs, N.J.: Prentice-Hall, 1969), p. 35.

62. News story in *The Milwaukee Journal*, May 28, 1971; the researcher being quoted here is Seymour S. Kety, professor of psychiatry at Harvard University and editor of the *Journal of Pediatric Research*.

63. Associated Press dispatch, *The Milwaukee Journal*, May 5, 1972; the researchers quoted here are Professors Jacques Gottlieb and Charles Frohman of Wayne State University.

64. Edward O. Wilson, *On Human Nature* (Cambridge, Mass.: Harvard University Press, 1978), p. 58.

65. Sybille Bedford, *Aldous Huxley: A Biography* (New York: Alfred Knopf and Harper & Row, 1974), p. 655.

66. Lucy Freeman and Julie Roy, *Betrayal* (New York: Stein & Day, 1976), p. 179.

67. Mark Vonnegut, *The Eden Express* (New York: Praeger Publishers 1975), p. 208.

68. For an example of Freudian analysis of homosexual behavior, see Sigmund Freud, *Dora: An Analysis of a Case of Hysteria* (New York: Collier Books, 1963).

69. News report, *New York Times*, November 17, 1972.

70. See Tennessee Williams, *Memoirs* (New York: Doubleday, 1975).

71. Del Martin and Phyllis Lyon, *Lesbian Woman* (New York: Bantam Books, 1972).

72. Laura Z. Hobson, *Consenting Adult* (New York: Doubleday, 1975).

73. Laud Hmphreys, *Out of the Closets* (Englewood Cliffs, N.J.: Prentice-Hall, 1972).

74. Psychiatrist Lawrence J. Hatterer of the Payne Whitney Clinic of New York Hospital, New York City, quoted in a *New York Times* dispatch, *Wisconsin State Journal*, February 21, 1971.

75. Report of a study at the University of California at Los Angeles, *Milwaukee Journal*, April 4, 1971.

76. Richard Green, "Sexual Identity of 37 Children Raised by Homosexual or Transsexual Parents," *American Journal of Psychiatry* 135 (1978), pp. 692–97.

77. Edward O. Wilson, *On Human Nature* (Cambridge, Mass.: Harvard University Press, 1978), pp. 146, 143.

78. Alan Bell, Morgan Weinberg, and Sue Hammersmith, *Sexual Preference: Its Development Among Men and Women* (Bloomington: Indiana University Press, 1981).

79. Max Lerner, "Researching Homosexual Issue," *Los Angeles Times*, reprinted in *The Lincoln Journal*, November 27, 1981, p. 6.

80. This behavior syndrome is fully described in James R. Morrison and Mark A. Stewart, "The Psychiatric Status of the Legal Families of Adopted Hyperactive Children," *Archives of General Psychiatry* 28 (1973) pp. 888–91.

81. "A Family Study of the Hyperactive Child Syndrome," *Biological Psychiatry* 3 (1971) pp. 189–95.

82. Morrison and Stewart, "The Psychiatric Status," p. 888.

83. Personal communication from Dr. Mark A. Stewart, Child Psychiatry Service, University of Iowa, Iowa City, Iowa, April 29, 1976.

84. Roger D. Freeman, "Minimal Brain Dysfunction, Hyperactivity, and Learning Disorders: Epidemic or Episode?" *The Hyperactive Child and Stimulant Drugs*, ed. James J. Bosco and Stanley S. Robin (Chicago: University of Chicago Press, 1977), pp. 5–30.

85. Marcel Kinsbourne and James M. Swanson, "Models of Hyperactivity: Implications for Treatment and Diagnosis," *Hyperactivity in Children: Etiology, Measurement, and Treatment Implications*, ed. Ronald L. Trites (Baltimore: University Park Press, 1979), pp. 1–20.

86. Helen Tryphonas, "Factors Possibly Implicated in Hyperactivity: Feinglod's Hypothesis and Hypersensitivity Reactions," *Hyperactivity in Children*, Trites, pp. 93–102.

87. For a discussion of the field of genetic counseling, see James R. Sorenson, *Social Aspects of Applied Human Genetics* (New York: Russell Sage Foundation, 1971).

88. For an exposition of the family-therapy treatment system evolved by the Palo Alto research group, see Virginia Satir, *Conjoint Family Therapy* (Palo Alto, Calif.: Science & Behavior Books, 1964). For a popularized view of family therapy, really the most engaging one we have seen to date, read Augustus Napier and Carl Whitaker, *The Family Crucible* (New York: Harper & Row, 1978).

89. See, for example, Gerald R. Patterson, *Families: Applications of Social Learning to Family Life* (Champaign, Ill.: Research Press, 1971).

90. For the failure of the daily press to give the general public an accurate picture of the modern world, see Ben Bagdikian, *The Effete Conspiracy and Other Crimes by the Press* (New York: Harper & Row, 1972). For efforts to do something about the reporting of behavioral science findings, see Orville G. Brim, Jr., et al., *Knowledge into Action: Improving the Nation's Use of the Social Sciences* (Washington, D.C.: National Science Foundation, 1969), pp. 29–32.

Chapter 4

1. See William O. Douglas, *Go East Young Man: The Early Years* (New York: Random House, 1974), p. 247. At one time or another Douglas was dean of the Yale University Law School, chairman of the securities and Exchange Commission, and justice on the United States Supreme Court.

2. The definitive source for role theory is Bruce J. Biddle and Edwin J. Thomas, eds., *Role Theory: Concepts and Research* (New York: John Wiley & Sons, 1966); see also Robin Williams, *American Society*, rev. ed. (New York: Alfred A. Knopf, 1960), pp. 55–73.

3. Biddle and Thomas have found over 250 different concepts used by role analysts; see "The Nature and History of Role Theory," *Role Theory*, chap. 1. For a good brief introduction to role analysis, see Edwin J. Thomas, ed., *Behavioral Science for Social Workers* (New York: Free Press, 1967), pp. 15–50.

4. This was during the famous crisis in October 1962 with the Soviet Union over the Russian nuclear missiles being installed in Cuba.

5. Carle C. Zimmerman, *Family and Civilization* (New York: Harper & Bros., 1947).

6. On the decline of authority in the father role, see E. E. LeMasters, "The Passing of the Dominant Husband-Father," *Journal of Impact of Science on Society* (Paris: UNESCO 21 [1971]).

7. When the first author played semiprofessional baseball in the 1930s, the players chewed tobacco. Today many of them chew bubble gum. See the discussion in Myron Brenton, "Notes on the Feminization of Society," *The American Male* (New York: Coward-McCann, 1966), chap. 3.

8. In 1964 a married couple of low income was prosecuted in Wisconsin for burying an infant without employing a mortuary (news story in the *Wisconsin State Journal*, April 10, 1964). Ancestors of the first author living in rural Ohio always buried their own dead without consulting authorities of any kind—unless a minister was called in to help with the burial rites.

9. In the 1960s a celebrated case in Minnesota resulted in a court order requiring that a university professor enroll his child in either a public or private elementary school approved by the state. The parents in this case had argued that they could give their child a superior education at home. We have lost the news story citations on this case, but it was widely publicized nationally. Compare this with the era of the poet Robert Frost, who sent his children to school only when he felt like it; see Lawrence Thompson, *Robert Frost* (New York: Holt, Rinehart, & Winston, 1966).

10. This word comes from Jerold Fennell, a private Omaha attorney who has spent a tremendous amount of time involved in abortion litigation. Fennell explained that only Utah and Massachusetts are enforcing legislation which makes it mandatory that a minor child inform parents before an abortion; Massachusetts goes a step further, making parental consent to the abortion mandatory. The question, of course, can be argued logically and vociferously from both viewpoints. Our point being, though, that parents can be left with the consequences of an abortion without any foreknowledge.

11. Rose Fitzgerald Kennedy, *Times to Remember* (New York: Doubleday 1974), p. 77.

12. UPI news report, *Wisconsin State Journal*, January 23, 1974.

13. Brim, Orville G. Jr., *Education for Child Rearing* (New York: Russell Sage Foundation), 1959; Max Lerner, *America as a Civilization* (New York: Simon & Schuster, 1957); see also David Riesman et al., *The Lonely Crowd* (New Haven: Yale University Press, 1961), pp. 37–65.

14. See Chapter 11, "Parents and Social Change," for further discussion of the problems of rural parents.

15. See Arthur Pearl, "The Poverty of Psychology—An Indictment," in *Psychological Factors in Poverty*, ed. Vernon L. Allen (Chicago: Markham Publishing, 1970), pp. 357–59.

16. Some of these possibilities are explored in Peter Schrag's study, *Village School Downtown* (Boston: Beacon Press, 1967); see also Benjamin Fine, *Underachievers: How They Can Be Helped* (New York: E. P. Duntton, 1967), chap. 11. There are also some interesting illustrations of new school programs in an

earlier study by James Conant, *Slums and Suburbs* (New York: McGraw-Hill, 1961).

17. See Dwight MacDonald, *Against the American Grain* (New York: Random House, 1962), p. 369.

18. From a study conducted for General Mills by a professional pollster. Parents representing 1,230 families with children under 13 nationwide were polled. Reported in the *Wisconsin State Journal*, April 21, 1977.

19. See E. E. LeMasters, *Blue-Collar Aristrocrats: Life-Styles at a Working-Class Tavern* (Madison: University of Wisconsin Press, 1975).

20. Alvin Toffler, *Future Shock* (New York: Random House, 1970), pp. 207–18.

21. E. E. LeMasters, "Parenthood as Crisis," *Marriage and Family Living* 19 (1957), 352–55.

22. Alice S. Rossi, "Transition to Parenthood," *Marriage and Family Living* 30 (1968), 26–39.

23. Desmond Morris, *The Naked Ape* (New York: McGraw-Hill, 1967), p. 103.

24. See Daniel Goleman's discussion, "Leaving Home: Is There a Right Time To Go?" *Psychology Today*, August 1980, pp. 52–61.

25. John Steinbeck, *The Grapes of Wrath* (New York: Alfred A. Knopf, 1937).

26. See Beatrice A. Wright, "Disability and Discrepance of Expectations," in *Role Theory*, ed. Biddle and Thomas, pp. 159–64.

27. For a discussion of the dyad and triad types of groups, see Theodore Caplow, *Two Against One: Coalitions in Triads* (Englewood Cliffs, N.J.: Prentice-Hall, 1968), p. vi: "In the primary triad of father, mother, and child, the foundation of a coalition may undermine paternal authority before the child is out of the cradle."

28. While serving as a dean of students, the first author was impressed with the number of complaints received from students assigned to three-person rooms. Quite often two of the occupants would gang up on the third person and that student would request a new room assignment. Conflict appeared to happen much less often in two-person rooms.

29. Walter Toman, *Family Constellations* (New York: Springer Publishing, 1964).

30. See Kathleen L. Dubas Jordan, "Parental Perceptions of the Effects of Marital Separation on Children in Nebraska" (Lincoln: University of Nebraska, 1978), p. 66. Similar results were found in Rod Eirick, "Coping as Divorced Single Parents: A Comparative Study of Fathers and Mothers" (Lincoln: University of Nebraska, 1979).

31. Green, *Middle-Class Male Child and Neurosis;* see also David F. Aberle and Kaspar D. Naegele, "Middle-Class Fathers' Occupational Role and the Attitudes toward Children," *American Journal of Orthopsychiatry* 22 (April 1952), pp. 366–78.

32. It would seem that young fathers in the middle class are especially prone to role conflicts in that they are attempting to establish themselves in their occupational role at the very moment when their wives and children need them most. One can see this clearly on the college campus in talking with the wives of junior faculty members. The young men are caught between the pressures "to publish or perish" on the one side, and their young wives' emerging feminism on the other, with feminism's implicit demand for men to be more actively involved with the children and housework.

33. We have reference to the material on parents found in survey studies such as Robert O. Blood, Jr., and Donald M. Wolfe, *Husbands and Wives* (New York:

Free Press, 1960); this is a valuable study but it does not delve into the depths of parental feelings and conflicts.

34. See Margaret Mead, *Male and Female* (New York: William Morrow, 1949).

35. John DeFrain and Rod Eirick, "Coping as Divorced Single Parents: A Comparative Study of Fathers and Mothers, *Family Relations* 30 (1981), 265–74.

36. Sharon Stitt's work was outlined in "Get Away, Parents Advised," *Wisconsin State Journal*, March 28, 1977. John DeFrain and his graduate students interviewed her via teleconference hook-up on April 30, 1981. "You really know your stuff," DeFrain told Ms. Stitt. "What's your background, anyway?" She replied, blushingly, "I'm a single parent with four children, and a high-school dropout." "Terrific!" DeFrain replied. "Education comes from lots of different bottles."

37. Blaine's book was reviewed in "Let Society Raise the Children," *Wisconsin State Journal*, April 7, 1973, section 1, p. 8. The book is *Are Parents Bad for Children?* (New York: Coward, McCann, & Geoghegan, 1973).

38. Lillian Carter, speaking on August 14, 1980, and quoted in *Parade* magazine, February 15, 1981, p. 14

39. Erma Bombeck, "The Family That Plays Together . . . (*Gets On Each Other's Nerves*)." (New York: Warner Brothers Records, 1977).

40. Robert Ardrey, *African Genesis* (New York: Atheneum Publishers, 1965), pp. 202–203.

41. According to a recent report from the U.S. Census Bureau the average number of births anticipated per married woman was 2.2. The study by Martin O'Connell and Carolyn C. Rogers is "Fertility of American Women: June 1979," *Current Population Reports* (Washington, D.C.: U.S. Government Printing Office, 1979). The 2.2 average was virtually unchanged from 1975, but down from 2.4 in 1971 and 2.9 in 1967. The authors said, "It is not certain whether the recent stability in birth expectations is transitional and will lead to further declines in fertility or whether it indicates a new demographic trend in the United States."

42. Ellen Peck and Judith Senderowitz, eds., *Pronatalism: The Myth of Mom & Apple Pie* (New York: Thomas Y. Crowell, 1974).

43. Ann Landers, "Parenthood: Is It All Pain, Little Joy?" *Wisconsin State Journal*, June 16, 1976.

44. The Newsday Service survey was reported in *The Milwaukee Journal*, June 17, 1976.

45. See Daniel R. Miller and Guy E. Swanson, *The Changing American Parent* (New York: John Wiley & Sons, 1958), p. 216.

46. Carole Baker, "Am I Parent Material?" National Alliance for Optional Parenthood, 2010 Massachusetts Avenue, NW, Washington, D.C. 20036.

47. Jean E. Veevers, "Researching Voluntary Childlessness: A Critical Assessment of Current Strategies and Findings," in *Contemporary Families and Alternative Lifestyles* ed. Eleanor Macklin and Roger Rubin (Beverly Hills, Calif.: Sage Publications in press). Also see Veevers' book, *Childless by Choice* (Toronto: Butterworths, 1980).

Chapter 5

1. Herbert Gans has an extensive analysis of social class subcultures and family life in his study *The Urban Villagers* (New York: Free Press, 1962); see also Robin Williams, *American Society*, 3d ed. (New York: Alfred A. Knopf, 1970).

2. On low-income families, see Lee Rainwater, *Behind Ghetto Walls* (Chicago: Aldine Publishing, 1970), also Salvador Minuchin et al., *Families of the Slums* (New York: Basic Books, 1967).

3. The homogenization theory that social class distinctions are disappearing in modern society has been questioned by a series of studies in recent years. See, for example, Gavin Mackenzie, *The Aristocracy of Labor* (New York: Cambridge University Press, 1973); an English study of affluent blue-collar workers by John Goldthorpe et al., *The Affluent Worker in the Class Structure* (New York: Cambridge University Press, 1969); also Gans, *Urban Villagers*.

4. Gerald Handel, "Parenthood and Social Class," in *Parenthood: Its Psychology and Its Psychopathology*, ed. E. James Anthony and Therese Benedek (Boston: Little, Brown, 1970), p. 90.

5. Rainwater has attempted to analyze the stance taken by the average American when he or she stops to think about the poverty group; see Lee Rainwater, "Neutralizing the Disinherited: Some Psychological Aspects of Understanding the Poor," in *Psychological Factors in Poverty*, ed. Vernon L. Allen (Chicago: Markham Publishing, 1970).

6. Michael Harrington, *The Other America* (New York: Macmillan, 1962); some people credit this book with having inspired the so-called war on poverty.

7. See Catherine S. Chilman, "Families in Poverty in the Early 1970s," *Marriage and Family Living* 37 (1975), pp. 49–60. One definition of poverty: half the median U.S. family income. This comes from Kirsten Groubjerg, David Street, and Gerald D. Suttles *Poverty and Social Change* (Chicago: University of Chicago Press, 1978), p. 67. Using this figure, in 1975, 19.4 percent of U.S. families were below the poverty level. Since 1947 the percentage has hovered around 20 percent, ranging from 18.9 to 20.9.

8. Martin Anderson, *Welfare: The Political Economy of Welfare Reform in the United States* (Stanford, Calif.: Hoover Institution Press, 1978).

9. Max Lerner, *America as a Civilization* (New York; Simon & Schuster, 1957), p. 558.

10. See William J. Goode, *After Divorce* (New York: Free Press, 1956), chap. 4.

11. See August B. Hollingshead and Frederick G. Redlich, *Social Class and Mental Illness* (New York: John Wiley & Sons, 1958); see also the analysis of Paul M. Roman and Harrison M. Trice, *Schizophrenia and the Poor* (Ithaca: New York School of Industrial Relations, 1967).

12. See James Conant, *Slums and Suburbs* (New York: McGraw-Hill, 1961).

13. See Marshall B. Clinard, *Sociology of Deviant Behavior*, rev. ed. (New York: Rinehart & Co., 1968), chaps. 6–9.

14. This material is summarized in Alvin L. Schorr, *Slums and Social Insecurity* (Washington, D.C.: U.S. Government Printing Office, 1963), pp. 13–14.

15. News release from Wisconsin Department of Public Health, Madison, Wisconsin, August 24, 1967.

16. For an analysis of alcoholism and social class, see Harrison M. Trice, *Alcoholism in America* (New York: McGraw-Hill, 1966), pp. 21–24.

17. Alfred C. Kinsey et al., *Sexual Behavior in the Human Male* (Philadelphia: W. B. Saunders, 1948), chap. 10; also Kinsey et al., *Sexual Behavior in the Human Female* (Philadelphia: W. B. Saunders, 1953), various chapters.

18. See Alvin L. Schorr, *Poor Kids* (New York: Basic Books, 1966).

19. Professionals who work in the area of child abuse are quick to point out that poor parenting pervades all strata of society: There are rich folks who beat up chil-

dren, just as there are poor folks who do so. But we would wager without flinching that if one were to pick 100 middle-class or above parents at random and compare them to 100 poor parents at random, that the percentage of parents who abuse their children would be much, much greater in the sample of poor parents. One treatment program for abusive and neglectful parents in Lincoln, for example, has 40 parents involved. Only 2 of the 40 parents make more than $10,000 per year; the average family income is $5400. Compare this to the average Lincoln family income of roughly $20,000 and you have a good idea that child abuse and neglect probably is much more common in low-income groups. A counterargument is that rich folks who beat up their childen can buy good counseling and lawyers to keep them out of trouble with the authorities. That is certainly a possiblity and probably happens on occasion. But it is a relatively cynical argument and has no data that we are familiar with to back it up.

20. Ibid.
21. New York Times News Service, "Study of Poor Families Paints Unexpected Picture," *Wisconsin State Journal*, July 17, 1977.
22. Lee Rainwater, *And the Poor Get Children* (Chicago: Quadrangle Books, 1960); also Leslie Westoff and Charles Westoff, *From Now to Zero* (Boston: Little, Brown, 1971).
23. Nathan Glazer and Daniel Patrick Moynihan, *Beyond the Melting Pot* (Cambridge, Mass.: Harvard University and M.I.T. Press, 1963).
24. Arthur Pearl and Frank Riessman, *New Careers for the Poor* (New York: Free Press, 1965).
25. St. Clair Drake and Horace R. Cayton, *Black Metropolis* New York: Harcourt, Brace, 1945). For a later study see Louis Kreisberg, *Mothers in Poverty* (Chicago: Aldine Publishing, 1970).
26. One problem facing these mothers is the lack of adequate daycare facilities for their preschool children; see *Report on Day Care*, Child Welfare Report, no. 14 (Washington, D.C.: U.S. Government Printing Office, 1964). This report shows that in the 1960s for 3 million children under the age of six whose mothers worked ouside of the home, there were only 185,000 places available in approved child-care centers for preschool children. There has been some improvement in this situation in the 1970s. By 1975 there were 326,000 children in daycare, but this represented only 1 percent of all children aged birth to six years old. Does supply meet demand? See M. J. Bane, "Child-care Arrangements of Working Parents." *Monthly Labor Review* 50–56.
27. For an excellent study of lower-class men, see Elliot Liebow, *Tally's Corner* (Boston: Little, Brown, 1967).
28. For a good summary of these problems, see Harry Caudill, "Appalachia: The Dismal Land," in *Poverty: Views from the Left*, ed. Jeremy Larner and Irving Howe (New York: William Morrow, 1968), pp. 264–79.
29. The writer is of the opinion that urban slums, bad as they are, offer some advantages over rural slums—chiefly in the superior welfare services offered in metropolitan areas; for an illustration, see Camille Jeffers, *Living Poor* (Ann Arbor, Mich.: Ann Arbor Publishers, 1967)—a participant-observation study of life in an urban low-income housing project.
30. Gans (*Urban Villagers*, chap. 11) says the lower class views the outside world with suspicion and distrust. In 1966 the median amount of formal schooling completed by nonwhites in the United States was 9.2 years for persons over 25 years of age, see *U.S. Book of Facts* (Washington, D.C.: U.S. Government Printing Office, 1968), p. 116, table 158.

31. Oscar Handlin, *The Uprooted* (Boston: Little, Brown, 1952).

32. August B. Hollingshead, *Elmtown's Youth* (New York: John Wiley & Sons, 1949).

33. For an analysis of the inferior health and inadequate medical services found among American black families, see Thomas F. Pettigrew, *A Profile of the Negro American* (Princeton, N.J.: D. Van Nostrand, 1964); also David R. Hunter, *The Slums* (New York: Free Press, 1964), chap. 7.

34. The other item mentioned most often involved the problem of rearing children when spouses disagree about how they should be reared.

35. Goode, *After Divorce*, chap. 4. Goode's thesis held up in later studies. See K. S. Renne, "Correlates of Dissatisfaction in Marriage," *Journal of Marriage and the Family* 32 (1970) pp. 54–76; and J. Scanzoni, *Sexual Bargaining* (Englewood Cliffs, N.J.: Prentice-Hall, 1972).

36. See William M. Kephart, *The Family, Society, and the Individual*, 3d ed. (Boston: Houghton Mifflin, 1972).

37. See Leonard Benson, "Fatherlessness," *Fatherhood: A Sociological Perspective* (New York: Random House, 1968), chap. 10.

38. See Jacobus Tenbroek, ed., *The Law of the Poor* (San Francisco: Chandler Publishing, 1966); also *The Extension of Legal Services to the Poor* (Washington, D.C.: U.S. Government Printing Office, 1965); also the *U.S. Riot Commission Report* (New York: Bantam Books, 1968).

39. There is a mass of material on the blue-collar family. Conveninent summaries will be found in Gans, *Urban Villagers* and E. E. LeMasters, *Blue-Collar Aristocrats: Life-Styles at a Working-Class Tavern* (Madison: University of Wisconsin Press, 1975).

40. Robert S. and Helen M. Lynd, *Middletown* (New York: Harcourt, Brace, & Co., 1929).

41. See Goldthorpe et al., *Affluent Worker in the Class Structure*.

42. For a brief summary of these trends, see George Meany, *Labor Looks at Capitalism*, AFL-CIO Publication, no. 139 (Washington, D.C., 1966). In 1956 the number of white-collar jobs exceeded blue-collar jobs for the first time in the United States; see Michael Harrington, "The Politics of Poverty," in *Poverty: Views from the Left*, ed. Jeremy Larner and Irving Howe (New York: William Morrow, 1968), p. 18.

43. These data are reviewed in F. Ivan Nye and Lois Wladis Hoffman, *The Employed Mother in America* (Chicago: Rand McNally, 1963), pp. 7–16.

44. LeMasters, *Blue-Collar Aristocrats*.

45. See Nathan Hurvitz, "Marital Strain in the Blue-Collar Family," in Arthur B. Shostak and William Gomberg, ed., *Blue-Collar World* (Englewood Cliffs, N.J.: Prentice-Hall, 1964), pp. 92–109; also Mirra Komarovsky, *Blue-Collar Marriage* (New York: Random House, 1964).

46. Reference is made to the CBS TV series, "All in the Family." Various labor leaders have been quoted in the daily press as not liking the character part of Archie Bunker.

47. *Wisconsin State Journal*, July 5, 1972.

48. See, for example; Arnold Green, "The Middle Class Male Child and Neurosis," *American Sociological review* 11 (1946), pp. 31–41; although based on very inadequate data, this paper has been widely cited as evidence that the middle-class family is "neurotic." See also Robert F. Winch, *The Modern Family* (New York: Holt, Rinehart & Winston, 1952); Winch's criticism of middle-class parents was considerably softened in later editions of this text.

49. Some of the features of the consumer society are discussed in John Kenneth Galbraith, *The Affluent Society* (Boston: Houghton Mifflin, 1958); see also Alvin Toffler, *Future Shock* (New York: Random House, 1970).

50. Lerner, *America as a Civilization*, pp. 488–95.

51. There is also a tendency for the father at this class level to moonlight (hold a second job) to achieve a decent standard of living.

52. See Goode, *After Divorce*, chaps. 4 and 5.

53. See E. E. LeMasters, "Social Class Mobility and Family Integration," *Marriage and Family Living* 16 (1954), pp. 226–32. For a different version of this matter, see Eugene Litwak, "Extended Kin Relations in an Industrial Society," in *Social Structure and the Family*, ed. Ethel Shanas and Gordon F. Streib (Englewood Cliffs, N.J.: Prentice-Hall, 1965), pp. 290–323.

54. See Gans, *Urban Villagers*, p. 264.

55. These observations are based on a survey of 540 upper-middle-class students attending an expensive private liberal arts college where the first author was teaching (unpublished study completed in the late 1950s).

56. Another study concluded that upper-middle-class and upper-class families are more concerned about status maintenance than they are about social class mobility. See Allan Schnaiberg and Sheldon Goldenberg, "Closing the Circle: The Impact of Children on Parental Status," *Marriage and the Family* 37 (1975), pp. 937–53.

57. In his penetrating analysis, Keniston argues that the center of the campus revolt in the 1960s was students from the upper-middle class. See Kenneth Keniston, *Youth and Dissent* (New York: Harcourt Brace Jovanovich, 1971); also Charles A. Reich, *The Greening of America* (New York: Random House, 1970).

58. Cat Stevens, "But I Might Die Tonight," from *Tea for the Tillerman* (Hollywood, Calif.: A & M Records, 1970).

59. See Melvin Kohn, *Class and Conformity* (Homewood, Ill.: Dorsey Press, 1969). Kohn's findings were confirmed by Viktor Gecas and F. Ivan Nye in "Sex and Class Differences in Parent-Child Interaction, A Test of Kohn's Hypothesis," *Marriage and the Family* 36 (1974), pp. 42–49. For an earlier study with similar conclusions, see Daniel R. Miller and Guy E. Swanson, *The Changing American Parent* (New York: John Wiley & Sons, 1958).

60. Paul M. Blumberg and P. W. Paul, "Upper-Class Families," *Marriage and the Family* 37 (1975), pp. 63–77.

61. Rose Fitzgerald Kennedy, *Times to Remember* (New York: Doubleday, 1974).

62. See the two-volume study of the life of Churchill's mother, *Jennie*, by Ralph G. Martin (Englewood Cliffs, N.J.: Prentice-Hall, Inc., 1969–71).

63. Anita Leslie, *The Marlborough House Set* (New York: Doubleday, 1973), p. 10.

64. See Edward VIII, *A King's Story* (New York: G. P. Putnam's sons, 1951).

65. See Lennard Bickel, *Rise Up to Life: The Man Who Made Penicillin and Gave it to the World* (New York: Charles Scribner's Sons, 1972).

66. Joseph P. Lash, *Franklin and Eleanor* (New York: W. W. Norton, 1971).

67. John Bartlow Martin, *Adlai Stevenson of Illinois* (New York: Doubleday, 1976).

68. Harold Acton, *Nancy Mitford: A Memoir* (New York: Harper & Row, 1975).

69. Jeffrey Potter, *Men, Money, and Magic: The Story of Dorothy Schiff* (New York: Coward, McCann, Geohegan, 1976), p. 30.

70. Sloan Wilson, *What Shall We Wear To the Party?* (New York: Arbor House, 1976), p. 23.

71. Steven Weed, *My Search for Patty Hearst* (New York: Crown Publishers, 1976).

72. Andrew Tobias, *Fire and Ice: The Story of Charles Revson* (New York: William Morrow, 1976).

73. Christina Crawford, *Mommie Dearest* (New York: William Morrow, 1978).

74. Barbara Goldsmith, *Little Gloria: Happy At Last* (New York: Alfred Knopf, 1980).

75. Doris Lilly, *Those Fabulous Greeks* (New York: Cowles, 1970).

76. Bernard Livingston, *Their Turf* (New York: Arbor House, 1973).

77. See Raymond B. Fosdick, *John D. Rockefeller, Jr.* (New York: Harper & Bros., 1956).

78. Elliot Roosevelt and James Brough, *An Untold Story: The Roosevelts of Hyde Park* (New York: G. P. Putnam's Sons, 1973).

79. George C. Kirstein, *The Rich: Are They Different?* (Boston: Houghton Mifflin, 1968).

80. This family ranks among the top families of Wisconsin. The family business has a worldwide reputation and one member of the family has been governor of the state.

81. C. G. McDaniel, Associated Press, "Super-Rich Kids Are Like the Poor, Doctor Reports." *Wisconsin State Journal*, August 9, 1978.

Chapter 6

1. See, for example, Leon H. Rottmann and William H. Meredith, "Indochinese Refugee Families: Their Strengths and Needs," *Family Strengths 4* ed., Nick Stinnett, John DeFrain, Kay King, Herbert Lingren, George Rowe, Sally Van Zandt, and Rosanne Williams (Lincoln: University of Nebraska Press, 1983). For a look at the problems inherent in resettling thousands of Cuban refugees, see "The Cuban Conundrum," *Newsweek*, September 29, 1980, pp. 30–31; and "The Welcome Wears Thin: Homeless and Jobless, Many Cuban Refugees Are Getting Restless," *Time*, September 1, 1980, pp. 8–10. Generally, as more and more refugee and immigrant families seek to enter the United States the search intensifies for ways to stem the tide. There is a good discussion of this in "Closing The Golden Door," *Time*, May 18, 1981, pp. 24–27. Any new group to enter the United States automatically becomes a minority, in a sense, especially if their cultural background is alien to Western industrial culture. Problems of acculturation versus maintenance of cultural identity abound.

2. For an analysis of the concept of minority group, see J. Milton Yinger, *A Minority Group in American Society* (New York: McGraw-Hill, 1965), chap. 3.

3. See Robert Staples, "Toward a Sociology of the Black Family," *Marriage and the Family 33* (1971), pp. 119–38. The quotation is from p. 133.

4. Marie Ferguson Peters, "The Black Family: Perpetuating the Myths," *The Family Coordinator 23* (1974), pp. 349–57.

5. Marie Peters, "Strengths of Black Families," *Family Strengths 3: Roots of Well-Being*, ed. Nick Stinnett, John DeFrain, Kay King, Patricia Knaub, and George Rowe (Lincoln: University of Nebraska Press, 1981), pp. 73–91.

6. Robert Hill, *The Strengths of Black Families* (New York: Emerson-Hall, 1972).

7. Harriette Pipes McAdoo, "Black Kinship," *Psychology Today*, May 1979, pp. 67–110.

8. For what appears to be the definitive account of the long black struggle for educational equality, see Richard Kluger, *Simple Justice* (New York: Alfred A. Knopf, 1975). Kluger notes that though we are a long way from desegregation of

our public schools, considerable progress has been made. For a look at the right-wing white counterrevolution to the black fight for educational equality, see Francis M. Wilhoit, *The Politics of Massive Resistance* (New York: George Braziller, 1973). In the 1950s, white southerners launched their massive resistance to the school desegregation movement. And, finally, see Barbara Jordan and Shelly Hearon, *Barbara Jordan* (Garden City, New York: Doubleday, 1979), for a good portrait of one black family that made it in spite of all its handicaps.

9. Of all white children 17 years old and under, 12.2 percent were living in poverty; of all black children 17 and under, 39.7 percent were living in poverty. "Table 11. Age and Sex—Persons by Poverty Status in 1977, Sex of Head, Family Relationship, Race, and Spanish Origin," *Current Population Reports*, Series P-60, No. 119 (Washington, D.C.: U.S. Department of Commerce, Bureau of the Census, 1979), p. 50.

10. The poverty syndrome is analyzed by Catherine S. Chilman, "Families in Poverty in the Early 1970s," *Marriage and the Family* 37 (1975), pp. 49–60.

11. See Andrew Billingsley, *Black Families in White America* (Englewood Cliffs, N.J.: Prentice-Hall, 1968).

12. The net migration of blacks from the South to other parts of the United States is estimated to have been about 5 million up to 1966; see the *U.S. Riot Commission Report* (New York: Bantam Books, 1968), p. 240.

13. In 1960, for example, nonwhite males in the United States were reported to have an average of 7.9 years of formal education. See Kenneth B. Clark and Talcott Parsons, eds., *The Negro American* (Boston: Beacon Press, 1966), p. 84.

14. See Angela Davis, *Angela Davis: An Autobiography* (New York. Random House, 1974).

15. Kenneth Keniston, *Youth and Dissent* (New York: Harcourt Brace Jovanovich, 1971). One of the first author's sons was arrested and charged with a felony in a campus battle between students and the police over the invasion of Laos; the second author, a youth in the 1960s, was active in many antiwar demonstrations.

16. This attempt to find African roots is documented by Richard Wright, the late black writer, in his personal journey back to the home of his ancestors. See Constance Webb, *Richard Wright* (New York: G. P. Putnam's Sons, 1968). Alex Haley, of course, touched a nationwide heartstring with the publication in 1976 of his widely acclaimed novel *Roots* (Garden City, N.J.: Doubleday), which traced six generations of his black family back to a village in Africa. The subsequent television productions reached more Americans than any other presentation in history. For an account of Haley's strong family ties and of how *Roots* came to be written, see his "Families in Black and White," *Family Strengths 3: Roots of Well-Being*, ed. Nick Stinnett, John DeFrain, Kay King, Patricia Knaub, and George Rowe (Lincoln: University of Nebraska Press, 1981), pp. 5–16.

17. "Reagan and the Blacks," *Newsweek*, July 13, 1981, pp. 20–21. "Goodbye to the Old Guard: The Civil Rights Movement Braces for an Uncertain Future," *Time*, September 21, 1981, pp. 20–21.

18. This material is summarized in William A. Brophy and Sophie D. Aberle, *The Indian: America's Unfinished Business* (Norman: University of Oklahoma Press, 1966); and Alan L. Sorkin, *The Urban American Indian* (Lexington, Mass.: Lexington Books, 1978).

19. On the precarious condition of the Menominee, see Joyce M. Erdman, *Wisconsin Indians* (Madison, Wisc.: Governor's Commission on Human Rights, 1966); problems of the Navaho are reviewed in Brophy and Aberle, *The Indian*.

20. The language problems of Indian school children are reviewed in Brophy and Aberle, *The Indian;* see also William T. Hagan, *American Indians* (Chicago: University of Chicago Press, 1961).

21. For a discussion of reservation Indians and urban Indians, see Vine Deloria, Jr., *Custer Died for Your Sins* (New York: Macmillan, 1969). The reservation versus nonreservation statistics are from the assistant director for financial management, Bureau of Indian Affairs, Department of the Interior, Washington, D.C., in a report entitled "Indian Population and Labor Force, April 1979."

22. On the failure of the reservation system, see Dale Van Every, *Disinherited* (New York: William Morrow, 1966).

23. For a discussion of culture conflict between Indians and white society, see Aberle and Brophy, *The Indian;* also Dee Brown, *Bury My Heart at Wounded Knee* (New York: Holt, Rinehart & Winston, 1970).

24. The poverty data on American Indians are discussed in Brophy and Aberle, *The Indian.*

25. See Michael Harrington, *The Other America* (New York: Macmillan, 1963).

26. Surveys of the Menominee Indians in Wisconsin have revealed that, in the late 1960s, at least 70 percent of the children in this group were in immediate need of dental care (Wisconsin Department of Health and Social Service, personal communication). In the book by Erdman, (*Wisconsin Indians,* p. 57) the statement is made: "Indian health is approximately a generation behind that of the non-Indian population in Wisconsin."

27. For an interesting discussion of identity problems among American Indians, see Erik H. Erikson, "Childhood in Two American Indian Tribes," *Childhood and Society,* 2d ed. (New York: W. W. Norton, 1963), part II.

28. A *Milwaukee Journal* news release, April 5, 1968, stated that the Indian suicide rate in Idaho is 100 times the national average. The first author has been unable to confirm this figure from other sources.

29. Brophy and Aberle (*The Indian,* pp. 162–63) state that the Indian birthrate is at least twice that of the national average and perhaps higher; also, see Alan L. Sorkin, *The Urban American Indian* (Lexington, Mass.: Lexington Books, 1978).

30. Brophy and Aberle (*The Indian*) discuss the problem of defining who is an Indian and of determining the number of Indians in American society.

31. "1980 Census Population Totals for Racial and Spanish Origin Groups in U.S. Announced by Census Bureau," *U.S. Department of Commerce News* (Washington, D.C.: Bureau of the Census, February 23, 1981), p. 1.

32. See Deloria, *Custer,* for a discussion of white stereotypes about Indians.

33. The poor people's march on Washington, in the summer of 1968, represented one of the first efforts of the American Indian to work with American blacks to solve or alleviate their mutual problems. See Stan Steiner, *The New Indians* (New York: Harper & Row, 1968), chap. 19.

34. Van Every, *Disinherited,* argues that the Indians could have defeated the Europeans when they first invaded America if the Indians had been united.

35. Deloria, *Custer,* and Steiner, *New Indians,* discuss the efforts to combine all Indians into one effective political force.

36. "1980 Census Population Totals for Racial and Spanish Origin Groups in U.S. Announced by Census Bureau," *U.S. Department of Commerce News* (Washington, D.C.: Bureau of the Census, February 23, 1981), p. 1.

37. Most of the problems of the Mexican-American family are discussed in Carey McWilliams, *North from Mexico: The Spanish-Speaking People in the United*

States (New York: Greenwood Press, 1968); also Stan Steiner, *La Raza: The Mexican Americans* (New York: Harper & Row, 1970).

38. Alfredo Mirandé, "The Chicano Family: A Reanalysis of Conflicting Views," *Journal of Marriage and the Family*, November 1977, pp. 747–56; and Alfredo Mirandé, "A Reinterpretation of Male Dominance in the Chicano Family," *The Family Coordinator*, October 1979, pp. 473–79.

39. Vicky L. Cromwell and Ronald E. Cromwell, "Perceived Dominance in Decision-Making and Conflict Resolution Among Anglo, Black and Chicano Couples," *Journal of Marriage and the Family*, November 1978, pp. 749–59.

40. Glenn R. Hawkes and Minna Taylor, "Power Structure in Mexican and Mexican-American Farm Labor Families," *Journal of Marriage and the Family* 37 (1975), pp. 807–11.

41. For a definitive discussion of Puerto Ricans in the United States, see Oscar Lewis, *La Vida* (New York: Random House, 1965).

42. About 80 percent of the Puerto Ricans in the United States are classified as white by the Bureau of the Census. See Clarence Senior, *The Puerto Ricans* (Chicago: Quadrangle Books, 1965), p. 46.

43. Oscar Lewis, *La Vida*, introduction.

44. See "1980 Census Population Totals for Racial and Spanish Origin Groups in U.S. Announced by Census Bureau," *U.S. Department of Commerce News* (Washington, D.C.: Bureau of the Census, February 23, 1981), p. 1. Also, Kal Wagenheim, "A Survey of Puerto Ricans on the U.S. Mainland in the 1970s" (New York: Prager Publishers, 1975), p. vi.

45. See Senior, *Puerto Ricans*, pp. 37–40, for a discussion of this point.

46. Lewis (*La Vida*, introduction) reports that 26 percent of the sample he studied in New York City had households headed by a woman; about half of the marriages in his New York sample were of the consensual or "free union" type.

47. A comparison of the kin network and its functions in Puerto Ricans in New York City may be found in Lewis, *La Vida*.

48. Senior (*Puerto Ricans*, p. 97) reports that Puerto Ricans in New York City are overrepresented in the poverty group by about two and a half times.

49. Wagenheim, "Survey of Puerto Ricans," p. 6.

50. Senior, *Puerto Ricans*, pp. 108–9.

51. Lloyd H. Rogler, *Migrant in the City: The Life of a Puerto Rican Action Group* (New York: Basic Books, 1972).

52. A good analysis of the three major religious groups in our society may be found in Will Herberg, *Protestant, Catholic, Jew* (New York: Doubleday, 1956). A very useful book on Jews in America is the work of Sidney Goldstein and Calvin Goldscheider, *Jewish Americans* (Englewood Cliffs, N.J.: Prentice-Hall, 1968).

53. See Michael Selzer, ed., *Kike!: Anti-Semitism in America* (New York: World Publishing 1972) for an extensive study of anti-Semitism in the United States.

54. See "Civil Liberties: Skokie and the Nazis," *Newsweek*, July 3, 1978, p. 31. Even though a long legal battle in the courts cleared the way for the Nazis' march through Skokie, they cancelled and chose to demonstrate in downtown Chicago instead. At their first appearance in front of the Federal Building, 25 uniformed Nazis were confronted by 5,000 angry counterdemonstrators and protected by 1,800 police.

55. Goldstein and Goldscheider, in *Jewish Americans*, have an analysis of three generations of Jewish families in Providence, Rhode Island. Judith R. Kramer and Seymour Leventman have a three-generation analysis of Jews in the St.

Paul-Minneapolis metropolitan area in the *Children of the Gilded Ghetto* (New Haven: Yale University Press, 1961). Milton Meltzer in *Taking Root: Jewish Immigrants in America* (New York: Farrar, Straus & Giroux, 1976) destroys the myth that Jews had money when they came to the United States. He outlines the terrible struggle Jewish parents had in this country to give their children an education and a chance for advancement.

56. George Cornell, "Divorce Among Jews Called Shocking Trend," *Wisconsin State Journal*, May 28, 1976, section 5, p. 4.

57. On the phenomenal success of the Japanese in America since World War II, see Albert Q. Maisel, *They All Chose America* (New York: Thomas Nelson & Sons, 1957), p. 133; on the Chinese-Americans see B. L. Sung, *Mountain of Gold* (New York: Macmillan 1967). Both of these minority groups have achieved college attendance records substantially above that of the general population. The Chinese, as most other minorities, have often been viewed in this country as being sneaky, mysterious, and untrustworthy. This image has slowly changed since the end of World War II. Two books that focus on the Chinese contributions to the building of this country and the white backlash to this perceived economic threat are Cheng-Tsu Wu (Ed.), *"Chink!": Anti-Chinese Prejudice in America* (New York: World Publishing, 1972); and Stan Steiner, *Fusang: The Chinese Who Built America* (New York: Harper & Row, 1979). Other good books on the topic are Paul K. T. Sih and Leonard B. Allen, eds., *The Chinese in America* (New York: St. John's University Press, 1976); Francis L. K. Hsu, *The Challenge of the American Dream: The Chinese in the United States* (Belmont, Calif.: Wadsworth, 1971); Harry H. L. Kitano, *Japanese Americans*, 2d ed. (Englewood Cliffs, N.J.: Prentice-Hall, 1976); Darrel Montero, *Japanese Americans: Changing Patterns of Ethnic Affiliation Over Three Generations* (Boulder, Colo.: Westview Press, 1980); and Stanford M. Lyman, *The Asian in North America* (Santa Barbara, Calif.: ABC-Clio, 1977).

58. "Homosexual Doctors," *Medical World News*, January 25, 1974, p. 41.

59. Bonnie M. Mucklow and Gladys K. Phelan, "Lesbian and Traditional Mothers' Responses to Adult Response to Child Behavior and Self-Concept," *Psychological Reports* 44 (1979), pp. 880–82.

60. Mildred D. Pagelow, "Heterosexual and Lesbian Single Mothers: A Comparison of Problems, Coping, and Solutions," *Journal of Homosexuality* 5 (1980), pp. 189–203.

61. Karen Gail Lewis, "Children of Lesbians: Their Point of View," *Social Work*, May 1980, pp. 198–203.

62. Brian Miller, "Gay Fathers and Their Children," *The Family Coordinator*, October 1979, pp. 544–52.

63. Bruce Voeller and James Walters, "Gay Fathers," *The Family Coordinator*, April 1978, pp. 149–57.

64. See Senior, *Puerto Ricans*, p. 18.

Chapter 7

1. Edward A. Strecker, M.D., *Their Mothers' Sons* (New York: J. B. Lippincott, 1946).

2. Philip Wylie, *A Generation of Vipers* (New York: Rinehart, 1942).

3. The writers have been unable to locate any research on the readership of controversial books such as this.

4. Geoffrey Gorer, *The American People*, rev. ed. (New York: W. W. Norton, 1964), p. 64.

5. See chapter 2 in Gorer's book.

6. Robert Ardrey, *African Genesis* (New York: Atheneum, 1965), p. 165.

7. Betty Friedan, *The Feminine Mystique* (New York: W. W. Norton, 1963); this book has been a continuous best seller for several years.

8. Alice S. Rossi, "Equality between the Sexes," *Daedalus* (Spring 1964), pp. 607–52.

9. See Norman A. Polansky et al., *Roots of Futility* (San Francisco: Jossey-Bass, 1972), reviewed by Catherine S. Chilman, *Social Work* 18 (1973), pp. 115–16.

10. Erik H. Erikson, *Childhood and Society*, 2d ed. (New York: W. W. Norton, 1963), p. 291.

11. Max Lerner, *America as a Civilization* (New York: Simon & Schuster, 1957), p. 551.

12. Erik H. Erikson, *Childhood and Society*, 2d ed. (New York: W. W. Norton, 1963), p. 289.

13. The first author has attempted to analyze this family revolution in a paper written for UNESCO; see E. E. LeMasters, "The Passing of the Dominant Husband-Father," *Impact of Science on Society* 21 (Paris, 1971), pp. 21–30.

14. A very readable analysis of social change in our society since 1900 may be found in Frederick Lewis Allen, *The Big Change* (New York: Harper & Bros., 1952).

15. For a discussion of how business kicks worn-out executives upstairs, see Alfred P. Sloan, Jr., *My Years with General Motors* (New York: Doubleday, 1964); also Peter F. Drucker, *Concept of the Corporation* (Boston: Beacon Press, 1946).

16. For a good, brief summary of the changing position of women in American society, see Margaret Mead and Frances Balgley Kaplan, *American Women* (New York: Charles Scribner's Sons, 1965), pp. 78–95.

17. For a detailed analysis of the role of the wife-mother in the economics of the modern American family, see Robert O. Blood, Jr., and Donald M. Wolfe, "The Economic Function," *Husbands and Wives* (New York: Free Press, 1960), chap. 4.

18. One has only to compare Freud's analysis of the father in Victorian society with that of Ackerman to see the startling change in the position of fathers since the 19th century; see Nathan Ackerman, *The Psychodynamics of Family Life* (New York: Basic Books, 1958).

19. See Eugene O'Neill, *Long Day's Journey into Night* (New Haven: Yale University Press, 1956). Other interesting material on O'Neill's parents may be found in Arthur and Barbara Gelb, *O'Neill* (New York: Harper & Bros., 1962).

20. See, for example, the description of the American father in Ackerman, *Psychodynamics of Family Life*, pp. 177–81.

21. For discussion of the American male, see Myron Brenton, *The American Male* (New York: Coward-McCann, 1966); Elaine Kendall, *The Upper Hand* (Boston: Little, Brown, 1965); also Charles W. Ferguson, *The Male Attitude* (Boston: Little, Brown, 1966).

22. See Midge Decter, *The New Chastity and Other Arguments against Women's Liberation* (New York: Capricorn Books, 1974); and Betty Friedan, *The Second Stage* (New York: Summit Books, 1981).

23. The basic research on the impact of the depression on families will be found in: Ruth Shonle Cavan and Katherine Howland Ranck, *The Family and the Depression* (Chicago: University of Chicago Press, 1938); Mirra Komarovsky, *The Unemployed Man and His Family* (New York: Dryden Press, 1940); Robert C. Angell, *The Family Encounters the Depression* (New York: Charles Scribner's Sons, 1936).

24. See Alvin Schorr, *Poor Kids* (New York: Basic Books, 1966); also a more recent study of public welfare policy and its impact on low-income families: *Explorations in Social Policy* (New York: Basic Books, 1968).

25. For an excellent discussion as to how mothers take over male roles when their husbands are in the armed forces, see the research reported in Reuben Hill, *Families under Stress* (New York: Harper & Bros., 1949).

26. See Strecker, *Their Mothers' Sons.*

27. Ferdinand Lundberg and Marynia A. Farnham, *Modern Women: The Lost Sex* (New York: Grosset & Dunlap, 1947). This is one of the most hysterical attacks on the American mother the writers have seen.

28. Ibid., p. 303.

29. For an extensive discussion of social class bias in clinic and private-practice case records, see August B. Hollingshead and Frederick C. Redlich, *Social Class and Mental Illness* (New York: John Wiley & Sons, 1958).

30. Lundberg and Farnham, *Modern Woman.*

31. Strecker, *Their Mother's Sons.*

32. On the use of control groups, see Claire Selltiz, Lawrence S. Wrightsman, and Stuart W. Cook, *Research Methods in Social Relations*, 3rd ed. (New York: Holt, Rinehart & Winston, 1976), pp. 128–129.

33. For a dramatic illustration of the value of good research controls, see how Clark Vincent's analysis of the unmarried mother in our society differs from that of Leontine Young. The two studies are Clark Vincent, *Unmarried Mothers* (New York: Free Press, 1961), and Leontine Young, *Out of Wedlock* (New York: McGraw-Hill, 1954).

34. A striking example of the value of a well-designed control group will be found in Henry J. Meyer, Edgar F. Borgatta, and Wyatt C. Jones, *Girls at Vocational High* (New York: Russell Sage Foundation, 1965).

35. See Karen Horney, *The Neurotic Personality of Our Time* (New York: W. W. Norton, 1937), for a discussion of the interaction of culture conflict and personality conflict.

36. A famous analysis of culture conflicts in American society is that of Robert S. Lynd, *Knowledge for What?* (Princeton, N.J.: Princeton University Press, 1948), pp. 60–63.

37. Lerner, *America as a Civilization*; David Riesman et al., *The Lonely Crowd* (New York: Yale University Press, 1961); Orville G. Brim, Jr., *Education for Child Rearing* (New York: Russell Sage Foundation, 1959).

38. Brim, *Education for Child Rearing*, p. 68.

39. Orville G. Brim, Jr., and Jerome Kagan, "Constancy and Change: A View of the Issues," *Constancy and Change in Human Development*, ed. Orville G. Brim, Jr., and Jerome Kagan (Cambridge, Mass.: Harvard University Press, 1980), pp. 1–25.

40. The full-time mother concept is discussed in Rossi, "Equality between the Sexes."

41. News story, *New York Times*, August 4, 1969.

42. This marital concept of "togetherness" is discussed in Lerner, *America as a Civilization.*

43. Herbert Gans' study of working-class couples in Boston concluded that these married couples did not subscribe to marital "togetherness." See *The Urban Villagers* (New York: Free Press, 1962); also E. E. LeMasters, *Blue-Collar Aristocrats* (Madison: University of Wisconsin Press, 1975).

44. See Chapter 4, "Role analysis of parenthood."

45. Associated Press, "Women Generally Oversee Finances." *Wisconsin State Journal,* August 25, 1977.

46. Richard Carter, *The Gentle Legions* (New York: Doubleday, 1961).

47. Ibid., "The Polio Triumph," chap. 4.

48. Ibid., p. 21.

49. Reuben Hill, "Sociological Frameworks for Family Study," paper presented at a meeting sponsored by the Department of Psychiatry, School of Medicine, University of Wisconsin, December 1967.

50. "Husbands and Wives as Earners: An Analysis of Family Data," *Monthly Labor Review,* February 1981, pp. 46–53. The figures of mothers' employment by race are instructive: white, 55.4 percent; black 66.3 percent; Hispanic, 53.9 percent.

51. Hedrick Smith, *The Russians* (New York: New York Times Quadrangle Books, 1976), p. 136. A related book of interest is Lionel Tiger and Joseph Shepher, *Women in the Kubbutz* (New York: Harcourt, Brace Jovanovich, 1975). The researchers concluded that the Israeli kibbutz or collective farm has failed in its efforts to achieve sexual equality, even though conditions for this were excellent. The authors, along the same line of Tiger's earlier writing, believe that bioorganic differences between males and females predispose social experiments such as the kibbutz to failure.

52. "The Superwoman Squeeze," *Time* Magazine, May 19, 1980, p. 73.

53. Claire Etaugh, "Effects of Nonmaternal Care on Children: Research Evidence and Popular Views," *American Psychologist,* April 1980, pp. 309–19.

54. Margaret M. Poloma, Brian F. Pendleton, and T. Neal Garland, "Reconsidering the Dual-Career Marriage: A Longitudinal Approach," *Journal of Family Issues* 2 (1981), p. 220.

55. Suzanne Model, "Housework by Husbands: Determinants and Implications," *Journal of Family Issues* 2 (1981), pp. 235–36.

56. Arland Thornton, University of Michigan Survey Research Center.

57. Colette Dowling, *The Cinderella Complex: Women's Hidden Fear of Independence* (New York: Summit Books, 1981). Dowling's remarks come from a teleconference dialog she had with faculty and students of the Department of Human Development and the Family, University of Nebraska-Lincoln in the spring of 1982.

58. A good source book on the Depression of the 1930s is David A. Shannon, ed., *The Great Depression* (Englewood Cliffs, N.J.: Prentice-Hall, 1960).

59. See Cavan and Ranck, *Family and the Depression;* Komarovsky, *Unemployed Man;* and Angell, *Family Encounters the Depression.*

60. See Susan Gettleman and Janet Markowitz, *The Courage to Divorce* (New York: Ballantine Books, 1975).

61. The divorce rate is actually not an accurate index of the amount of marital

failure in our society. It fails to include many separations, desertions, and "holy deadlock" marriages that are failures but have not been terminated.

62. See Murray A. Straus, Richard J. Gelles, and Suzanne K. Steinmetz, *Behind Closed Doors: Violence in the American Family* (Garden City, New York: Anchor Press/Doubleday, 1980).

63. Besides the 11.7 percent of the households headed by a single female, another 5.6 percent are headed by a single male for a total of 17.3 percent. U.S. Bureau of the Census, *Current Population Reports*, Series P-20, No. 349, Table 55, 1979.

64. Some of the problems of the American male are discussed in Myron Brenton, *The American Male* (New York: Coward-McCann, 1966); see also Warren Farrell, *The Liberated Man* (New York: Bantam Books, 1975).

65. Ashley Montagu, *The Natural Superiority of Women* (New York: Macmillan, 1968).

66. These studies will be reviewed in Chapter 8, "The American father."

67. William O'Neill, *Everyone was Brave: The Rise and Fall of Feminism in America* (Chicago: Quadrangle Books, 1969). By the word "fall" in the title, O'Neill means that the first feminine revolution after World War I was only partially successful.

68. For descriptions of how English upper-class boys are sent away to boarding schools, see the autobiography of Harold Macmillan, *Winds of Change* (New York: Harper & Row, 1966); also Randolph S. Churchill, *Winston S. Churchill* (New York: Houghton Mifflin, 1966). This first volume deals with the childhood of Winston Churchill. For an account of how Franklin D. Roosevelt was saved from a doting mother, see the account of his years at Groton in John Gunther, *Roosevelt in Retrospect* (New York: Harper & Bros., 1950).

69. On the Jewish mother, see Martha Wolfenstein, "Two Types of Jewish Mothers," in *The Jews: Social Patterns of an American Group*, ed. M. Sklare (New York: Free Press, 1958).

70. On the Italian mom, see Irving R. Levine, *Main Street, Italy* (New York: Doubleday, 1963), p. 24. Levine, a foreign correspondent for one of the national television networks in the United States, who was stationed in Rome, claims that no mothers anywhere spoil their sons as do the Italian mothers. For another treatment of the Italian mother, this one by an Italian, see Luigi Barzini, *The Italians* (New York: Atheneum Publishers, 1964), especially chapter 11, "The Power of the Family."

71. Sylvia Porter, "What's a Housewife Worth?" *Wisconsin State Journal*, October 9, 1978.

72. See Shirley Radl, *Mother's Day Is Over* (New York: Charterhouse Publishers, 1973); Ellen Peck, *The Baby Trap* (New York: Pinnacle Books, 1973); Anna and Arnold Silverman, *The Case against Having Children* (New York: David McKay, 1971); Ellen Peck and Judith Senderwitz, eds., *Pronatalism: The Myth of Mom & Apple Pie* (New York: Thomas Y. Crowell, 1974).

73. Marilyn French, *The Women's Room* (New York: Jove/Harcourt Brace Jovanovich, 1979), pp. 68–69.

74. Jessie Bernard, *The Future of Motherhood* (New York: Penguin Books, 1975); Jane Howard, *A Different Woman* (New York: E. P. Dutton, 1973).

75. Jane Howard, *A Different Woman*, p. 27.

76. James D. Wright, "Are Working Women *Really* More Satisfied? Evidence From

Several National Surveys," *Journal of Marriage and the Family*, May 1978, pp. 301–13.

77. Nick Stinnett, Greg Sanders, and John DeFrain. "A Nation-Wide Study of Strong Families," in *Family Strengths 3: The Roots of Well-Being*, ed. Nick Stinnett, John DeFrain, Kay King, Patricia Knaub, and George Rowe (Lincoln: University of Nebraska Press, 1981).

78. Betty Friedan, *The Second Stage* (New York: Summit Books, 1981). Quotes by Friedan and Jong taken from John Leo, "New Frontier for Feminism: Friedan Says the Family Needs Attention," *Time* Magazine, October 12, 1981, p. 118.

Chapter 8

1. Charles W. Ferguson, *The Male Attitude* (Boston: Little, Brown, 1966).

2. Elaine Kendall, *The Upper Hand* (Boston: Little, Brown, 1965).

3. Myron Brenton, *The American Male* (New York: Coward-McCann, 1966).

4. Margaret Mead, *Male and Female* (New York: William Morrow, 1949).

5. Desmond Morris, *The Naked Ape* (New York: McGraw-Hill, 1967).

6. Leonard Benson, *Fatherhood: A Sociological Perspective* (New York: Random House, 1968).

7. Robert R. Sears et al., *Patterns of Child Rearing* (Evanston, Ill.: Row, Peterson, 1957).

8. Daniel R. Miller and Guy E. Swanson, *The Changing American Parent* (New York: John Wiley & Sons, 1958).

9. Robert O. Blood, Jr., and Donald M. Wolfe, *Husbands and Wives* (New York: Free Press, 1960).

10. William J. Goode, *After Divorce* (New York: Free Press, 1956).

11. Clark Vincent, *Unmarried Mothers* (New York: Free Press, 1961).

12. David A. Goslin, ed., *Handbook of Socialization Theory and Research* (Chicago: Rand McNally, 1969). Goslin has not updated his handbook, so we have no comparative figures for today.

13. B. J. Ruano, J. D. Bruce, and M. M. McDermott, "Pilgrim's Progress II: Recent Trends and Perspectives in Family Research," *Journal of Marriage and the Family* 31 (1969), pp. 688–98.

14. Otto Pollak, *Social Science and Psychotherapy for Children* (New York: Russell Sage Foundation, 1952); see also Pollak, *Integrating Sociological and Psychoanalytic Concepts* (New York: Russell Sage Foundation, 1956).

15. Kendall, *Upper Hand*, p. 4.

16. Pauline Bart, "Divorced Men and Their Children: A Study of Emerging Roles," paper given at the annual meeting of the American Sociological Association, Washington, D.C., 1970, p. 1.

17. Benjamin Spock, *Raising Your Child in a Difficult Time* (New York: W. W. Norton, 1974).

18. Joseph Church, *Understanding Your Child from Birth to Three: A Guide to Your Child's Psychological Development* (New York: Random House, 1973).

19. John DeFrain, "Sexism in Parenting Manuals," *Family Coordinator*, July 1977, pp. 245–51.

20. Melvin L. Kohn, *Class and Conformity* (Homewood, Ill.: Dorsey Press, 1969).

21. David Fanshel, *Foster Parenthood: A Role Analysis* (Minneapolis: University of Minnesota Press, 1966).

22. John R. Seeley et al., *Crestwood Heights* (New York: Basic Books, 1956).

23. John O'Brien, "The Decision to Divorce" (Ph.D. diss., University of Wisconsin, 1970).

24. Jeanne Mueller, "Reconciliation or Resignation: A Case Study," *Family Coordinator* (October 1970), pp. 345–52.

25. Adrian de Winter, "Family Planning in Uruguay" (Ph.D. diss., University of Wisconsin, 1971).

26. Details on this unpublished research may be obtained from John DeFrain, Department of Human Development and the Family, University of Nebraska-Lincoln 68583.

27. John DeFrain, "Sexism in Parenting Manuals," *The Family Coordinator*, July 1977, pp. 245–51.

28. Claybaugh and McCoy classified the following books as having serious discussions of fathers as nurturant beings: Benjamin Spock, *Baby and Child Care* (1977); Letty Cottin Pogrebin, *Growing Up Free* (1980); Elizabeth M. Whelan, *"A Baby? Maybe"* (1975); Edward Tronick and Lauren Adamson, *Babies as People* (1980); Catherine Milinarie, *Birth* (1974); Sam Bittman and Sue Rosenburg Zalk, *Expectant Fathers* (1978); Louise Bates Ames, *How To Father* (1974); S. Adams Sullivan, *The Father's Almanac* (1980); Marian Howard, *Only Human* (1979); Alison Cragin Herzig and Jane Lawrence Mali, *"Oh, Bob! Babies"* (1980).

29. See Theodore C. Sorensen, *Kennedy* (New York: Harper & Row, 1965), p. 381.

30. For a discussion of some of these points, see Fred Best, ed., *The Future of Work* (Englewood Cliffs, N.J.: Prentice-Hall, 1973).

31. E. E. LeMasters, *Blue-Collar Aristocrats: Life-Styles at a Working-Class Tavern* (Madison: University of Wisconsin Press, 1975).

32. Gene Marine, *A Male Guide to Women's Liberation* (New York: Holt, Rinehart and Winston, 1972); Warren Farrell, *The Liberated Man* (New York: Bantam Books, 1975).

33. John DeFrain, "The Nature and Meaning of Parenthood" (Ph.D. dissertation, University of Wisconsin, Madison, 1975).

34. Alan Booth, "Does Wives' Employment Cause Stress for Husbands?" *Family Coordinator*, October 1979, p. 447.

35. George P. Murdock, *Social Structure* (New York: Macmillan, 1949). In a survey of 250 human societies, Murdock found that a majority of them permit a man to have more than one mate.

36. See Oscar Lewis, *Five Families* (New York: Basic Books, 1959).

37. Herbert Gold, *The Age of Happy Problems* (New York: Dial Press, 1962), pp. 27–33.

38. See, for example, George Schaller, *The Mountain Gorilla* (Chicago: University of Chicago Press, 1963); also Jane Goodall, *In the Shadow of Man* (Boston: Houghton Mifflin, 1971).

39. Elaine Morgan, *The Descent of Woman* (New York: Stein & Day, 1972).

40. Morgan, *Descent of Woman*, p. 168.

41. Kingsley Davis, *Human Society* (New York: Macmillan, 1949), p. 400.

42. See Morris, *Naked Ape*.

43. See Marine, *A Male Guide to Women's Liberation*, pp. 64–97, for an extensive discussion of differential socialization of girls and boys for parenthood in our society.

44. Michael E. Lamb and Jamie E. Lamb, "The Nature and Importance of the Father-Infant Relationship," *Family Coordinator*, October 1976, p. 379.

45. Michael E. Lamb, ed., *The Role of the Father in Child Development* (New York: John Wiley & Sons, 1976), p. 25.

46. Ross D. Parke and Douglas B. Sawin, "The Father's Role in Infancy: A Re-Evaluation," *Family Coordinator*, October 1976, p. 365.

47. Ross D. Parke and Douglas B. Sawin, "Fathers," *Psychology Today*, November 1977, p. 112.

48. Between 1970 and 1980, for example, total U.S. unemployment ran between a low of 4.9 percent in 1970 to a high of 8.5 percent during the recession of 1975. Unemployment for married men with wives present during this time was considerably lower, of course: a low of 2.3 percent in 1973 and a high of 5.1 percent in 1975. As this book goes to press in late 1982, U.S. unemployment hovers around 10 percent, and the media daily tells us that this is the worst rate since World War II. For unemployment data, see the U.S. Bureau of the Census, *Statistical Abstract of the U.S.* (Washington, D.C.).

49. For an excellent analysis of poverty in our society, see the collection of essays, *Poverty: Views from the Left*, ed. Jeremy Larner and Irving Howe (New York: William Morrow, 1968).

50. See Alfred Kinsey et al., *Sexual Behavior in the Human Male* (Philadelphia: W. B. Saunders, 1948), p. 585.

51. These are estimates by Bob and Margaret Blood who are extrapolating from research by Morton Hunt. See the Bloods' *Marriage*, 3d ed. (New York: Free Press, 1978), p. 241.

52. William Masters and Virginia Johnson, *Human Sexual Inadequacy* (Boston: Little, Brown, 1970).

53. President Harding apparently was married to a sexless woman who knew that he had had at least two affairs with other women; see Francis Russell, *The Shadow of Blooming Grove: Warren G. Harding in His Times* (New York: McGraw-Hill, 1968).

54. "Has liquor ever been a cause of trouble in your family?" Yes, 17 percent; no, 81 percent; don't know, 2 percent. Figures from George H. Gallup, *The Gallup Poll: Public Opinion 1972–1977* (Wilmington, Delaware: Scholarly Resources, 1977), p. 972.

55. Harrison M. Trice, *Alcoholism in America* (New York: McGraw-Hill, 1966), chap. 5.

56. See their book, *Behind Closed Doors: Violence in the American Family* (Garden City, N.Y.: Doubleday, 1980).

57. Herbert J. Gans, *The Urban Villagers* (New York: Free Press, 1962).

58. LeMasters, *Blue-Collar Aristocrats*.

59. Erik H. Erikson, *Childhood and Society*, 2d ed. (New York: W. W. Norton, 1963), p. 295.

60. Henry B. Biller and Dennis L. Meredith, *The Invisible American Father* (Kingston: University of Rhode Island, 1972), p. 1.

61. Hans Peter Dreitzel, *Family, Marriage, and the Struggle of the Sexes* (New York: Macmillan, 1972), p. 10.

62. E. E. LeMasters, "The Passing of the Dominant Husband-Father," *Impact of Science on Society* 21 (1971), pp. 21–30 (UNESCO, Paris). This paper is reprinted in Dreitzel, *Family, Marriage, and the Struggle of the Sexes.*

63. See Mel Krantzler, *Creative Divorce* (New York: Evans, 1974); Joseph Epstein, *Divorced in America* (New York: E. P. Dutton, 1974).

64. Elaine Steinbeck and Robert Wallsten, eds., *Steinbeck: A Life In Letters* (New York: Viking Press, 1975), p. 661.

65. LeMasters, *Blue-Collar Aristocrats.*

66. News story, *New York Times*, February 7, 1974.

67. Epstein, *Divorced in America*, p. 259.

68. These studies are reviewed in Reuben Pannor et al., *The Unmarried Father* (New York: Springer Publishing, 1971).

69. H. Krause, "Child Welfare, Parental Responsibility and the State," *Family Law Quarterly* 6 (1972), pp. 372–404.

70. A. Hayman, "Legal Challenges to Discrimination Against Men," in *The Forty-Nine Percent Majority: The Male Sex Role*, ed. D. David and R. Brannon (Reading, Mass.: Addison-Wesley, 1976).

71. F. Schafrick, "The Emerging Constitutional Protection of the Putative Father's Parental Rights," *Family Law Quarterly* 7 (1973), pp. 75–111.

72. Miriam Aberg, Patricia Small, and J. Allen Watson, "Males, Fathers and Husbands: Changing Roles and Reciprocal Legal Rights," *Family Coordinator*, October 1977, pp. 327–31.

73. Jessie Bernard, *The Future of Motherhood* (New York: Dial Press, 1974); and *The Future of Marriage* (New York: Bantam Books, 1972).

74. Nearly 85 percent of American men feel family life is very important for a happy and satisfied life, according to Lou Harris and Associates, "The Playboy Report on American Men" (Chicago: Playboy Press, 1979), p. 6.

75. See John DeFrain, "Androgynous Parents Tell Who They Are and What They Need," *The Family Coordinator*, April 1979, pp. 237–43.

76. Jessie Bernard, "The Good-Provider Role: Its Rise and Fall," *American Psychologist*, January 1981, p. 12.

Chapter 9

1. Associated Press, "One-Parent Home Chances Rise," *Wisconsin State Journal*, March 12, 1979. This article cites the predictions of Paul Glick and Arthur Norton, Census Bureau analysts.

2. U.S. Bureau of the Census Report, Associated Press, *Lincoln* (Nebraska) *Journal*, June 22, 1980.

3. KFC National Co-op, "Single Parent Study," August 1979, p. 1. A survey of single parents conducted nationwide by National Family Opinion, Inc., for the Kentucky Fried Chicken Time Out Institute; and Sandra Stencel, Editorial Research Reports, "Single Parents: A Problem Grows," *Wisconsin State Journal*, September 30, 1976, section 5, p. 1.

4. KFC National Co-op, "Single Parent Study," p. 3.

5. On the financial problems of divorced women, see William J. Goode, "Postdivorce Economic Activities," *After Divorce* (New York: Free Press, 1956), chapter 16. A more recent sourcebook for understanding divorce is a book of articles

edited by George Levinger and Oliver C. Moles, *Divorce and Separation* (New York: Basic Books, 1979).

6. Goode, *After Divorce;* see chapter 16 for a discussion of the problem of support payments after divorce.

7. The financial problems of the divorced man were analyzed in a 1968 study (unpublished) conducted by the writer and several graduate students from the School of Social Work, University of Wisconsin. Eighty divorced men were interviewed at length. Financial problems were one of the constant complaints of these men.

8. On the employment of wives at the point of divorce, see Goode, *After Divorce,* pp. 71–74.

9. A discussion of the financial crises of AFDC mothers may be found in Sydney E. Bernard, *Fatherless Families: Their Economic and Social Adjustment* (Waltham, Mass.: Brandeis University, 1964); see also Louis Kriesberg, *Mothers in Poverty* (Chicago: Aldine Publishing, 1970).

10. For an analysis of the employment of mothers with minor children, see F. Ivan Nye and Lois Wladis Hoffman, *The Employed Mother in America* (Chicago: Rand McNally, 1963), pp. 7–15.

11. David Knox, *Exploring Marriage and the Family* (Glenview, Ill.: Scott, Foresman, 1979), p. 540.

12. See Reuben Hill, *Families Under Stress* (New York: Harper & Bros., 1949); also, Pauline Boss, "A Clarification of the Concept of Psychological Father Presence in Families Experiencing Ambiguity of Boundary," *Journal of Marriage and the Family* 39 (1977), pp. 141–51.

13. Goode (*After Divorce,* chap. 21) discusses some of the postdivorce problems of the father and his children.

14. In the 1968 unpublished study of 80 divorced men cited earlier (see note 7), the lack of contact with their children was one of the problems most often referred to by these fathers.

15. John DeFrain, Kathy Jordan, Kendra Summers, and Patricia Welker, "The Child Experiencing Marital Separation and Divorce: A Longitudinal Study of Parents' and Children's Perceptions" (Lincoln: Department of Human Development and the Family, University of Nebraska, 1980).

16. This woman was a professional social worker—hence some of her language is a bit technical.

17. For a discussion of the concept of social deviation, see Marshall B. Clinard, *Sociology of Deviant Behavior* (New York: Rinehart, 1968), pp. 3–27.

18. On the attitudes of people toward the divorced person in our society, see Morton M. Hunt, *The World of the Formerly Married* (New York: McGraw-Hill, 1966); Jan Fuller, *The Scrapbook of My Divorce* (New York: Arthur Fields Books 1973); and Morton and Bernice Hunt, *The Divorce Experience* (Hightstown, N.J.: McGraw-Hill, 1977).

19. It is possible, of course, for a woman who was once married to become an unmarried mother at a later date—as a widow or as a divorced woman.

20. Alvin Schorr explores the inadequacy of the AFDC welfare program in his study, *Explorations in Social Policy* (New York: Basic Books, 1968).

21. For an extensive study of this, see John Woodward, Jackie Zabel, and Cheryl DeCosta, "Loneliness and Divorce," *Journal of Divorce* 4 (1) (1980).

22. In the 1968 study of divorced men, conducted at the University of Wisconsin, there was frequent concern expressed by the men about the welfare of their

children after the divorce (see note 7). Excellent discussions of the divorced father and his children will be found in Mel Krantzler, *Creative Divorce* (New York: Evans, 1974); also *Steinbeck: A Life in Letters,* ed. Elaine Steinbeck and Robert Wallsten (New York: Viking Press, 1975), and E. Mavis Hetherington, Martha Cox, and Roger Cox, "Divorced Fathers," *The Family Coordinator,* 25 (1976), 417–28.

23. See Goode, *After Divorce,* chap. 21, for a discussion of how the divorced women in his sample felt about rearing children after the marriage had been terminated.

24. Maggie P. Hayes, Nick Stinnett, and John DeFrain, "Learning About Marriage from the Divorced," *Journal of Divorce* 4 (1) (1980).

25. Murray Straus, "Preventing Violence and Strengthening the Family" (Paper presented at the Third National Symposium on Building Family Strengths, University of Nebraska-Lincoln, May 1980).

26. Morton Hunt, personal communication, February 16, 1979.

27. One of the better discussions of desertion is the paper by William M. Kephart, "Occupational Level and Marital Disruption," *American Sociological Review* (August 1955). Among other things Kephart believes desertion to be more common than is generally thought. He also found that desertion was by no means limited to the lower socioeconomic levels.

28. The writers have been unable to find any empirical research that compares the psychological trauma of divorce with that of desertion.

29. On the courtship problems of divorced and separated women, see Susan Gettelman and Janet Markowitz, *The Courage to Divorce* (New York: Ballantine Books, 1975).

30. See DeFrain, Jordan, Summers, and Welker, "Child Experiencing Marital Separation and Divorce."

31. Robert Weiss, *Marital Separation* (New York: Basic Books, 1975).

32. On some of the problems of widows in our society, see Jessie Bernard, *Remarriage* (New York: Dryden Press, 1956).

33. Two comprehensive studies of the never-married mother in our society are Clark Vincent, *Unmarried Mothers* (New York: Free Press, 1961); and Robert W. Roberts, ed., *The Unwed Mother* (New York: Harper & Row, 1966).

34. Bernstein found that most never-married mothers in the United States eventually marry. See Rose Bernstein, "Are We Still Stereotyping the Unmarried Mother?" *Social Work* 5 (January 1960), pp. 22–38.

35. Thomas Holmes and R. H. Rahe, "The Social Readjustment Rating Scale," *Journal of Psychosomatic Research* 11 (1967), pp. 213–18.

36. Jack C. Horn, "Life With (Single) Father," *Psychology Today,* February 1980, p. 104.

37. Arnold J. Katz, "Lone Fathers: Perspectives and Implications for Family Policy," *The Family Coordinator* 28 (1979), pp. 521–528.

38. Besides Katz, see John DeFrain and Rod Eirick, "Coping as Divorced Single Parents: A Comparative Study of Fathers and Mothers," *Family Relations* 29 (April 1980); Helen Mendes, "Single Fathers," *The Family Coordinator* 25 (1976), pp. 439–644; and Dennis Orthner, T. Brown, and D. Ferguson, "Single Parent Fatherhood: An Emerging Lifestyle," *The Family Coordinator* 25 (1976), pp. 423–638.

39. Robert R. Bell, *Marriage and Family Interaction*, 4th ed. (Homewood, Ill.: Dorsey Press, 1975), p. 554.

40. J. Louise Despert, *Children of Divorce* (New York: Doubleday, 1962).

41. Statement from the dust cover of the Despert volume.

42. Krantzler, *Creative Divorce*.

43. "Study Reveals Parents' Ideas," Associated Press, *Wisconsin State Journal*, April 21, 1977. The survey of 1,230 families with children under age 13 was sponsored by General Mills.

44. Conference on the one-parent family sponsored by the Wisconsin Department of Public Instruction, reported in *The Milwaukee Journal*, August 19, 1976.

45. Philippe Aries, *Centuries of Childhood* (New York: Vantage Press, 1962).

46. Bernard Farber, *Family Organization and Interaction* (San Francisco: Chandler Publishing, 1964), p. 457.

47. Alfred Kadushin, "Single-Parent Adoptions: An Overview of Some Relevant Research," *Social Service Review* 44 (1970), pp. 263–74. The quote is from p. 271.

48. Ibid. See also Elizabeth Herzog and Cecelia Sudia. "Fatherless Homes: A review of the research," *Children* 15 (1968), pp. 79–81.

49. Joan Aldous, "Children's Perceptions of Adult Role Assignment," *Marriage and the Family* 34 (1972), pp. 55–65.

50. See E. E. LeMasters, "Illusions about the Two-Parent Family," *The One-Parent Family* (Iowa City: University of Iowa Extension, 1976).

51. See Leona and Jerrold Schecter, *An American Family in Moscow* (Boston: Little, Brown, 1975).

52. Mavis Hetherington, "Divorce: A Child's Perspective," *American Psychologist* 34 (1979), p. 857.

53. DeFrain, Jordan, Summers, and Welker, "A Child Experiencing Marital Separation and Divorce."

54. Hetherington, "Divorce."

55. Gary W. Peterson, and Helen K. Cleminshaw, "The Strength of Single-Parent Families During the Divorce Crisis: An Integrative Review with Clinical Applications," *Family Strengths: Positive Models for Family Life*, ed. Nick Stinnett, Barbara Chesser, John DeFrain, and Patricia Knaub (Lincoln: University of Nebraska Press, 1980).

56. Information on this research may be obtained by writing Dr. John DeFrain, Department of Human Development and the Family, University of Nebraska-Lincoln, 68583.

57. Howard H. Irving, *Divorce Mediation* (New York: Universe Books, 1981), pp. 62–63.

58. Paul C. Glick, "A Demographer Looks at American Families," *Journal of Marriage and the Family* 37 (1975), pp. 15–26.

59. Anne W. Simon, *Stepchild in the Family* (New York: Odyssey Press, 1964), p. 59.

60. E. M. Rallings, "The Special Role of the Stepfather," *The Family Coordinator* 25 (1976), p. 445–449.

61. Some very useful suggestions from stepparents will be found in Helen Thomson, *The Successful Stepparent* (New York: Harper & Row, 1966).

62. Simon, *Stepchild in the Family*.

63. Jessie Bernard, *Remarriage: A Study of Marriage* (New York: Dryden Press, 1956).

64. L. Duberman, "Step-Kin Relationships," *Journal of Marriage and the Family* 35 (1973), pp. 283–92.

65. Sharon Hanna and Patricia Knaub, "Strengths Within Families of Remarriage" (Manuscript, Department of Human Development and the Family, University Nebraska-Lincoln, 1980).

66. John W. Santrock, Richard Warshak, Cheryl Lindbergh, and Larry Meadows, "Children's and Parents' Observed Social Behavior in Stepfather Families," *Child Development* 53 (1982), p. 472–80.

67. Ruth Roosevelt and Jeannette Lofas, *Living In Step: A Remarriage Manual for Parents and Children* (New York: McGraw-Hill, 1976).

68. Norval D. Glenn, "The Well-Being of Persons Remarried after Divorce," *Journal of Family Issues* 2 (1981), p. 70.

69. Alfred Kadushin, *Child Welfare Services*, 2d ed. (New York: Macmillan, 1974), p. 523.

70. Arthur D. Sorosky, Annette Baran, and Reuben Pannor, *The Adoption Triangle* (Garden City, N.Y.: Anchor/Doubleday, 1978).

71. Katrina Wehking Johnson reviewed the book in the *Journal of Marriage and the Family*, November 1978, pp. 842–43.

72. Some of these problems are discussed by H. David Kirk in *Adoptive Kinship: A Modern Institution in Need of Reform* (Toronto: Butterworth, 1981).

73. Alfred Kadushin and Fred Seidl, "Adoption Failure: A Social Work Postmortem," *Social Work* 16 (1971), pp. 32–38.

74. Rita James Simon and Howard Altstein, *Transracial Adoption* (New York: John Wiley & Sons, 1977), p. 45.

75. David Fanshel, *Far from the Reservation* (Metuchen, N.J.: Scarecrow Press, 1972).

76. Simon and Alstein, *Transracial Adoption*, p. 187.

77. Constance Abraham and John DeFrain, "A Look at Transracial and Same-Race Adoptive Parents" unpublished manuscript, Department of Human Development and the Family, University of Nebraska-Lincoln, 1976).

78. Simon and Altstein, *Transracial Adoptions*.

79. Most of these topics are discussed in Kadushin, *Child Welfare Services*.

80. Kadushin, *Child Welfare Services*, p. 401.

81. Kadushin, chap. 9.

82. Ibid.

83. Ibid.

84. For a good analysis of the foster-parent role, see David Fanshel, *Foster Parenthood* (Minneapolis: University of Minnesota Press, 1966).

Chapter 10

1. Paper presented by Dr. Gerald Looney of the University of Arizona at the annual meeting of the American Academy of Pediatricians, Chicago, reported in the *New York Times*, October 1, 1971.

2. Ibid.

3. Associated Press report, *Wisconsin State Journal*, January 21, 1975.

4. Survey of research by Joan Beck, *Chicago Tribune*, April 20, 1972.

5. Interview with United Press, *Wisconsin State Journal*, May 26, 1974.

6. Address to the American Psychological Association, *New York Times*, September 3, 1968.

7. *Television and Violence*, symposium at the Stanford University College of Medicine, November 17, 1968.

8. Professor Cline has been running controlled experiments on the reaction of children to violence on film.

9. For a reply to the critics of commercial television, see Norman S. Morris, *Television's Child* (Boston: Little, Brown, 1971).

10. Robin Wight, *The Day the Pigs Refused to be Driven to Market* (New York: Random House, 1974).

11. Robert Metz, *CBS: Reflections in a Bloodshot Eye* (Chicago: Playboy Press, 1975).

12. United Press International, "AMA Ties Violence To TV," *Wisconsin State Journal*, June 22, 1977.

13. Associated Press, "Teen Charged With Murder Will Plead TV Insanity," *Wisconsin State Journal*, August 20, 1977.

14. Vincent Bugliosi and Curt Gentry, *Helter Skelter: The True Story of the Manson Murders* (New York: W.W. Norton, 1974), p. 460.

15. Muriel G. Cantor, *The Hollywood TV Producer* (New York: Basic Books, 1971), p. 147.

16. John P. Murray and Barbara Lonnborg, *Children and Television: A Primer for Parents*. Single copies of this beautiful pamphlet are available for free from the Boys Town Center, Boys Town, Nebraska 68010.

17. For material on the Soviet Union, see Leona and Jerrold Schecter, *An American Family in Moscow* (Boston: Little, Brown, 1975); also Urie Bronfenbrenner, *Two Worlds of Childhood: U.S. and U.S.S.R.* (New York: Russell Sage Foundation, 1970).

18. Martin Abrahamson, United Press Hollywood columnist, *Milwaukee Journal*, September 10, 1968.

19. *Milwaukee Journal*, September 15, 1974.

20. For a bitter analysis of commercial television, see Milton Mayer, *About Television* (New York: Harper & Row, 1972); also Metz, *CBS*. Metz is television commentator for the *New York Times* and has devoted his professional career to a study of mass media.

21. See David Dalton, *James Dean* (San Francisco, Straight Arrow Books, 1974).

22. Grace and Fred Hechinger, *Teen-Age Tyranny* (New York: William Morrow, 1963), pp. 151–52.

23. Paul Woodring, *Saturday Review*, March 23, 1963, p. 72.

24. Paper given by S. I. Hayakawa to the American Psychological Association.

25. *Webster's New World Dictionary of the American Language*, college ed. (Cleveland: World Publishing, 1956), p. 672.

26. See David Riesman et al., *The Lonely Crowd* (New Haven: Yale University Press, 1961), chap. 2.

27. Margaret Mead, *And Keep Your Powder Dry* (New York: William Morrow, 1965).

28. George Gallup, "Most Parents See TV-Crime Link," *Milwaukee Journal*, February 17, 1977.

29. See Mayer, *About Television*.

30. Schecter and Schecter, *American Family in Moscow.*

31. E. E. LeMasters, *Blue-Collar Aristocrats: Life-Styles at a Working-Class Tavern* (Madison: University of Wisconsin Press. 1975).

32. For a scholarly and readable discussion of marriage in contemporary America, see Jessie Bernard, *The Future of Marriage* (New York: Bantam Books, 1973).

33. Fred Friendly, *Due to Circumstances beyond Our Control* (New York: Random House, 1967), p. xii. Friendly is a former director of CBS news.

34. *Chicago Tribune* report, August 12, 1975.

35. Mayer, *About Television*, p. 9

36. Riesman et al., *The Lonely Crowd*, p. 82.

37. James S. Coleman, *The Adolescent Society* (New York: Fress Press, 1961), p. 9.

38. Ralph Keyes, *Is There Life After High School?* (Boston: Little, Brown, 1976). From an interview in the Chicago *Tribune*, June, 28, 1976.

39. Coleman, *Adolescent Society*, p. 312.

40. See Salvador Minuchin et al., *Families of the Slums* (New York: Basic Books, 1967), p. 219.

41. Alvin Toffler, *Future Shock* (New York: Random House, 1970), p. 249.

42. Kenneth Keniston, *Youth and Dissent: The Rise of a New Opposition* (New York: Harcourt Brace Jovanovich, 1971).

43. George Gallup, "Many Youths Want Different Lifestyle," *Lincoln Journal*, October 5, 1981, p. 6.

44. See Jesse Pitts, "The Family and Peer Group," in *The Family*, ed. Norman Bell and Ezra Vogel, (New York: Free Press, 1960), pp. 290–310.

45. On counterculture, see Theodore Roszak, *The Making of a Counter Culture* (New York: Doubleday, 1968); Charles A. Reich, *The Greening of America* (New York; Random House, 1970); and Keith Melville, *Communes in the Counter Culture* (New York: William Morrow, 1972). Parents will find the Reich volume especially helpful in understanding the nature of the youth revolt.

46. A study of approximately 1,000 young persons who took refuge in the Haight-Ashbury section of San Francisco concluded that a majority were from upper-middle-class homes; see David E. Smith and John Luce, *Love Needs Care* (Boston: Little, Brown, 1971).

47. "Communes: A More Businesslike Style," *U.S. News & World Report*, March 3, 1980, p. 67.

48. Judith K. Balswick and Jack Balswick, "Where Have All the Alienated Students Gone?" *Adolescence*, Fall 1980, p. 691.

49. Jessie Bernard, "Teen-Age Culture: An Overview," *Annals of the American Academy of Political and Social Science* 338 (November 1961), pp. 1–12.

50. John Barbour, Associated Press, "Teen Years Going Up in Smoke?" *Lincoln Journal*, October 4, 1981, section C, p. 1.

51. Henry Wechsler and Mary McFadden, "Drinking Among College Students in New England," *Journal of Studies on Alcohol* 40 (1979), pp. 969–96.

52. This withdrawal pattern is explored at length in the Haight-Ashbury study (Smith and Luce, *Love Needs Care*); see also the discussion in Melville's study *Communes in the Counter Culture.*

53. Statement in the *Chicago Tribune*, April 4, 1971.

54. Joseph Adelson, "Adolescence and the Generalization Gap." *Psychology Today*, February 1979, pp. 33–37.

55. For a review of the so-called sexual revolution, see Robert R. Bell, *Premarital Sex Codes in a Changing Society* (Englewood Cliffs, N.J.: Prentice-Hall, 1966).

56. U.S. Bureau of the Census, *Statistical Abstract of the U.S.: 1980* (Washington, D.C., 1980), p. 66.

57. Ollie Pocs and Annette G. Godow, "Can Students View Parents as Sexual Beings?" *The Family Coordinator*, January 1977, pp. 31–36.

58. Murray and Lonnborg. *Children and Television.*

Chapter 11

1. Kingsley Davis, "The Sociology of Parent-Youth Conflict," *American Sociological Review* 5 (August 1940), pp. 523–35. For extensive analysis of the process of social change, see Amitai and Eva Etzioni, eds., *Social Change* (New York: Basic Books, 1964).

2. Davis, "Parent-Youth Conflict," p. 523.

3. A useful book on recent social change and the family is John Rothchild and Susan Wolfe, *The Children of the Counterculture* (New York: Doubleday, 1976).

4. Alvin Toffler, *Future Shock* (New York: Random House, 1970), p. 259.

5. Toffler, *Future Shock*, p. 13.

6. In a study of men and women who frequent a blue-collar tavern, the writer found the women to be more contemporary than the men. See E. E. LeMasters, *Blue-Collar Aristocrats: Life-Styles at a Working-Class Tavern* (Madison: University of Wisconsin Press, 1975).

7. See Alvin Schorr, *Explorations in Social Policy* (New York: Basic Books, 1968).

8. For a good analysis of the impact of prohibition on American society, see Andrew Sinclair, *Prohibition: The Era of Excess* (Boston: Little, Brown, 1962).

9. On changes in the dating system after World War II, see Robert D. Herman, "The Going Steady Complex," *Marriage and Family Living* 17 (1955), pp. 36–40.

10. On the increase in divorce, see Paul C. Glick, "A Demographer Looks at American Families," *Marriage and the Family* 37 (1975), pp. 15–26.

11. Max Lerner, *America as a Civilization* (New York: Simon & Schuster, 1957). p. 569.

12. For an excellent discussion of American immigrant parents and their child-rearing problems, see Oscar Handlin, *The Uprooted* (Boston: Little, Brown, 1952), especially chap. 9.

13. An excellent analysis of the deficiencies of the urban school may be found in Peter Schrag, *Village School Downtown* (Boston: Beacon Press, 1967).

14. These data were analyzed in the preceding chapter, and the references will be found there.

15. Bernard Farber, *Family: Organization and Interaction* (San Francisco: Chandler Publishing, 1964), pp. 493–95.

16. For a discussion of housing in the ghetto, see the *U.S. Riot Commission Report* (New York: Bantam Books, 1968), pp. 467–82; also Lee Rainwater, *Behind Ghetto Walls* (New York: Free Press, 1970).

17. Some of these positive features of urban life are discussed in Herbert J. Gans, *The Urban Villagers* (New York: Free Press, 1962).

18. Some of the superior features of the urban welfare system are discussed by Schorr, *Explorations in Social Policy.*

19. A good analysis of some of the problems faced by Jewish parents in America may be found in Nathan Glazer and Daniel Patrick Moynihan, "The Jews," *Beyond the Melting Pot* (Cambridge, Mass.: MIT Press, 1963), chap. 3.

20. U.S. Department of Commerce, *Statistical Abstract of the United States*, 101st ed. (Washington, D.C.: U.S. Government Printing Office, 1980), p. 685.

21. One of the best accounts of the farm revolution is Lauren Soth's *An Embarrassment of Plenty* (New York: Thomas Y. Crowell, 1965). See also the paper by Lee G. Burchinal, "The Rural Family of the Future," in *Our Changing Rural Society*, ed. James H. Copp (Ames: Iowa State University Press, 1964), pp. 159–97. Also take a look at Suzanne Fremon and Morrow Wilson, eds., *Rural America* (New York: H. W. Wilson, 1976).

22. We find that most college students are unaware of the fact that the poverty rate is higher in rural America than in our cities. They also do not realize that about three fourths of the rural poor are white; see *White Americans in Rural Poverty*, Agricultural Economics Report, no. 124, (Washington, D.C.: U.S. Government Printing Office, 1967).

23. David Riesman et al., *The Lonely Crowd*, rev. ed. (New Haven: Yale University Press, 1961), pp. 45–55.

24. William H. Whyte, Jr., *The Organization Man* (Garden City, N.Y.: Doubleday, 1957), especially chapter 29, "Conclusion."

25. Riesman et al., *Lonely Crowd*, pp. 40–45.

26. Riesman et al., *Lonely Crowd*, p. 42. For the non-Greek scholars it might be pointed out that Icarus crashed into the sea and never made it back home.

27. This survey was done in a metropolitan "liberal" Protestant church in the Midwest in 1967.

28. Some American bishops have asked for a reappraisal of the church's stand on birth control, citing surveys which indicated that 76.5 percent of American Catholic women use some type of artificial birth control, and that only 29 percent of the priests in the United States believe some measures are immoral. Pope John II refused to back down on the church's ban on artificial birth control. Truth, he argued, "is not always the same as the majority opinion." From Associated Press, "Pope Upholds Birth-Control Ban," *The Lincoln Journal*, December 15, 1981.

29. Riesman et al., *Lonely Crowd*, p. 47.

30. For an interesting discussion of modernity among fathers and mothers in their parental roles, see John R. Seeley et al., "Parent Education," *Crestwood Heights* (New York: Basic Books, 1956), chap. 9; also, look at LeMasters, *Blue-Collar Aristocrats*.

31. In one of the more elaborate modern studies of parents, almost half of the mothers reported disagreements with their husbands over discipline problems with children, with the father reported to be "tougher." See Daniel R. Miller and Guy E. Swanson, *The Changing American Parent* (New York: John Wiley & Son, 1958), p. 225.

32. Davis, "Parent-Youth Conflict," p. 524.

33. For an analysis of the process of resocialization, see Orville G. Brim, Jr., and Stanton Wheeler, *Socialization after Childhood* (New York: John Wiley & Sons, 1966).

34. Ruth Benedict, "Continuities and Discontinuities in Cultural Conditioning," *Psychiatry* 1 (May 1938), pp. 161–67.

35. An interesting paper is that by Kenneth Keniston, "Social Change and Youth in America," in *The Challenge of Youth*, ed. Erik Erikson (New York: Doubleday, 1968), pp. 191–222.

36. Toffler, *Future Shock*.

37. For a similar incident in a popular novel, see Laura Z. Hobson, *Consenting Adult* (Garden City, N.Y.: Doubleday, 1975).

38. Lewis S. Feuer, *The Conflict of Generations* (New York: Basic Books, 1969).

39. Edwin Newman, *Strictly Speaking* (New York: Bobbs-Merrill, 1974), p. 11.

40. Eleanor Macklin, "Heterosexual Cohabitation among Unmarried College Students." *Family Coordinator* 21 (1972), pp. 463–72.

41. Robert Coles, *Farewell to the South* (Boston: Little, Brown, 1972), pp. 216–17.

42. Edgar Z. Friedenberg, *The Vanishing Adolescent* (New York: Dell Publishing, 1962).

43. Peter Collier and David Horowitz, *The Rockefellers: An American Dynasty* (New York: Holt, Rinehart & Winston, 1976).

44. North American Newspaper Alliance, "Youth Closing Generation Gap," *Milwaukee Journal*, January 29, 1974.

45. Toffler, *Future Shock*, p. 220.

Chapter 12

1. Eric Berne, *Games People Play* (New York: Grove Press, 1964), p. 171.

2. See Herbert J. Gans, *The Urban Villagers* (New York: Free Press, 1962); E. E. LeMasters, *Blue-Collar Aristocrats: Life-Styles at a Working-Class Tavern* (Madison: University of Wisconsin Press, 1975).

3. Berne, *Games People Play*, pp. 104–7.

4. Sean O'Faolain, *Vive Moi!* (Boston: Little, Brown, 1964), p. 108.

5. Robert R. Bell, *Marriage and Family Interaction*, 4th ed. (Homewood, Ill.: Dorsey Press, 1975), p. 499.

6. For an analysis of the problems in working with teenage gangs (infiltrating the group), see Irving Spergel, *Street Gang Work: Theory and Practice* (Reading, Mass.: Addison-Wesley, 1966). One of Spergel's points is that this work requires courage.

7. For an interesting analysis of the generation gap, see Richard Lorber and Ernest Fladell, *The Gap* (New York: McGraw-Hill, 1968).

8. The observations on officer models in the U.S. Naval Air Corps are based on the first author's three years of service during World War II.

9. George R. Bach and Peter Wyden, *The Intimate Enemy* (New York: William Morrow, 1969), p. 288.

10. See, for example, Arthur Niederhoffer, *Behind the Shield: The Police in Urban Society* (New York: Doubleday, 1967).

11. In a university city in which the first author was teaching, a group of young people watched passively while a patrolman was beaten up by three men he had tried to arrest for creating a disturbance.

12. Max Lerner, *America as a Civilization* (New York: Simon & Schuster, 1957), pp. 560–70.

13. One of the major findings of the *U.S. Riot Commission Report* (New York: Bantam Books, 1968), was the feeling of hostility (if not hatred) that the urban racial minorities have toward the police; see chapter 11, "The Police and the Community."

14. Daniel R. Miller and Guy E. Swanson, "Child Training in Entrepreneurial and Bureaucratic Families," *The Changing American Parent* (New York: John Wiley & Sons, 1958), chap. 4.

15. On conformity in our society, see David Riesman et al., *The Lonely Crowd* (New Haven: Yale University Press, 1961), also William H. Whyte, Jr., *The Organization Man* (New York: Doubleday, 1957), especially pt. 1, "The ideology of Organization Man."

16. Melvin L. Kohn, *Class and Conformity: A Study of Values* (Homewood, Illinois: Dorsey Press, 1969), p. 89.

17. For a discussion of the functionality of the two systems of child rearing analyzed in their study, see Miller and Swanson, *Changing American Parent*, pp. 109–18.

18. For a delineation of the child-development model, see Evelyn Millis Duvall, *Family Development*, 5th ed. (Philadelphia: J. B. Lippincott, 1977).

19. See Lerner, *America as a Civilization*, pp. 562–68, for a discussion of how American parents spoil their children.

20. Lerner, *America as a Civilization*, pp. 562–63.

21. On the production of guilt in parents, see Orville G. Brim, Jr., *Education for Child Rearing* (New York: Russell Sage Foundation, 1959).

22. The athletic coach model used here was derived from several weeks the first author once spent with a group of coaches at Ohio State University. This group included two men who later became nationally famous for their winning teams—Paul Brown and Woody Hayes.

23. Athletic banquet speech reported in the *Milwaukee Journal*, November 14, 1965.

24. Brim, *Education for Child Rearing*, p. 98.

25. Ibid.

26. See Carl Rogers, *Client-Centered Therapy* (Boston: Houghton Mifflin, 1951). For a good analysis of the Rogerian counseling system, see Calvin S. Hall and Gardner Lindzey, *Theories of Personality* (New York: John Wiley & Sons, 1957), pp. 467–502.

27. Some of the principles of communication therapy will be found in Virginia Satir, *Conjoint Family Therapy* (Palo Alto, Calif.: Science & Behavior Books, 1964), and Jay Haley, *Strategies of Psychotherapy* (New York: Grune & Stratton, 1963). For a highly readable picture of how to change communication patterns in any family, see Virginia Satir, *Peoplemaking* (Palo Alto: Science Behavior Books, 1972).

28. See Sheldon D. Rose, "A Behavioral Approach to the Group Treatment of Parents," *Social Work* 14 (1969), pp. 21–29; also Harry Lawrence and Martin Sundel, "Behavior Modification in Adult Groups," *Social Work* 17 (1972), pp. 24–43.

29. For a detailed explication of behavior-modification concepts and techniques, see Sheldon D. Rose, *Treating Children in Groups* (San Francisco: Jossey-Bass, 1972); also Lawrence and Sundel, "Behavior Modification," p. 34.

30. Norman Epstein, "Brief Group Therapy in a Child Guidance Clinic," *Social Work* 15 (1970), pp. 33–38.

31. See Marshall L. Hamilton, *The Father's Influence on Children* (Chicago: Nelson-Hall Publishers, 1977).

32. From an excerpt of James C. Dobson's *Straight Talk to Men and Their Wives* (Waco, Texas: Word Books, 1980), printed in *Guideposts*, February 1981, p. 23.

33. See, for example, Susan D. Bean, "The Parent Aide Support Service: How Volunteers Effect Growth in Abusive and Neglectful Parents," in *Family Strengths: Positive Models for Family Life*, ed. Nick Stinnett, Barbara Chesser, John DeFrain, and Patricia Knaub (Lincoln: University of Nebraska Press, 1980), pp. 369–82.

34. Mary Koch, Associated Press, "Runaway Parents Get Away from It All," *Wisconsin State Journal*, January 23, 1979, section 3, p. 1.

35. Thomas Gordon, *Parent Effectiveness Training* (New York: New American Library Edition, 1975), p. ix.

36. From a personal conversation with Don Dinkmeyer in July 1981.

37. James W. Croake and Kenneth E. Glover, "A History and Evaluation of Parent Education," *The Family Coordinator*, April 1977, pp. 151–158.

38. Kelley M. L. Brigman, "Positive Aspects of Problems in Family Relationships: A Survey of Expert Opinion," in *Family Strengths 4: Positive Support Systems*, ed. Nick Stinnett, John DeFrain, Kay King, Herbert Lingren, George Rowe, Sally Van Zandt, and Rosanne Williams (Lincoln: University of Nebraska Press, 1983).

Index

This book has been set VIP in 10 and 9 point Memphis Light, leaded 3 points. Chapter numbers and titles are 18 point Helvetica Light. The size of the type page is 26 by 46 picas.